Shakespeare's cinema of love

Manchester University Press

Shakespeare's cinema of love

A study in genre and influence

R. S. WHITE

Manchester University Press

Copyright © R. S. White 2016

The right of R. S. White to be identified as the author of this work has been asserted by him in accordance with the Copyright, Designs and Patents Act 1988.

Published by Manchester University Press
Altrincham Street, Manchester M1 7JA, UK
www.manchesteruniversitypress.co.uk

British Library Cataloguing-in-Publication Data is available

ISBN 978 0 7190 9974 8 hardback
ISBN 978 1 5261 4362 4 paperback

First published by Manchester University Press in hardback 2016

This edition published 2020

The publisher has no responsibility for the persistence or accuracy of URLs for any external or third-party internet websites referred to in this book, and does not guarantee that any content on such websites is, or will remain, accurate or appropriate.

Typeset by Out of House Publishing

Contents

Acknowledgements	*page* vi
Introduction: Shakespeare shaping modern movie genres	1
1 'Madly mated': *The Taming of the Shrew* and odd-couple comedy	39
2 Dreams in the forest: romantic comedy	71
3 'The guy's only doing it for some doll': musical comedy	109
4 Of errors and Eros: a brief digression on twins	140
5 Comedy of disguise and mistaken identity	148
6 'Star-crossed lovers': *Romeo and Juliet* and romantic tragedy	178
Conclusion	223
Bibliography	227
Index	238

Acknowledgements

The edition used for quotations is *William Shakespeare: The Complete Works*, 2nd edn, ed. Stanley Wells and Gary Taylor (Oxford: Clarendon Press, 2005). I am grateful to the two anonymous readers for Manchester University Press for seeing enough merit in this book to be published. Matthew Frost at the Press has been generous in his tactful encouragement. The British Film Institute allowed me unlimited use of their wonderful resources. The Australian Research Council awarded me an Australian Professorial Fellowship (Project number DP0877846) to carry out research on 'Shakespeare and Film Genres', which so far has resulted in three books and many articles that otherwise would be unlikely to have been written. The book is also intended as a contribution to the 'Shaping the Modern' Programme in the Australian Research Council Centre of Excellence for the History of Emotions 1100–1800 (Project number CE110001011), with which I have the pleasure of association.

Others have helped with specific information or more general conceptual advice: Bruce Babington, Peta Beasley, Tim Carter, Deborah Cartmell, Marina Gerzic, Indira Ghose, Lisa Hopkins, Philippa Kelly, Scott Newstok, Katrina O'Loughlin, Shalmalee Palekar, Elinor Parsons, Olga Sankey, Poonam Trivedi, Penelope Woods, Li Lan Yong, and many others who opened up windows of insight. Having taught 'Shakespeare at the Movies' for many years, I have been given countless ideas by my students, for which I am grateful. All those who attended various 'Shakespeare and Film' seminars at conferences over the years in places like Los Angeles, Paris, Stratford, Prague, Valencia, and elsewhere, have generously shed light on the whole area. My daughters Marina and Alana were intrigued by my determination to find Shakespeare hidden in films we watched together, and contributed some valuable insights from their own interests in movies. They suggested I should name the book *Where's Willy*, on the model of the children's cartoon puzzle books entitled *Where's Wally*, in which a tiny figure is hidden somewhere in a large, maze-like crowd – just look hard enough and eventually you will find him.

Introduction: Shakespeare shaping modern movie genres

First a Girl is a neglected but charming British movie made in 1935. Its significance in cinema history, when noticed at all, is that it was sourced from a more well-known and oft-adapted German film of 1933, *Viktor and Viktoria*, and was later studied by Julie Andrews in rehearsing the Broadway musical made into a film, *Victor Victoria* (1982), which turned Mary Poppins into a gay icon. Elizabeth (Jessie Matthews) delivers clothes for a fashion house, yearns to be a singer, but fails an audition. So does aspiring Shakespearean actor Victor (Sonnie Hale), who introduces the first of numerous Shakespearean quotations with a speech from *Julius Caesar* delivered in a failed audition. A born loser, Victor is offered a part as a female impersonator in a music hall, but is afflicted by laryngitis. An accidental meeting with Elizabeth gives him an idea: 'You can do something for me. [*She*] Can I? [*He*] Take off those pyjamas. [*She, shocked*] What? [*He*] Put this on …'. And so Elizabeth becomes Bill, a woman pretending to be a young man impersonating a woman called Victoria in performances. Victor, again quoting from *Julius Caesar*, 'There is a tide in the affairs of men', takes on the role of mentor as 'Bill/Victoria' embarks on a dazzling career. 'She' is of course a smash-hit in the apparently cross-dressed role, and Jessie Matthews's singing and dancing skills are fully showcased. What stretches credulity is how everybody is taken in, since only a myopic Mr Magoo would fail to see the figure as anything but that of a voluptuous woman. It takes nothing less than a nude bathing close encounter to convince the intrigued lothario, Robert, consort of Princess Helen Mironoff, that there is something noticeably unusual about this boy. Wary of making the princess jealous, he maintains the pretence against the evidence of his eyes: 'I'm glad he's a boy.' Now he realises why he had been strongly attracted when putting Bill through the male social rituals of drinking heavily and smoking a cigar in the bar, a scene milked for comedy. 'I can't be a man all my life', Elizabeth laments ruefully to Victor, and elsewhere she declares in a context that is full of gay overtones, 'I'm in love with Robert'. The word 'gay' occurs several times with at least some ambiguity – the refrain of the final song is 'The world is happy and gay' – and androgyny is the obvious, recurrent source for jokes – 'I'm not staying like this all my life', 'Don't you like me as a girl?' – and problematical identity in Victor's rueful 'I've been father, mother, brother, sister to that boy.' Just as suspicions grow and the police are called to attend to the deception encapsulated in the stage conundrum 'He's a girl', Victor recovers his voice and public ignominy is averted. The final performance on stage presents Victor as the female impersonator, thus preventing exposure of the cross-dressed pretender. Later, when a passport is produced for confirming identity, the dialogue runs, 'This passport is for a man' ... 'Yes, but first a girl' ... 'And always a girl'.

The film is replete with Shakespearean lines, from *Romeo and Juliet*, *Hamlet*, *Richard II*, *The Merchant of Venice*, *As You Like It*, and even *The Rape of Lucrece*. More pertinently, Shakespeare's use of boy actors is drawn by implication into the comedy of paradoxes based on gender, as evidenced in the exchange with Victor: '[She] But wait until they see your Hamlet' ... '[He] Hamlet? I'll be the greatest Cleopatra the world has ever seen.' There are unmistakable analogies with the figure of Rosalind in *As You Like It*, a boy actor playing a woman pretending to be a youth, while the scenes between Bill and Robert (before he twigs), and Bill and the princess (who intuits the deception), hold the homoerotic overtones of those between, respectively, Viola and Orsino, and Cesario and Olivia in *Twelfth Night*. In filmic terms *First a Girl* is a romantic comedy, a musical comedy, and a backstage musical. But what is its relation to Shakespeare? It is less than an adaptation or an offshoot of a specific play, yet it seems more than a vehicle for just opportunistic quotations. The answer to be pursued in this book is that there is a deeper, structural analogy at work, and that the playfully developed, capacious genre is a composite kind of Shakespearean comedy, taking that term as descriptive of a group of plays whose dominant attitudes to love, motifs, and generic expectations adhere to each other. From *Twelfth Night*, *As You Like It*, *The Merchant of Venice*, and *The Two Gentlemen of Verona* it borrows the disguised heroine, and from these plays combined with *A Midsummer Night's Dream* it borrows the concept of an alternative play-world, in which identity and love become subjects for confusion, contemplation, and eventual clarification. In Shakespearean comedy this has been analysed as the 'green world', and the alternation of 'real' and 'play' spaces equates to the distinction in filmic romantic comedy between 'backstage' action and musical performance. In this sense, Shakespearean comedy can be said to lie behind cinematic comedy of love and its various sub-genres, including musical comedy. It can be further argued, though it will only be alluded to in this book, that the infusion of Shakespearean romantic comedy into the modern popular mode of cinema has provided a channel for certain conventions of love to take prominence in our own world, suggesting that Shakespeare, both directly and indirectly, has helped create some of our own cultural and psychological paradigms of fulfilled love. At the same time, there is a different, rival conception of love as the product of inter-personal conflict, which feeds into movies from *The Taming of the Shrew* and *Much Ado About Nothing*, inviting separate treatment.

Deborah Cartmell and Imelda Whelehan point out that 'the Internet Movie Database now labels Orson Welles's *Othello* (1952) as "drama", and Tim Blake Nelson's adaptation of the same play, O (2001) as "drama/romance/thriller"'.[1] However, another way of looking at the genre of these films could be to classify both as lying within an 'Othello genre'. By extension, other 'drama/romance/thrillers', which contain some common elements from a list including love triangle, constructed jealousy, deception, voyeurism, and racial difference, and some element of 'crime of passion' (*A Double Life* (1947), *All Night Long* (1962), the theatrical sub-plot in *Les Enfants du Paradis* (1945), and even *Sex, Lies, and Videotape* (1989)) might be classified likewise, rather than 'drama/romance/thrillers', even when Shakespeare's play is not necessarily named or directly visible as a source. I shall not be considering *Othello* itself in this book, but extending the analogy to films that bear a resemblance to Shakespeare's comedies or to *Romeo and Juliet*, where the plays provide narrative structures for recognisable and influential genres around the subject of love in modern movies. This book argues that Shakespeare's plays on love significantly influenced and helped to shape some movie genres in the twentieth century, and that the nature of this indebtedness has not gained recognition because it is not always easy to identify or describe. Books proliferate about adaptation of Shakespeare's plays into films, but very few concentrate on the subject of genre. Part of Shakespeare's ubiquitous legacy lies in the ways the structural expectations in his plays anticipate, can be adapted into, a range of film genres dealing with love, and in some cases can be claimed as cinematic sub-genres in their own right.

Making such claims risks the twin dangers of overstating or underestimating such an influence and I try to steer a middle course between the two. On the one hand, I certainly do not want to give the impression that every film genre, let alone every film, is influenced by the genres used and partially created by a dramatist who was writing over four hundred years ago. To claim anything like this would run the risk of ignoring the advice of 'Sam Wo-Toi' in the Mike Hammer film noir television series, *Tattoo Brute* (1958), his very existence a small part of the process I am observing: 'It was Shakespeare who so sagely observed the bad effects of protesting too much.' The allusion to *Hamlet* suggests audience recognition even in such an unpromising context, but more to the point is the sentiment itself, since exaggerating the degree of Shakespearean referencing would be as neglectful as ignoring it altogether. Some film genres show more signs of influence than others in terms of their narrative logic. There are a number of movies that evidence important generic similarities, whether these are consciously known to the film-makers or not, while other groups show a pervading, atmospheric, structural, or stylistic influence, suggesting a Shakespearean genre, without necessarily making overt reference to one particular play as model. On the other hand, it would be misleading to follow in the footsteps of some film historians and theorists who at least tacitly give the impression that film is a completely separate medium from theatre, with its own circumscribed history and theoretical grounding, owing little or nothing to earlier dramatic innovations or stage history. We need a corrective to such a view, a mediating account, if only because Shakespeare has been such a central and abiding cultural figure in the history of entertainment that some oblique or direct influences must have entered the dominant mass medium of movies from the 1890s onwards. Sergei Eisenstein, in some ways the father of film criticism and closer historically to the medium's inception than recent theorists, lends some strong support for this view, in his own genial style:

> I do not know about the reader, but I have always derived comfort from repeatedly telling myself our cinema is not entirely without an ancestry and a pedigree, a past or a rich cultural heritage from earlier epochs. It is only very thoughtless or arrogant people who could construct laws and aesthetic for cinema, based on the dubious assumptions that this art came out of thin air![2]

Eisenstein continues:

> Let Dickens and the whole constellation of ancestors, who go as far back as Shakespeare or the Greeks, serve as superfluous reminders that Griffith and our cinema alike cannot claim originality for themselves, but have a vast cultural heritage; ... Let this heritage serve as a reproach to these thoughtless people with their excessive arrogance towards literature, which has contributed so much to this apparently unprecedented art, and most important to the art of viewing – and I mean *viewing*, in both the senses of this term – not *seeing*.

Introduction 5

Allardyce Nicoll, in *Film and Theatre*, a book that was pioneering and remarkably comprehensive for its time in the 1930s, points out that it was eight years after the invention of movies in 1895 that attempts were made simply to tell a story in the new medium, let alone group them in genre categories.[3] To quote Cartmell and Whelehan's book again, they suggest that 'In the early period of cinema, when film genres were newly emergent, movies were not identified, as they are today, in relation to a specific generic identity'.[4] Genres emerged later, drawing inevitably on theatre practice, although gradually independent movie genres developed. These have been in a state of flux and modification ever since, with new sub-genres and hybrid genres emerging regularly.

Douglas Lanier, in a brief but penetrating essay, has anticipated some of the problems faced in this book.[5] In an age when 'Shakespeare on film' is a virtually universal way of teaching the plays, Lanier points out the twin dangers relating to genre study, either of implying an ideological dominance of modern cultural forms such as movies and imposing them inappropriately on an early modern dramatist, or alternatively of giving Shakespeare a transhistorical status that acts as an invidious, qualitative comparison with contemporary culture. This points to the fact that Shakespearean adaptation has always had an ambiguous place in cinema history. Lanier's eminently sensible solution is to resist the pulls in both directions and instead respect the differences between the two areas, the historical and current, refusing to accept one or the other as normative. Perhaps recklessly, my approach will suggest there is a tighter connection between the two than is commonly noticed, and that in many ways Shakespeare can be seen to have laid down in his self-evidently enduring and innovative plays a set of historical 'templates' for genres, which the film industry has adopted without systematically intending it. Even if some of my suggestions may seem offered in a spirit of special pleading, I take the opportunity to advance them, problems and all, to open up a discussion on genre history that links Elizabethan drama with the modern world of movies, for others to explore and perhaps more satisfactorily to trace. This is offered as an 'ideas' book rather than a reference work on 'Shakespeare adaptations' or a comprehensive study in film history. In the words of Keats's 'Ode on a Grecian Urn', 'Heard melodies are sweet, but those unheard / Are sweeter', and it is my hope to bring the 'unheard' to a threshold of hearing.

For those who wish to explore other aspects of Shakespearean adaptation into movies, Richard Burt's capacious two-volume *Shakespeares after Shakespeare* offers comprehensive and fascinating guidance,[6] and pioneering works by Kenneth Rothwell, Samuel Crowl, Russell Jackson, Lanier himself, and many others have been published on filmed versions of Shakespeare. Burt's work in particular seeks primarily to establish direct Shakespearean sources for adaptations and offshoots in a variety of media, whereas I hope to trace other, indirect lines of influence into movies, relating to narrative shape and genre. It seems desirable to break down boundaries between Shakespeare and modern popular media, returning his works to their intended place as mass entertainment. It seems a good time to remind ourselves of the popular roots of Shakespeare's plays, in a year dominated internationally by events commemorating the 400th anniversary of the death of the 'Man of the Millennium' declared in 2000. I hope that layers of recognition can add richness to response, whether in the context of Shakespeare's plays or of popular movies. Moreover, the matter of influence between Shakespeare and movies is in some senses mutual. While we trace the influence of Shakespeare on film genres, we can also gain an awareness from the derivative films of potential new readings of Shakespeare's plays for contemporary audiences. I seek readers willing to accept a degree of lateral thinking and imaginative leaps, willing to follow some quite speculative trails, and, I hope, to contribute their own suggestions along similar lines, drawing on their individual experience of movies. The benefit may lie in an enhanced understanding of the way literary and dramatic genres interpenetrate with the history of cinema through complex avenues of cultural transmission and adaptation. Given the complexity of the process of following such a trail, it has been difficult to avoid using the word 'elusive' more frequently than is comfortable, and I find myself pleading like Bernardo in *Hamlet*, 'Is not this something more than fantasy?', aware that some will probably answer coldly, 'No'. I plead for generous readers, hoping that the study will illuminate some aspects of both film history and Shakespearean studies that have not received sustained attention, and which may set chiming bells of recognition:

> I must have liberty
> Withal, as large a charter as the wind,
> To blow on whom I please, for so fools have;
> And they that are most gallèd with my folly,
> They most must laugh. (*As You Like It*, 2.7.47–51)

After all, my twin subjects, Shakespearean works dealing with love and cinematic comedy and tragedy of love, are in essence both centred on the follies of love.

It should also be made clear at the outset that this book does not focus exclusively or even predominantly on 'the Shakespeare film' as such, defined as a movie clearly signalled as a filmed version of a particular play by Shakespeare. This territory can be categorised as a genre in its own right, or as a sub-genre of the 'heritage film', or what Timothy Corrigan calls the 'literary film'. Such a movie 'draws attention to the literary work from which it is derived, presuming either familiarity with that work or at least cultural recognition of its literary status'.[7] Some of my examples will fall into this category, but by no means all. Nor do I dwell exclusively on works that are known in Shakespeare studies as 'offshoots' or 'derivatives', those films that adapt Shakespearean material – sometimes drastically but still recognisably – in ways that are designed to be noticed as revisions of the plays.[8] Such terms openly proclaim that the film-makers are aware of a Shakespearean source text, and although in many cases this will be true, in just as many they do not draw attention to a source, and may indeed be completely unaware of a Shakespearean precedent, mediated as it is through other films. Although inevitably there will be many deliberate 'offshoots' cropping up in the discussion, this is not the primary reason for using them in the analysis. Rather, such movies are part of the broader evidence that film genres are influenced or even created by generic blueprints initiated in plays by Shakespeare, sometimes adapted knowingly but often without acknowledgement from the makers or recognition by their audiences. In this sense, influence is seen as an essential part of all culture that has evolved intertextually from historical antecedents and models that themselves have receded from direct view. It also raises the possibility of claiming Shakespeare's romantic genres – comic and tragic – as mediated influences on our ways of thinking about love in the modern world, despite the fact that other 'intermediaries' lie between the source and the output.[9] Many of our attitudes and conventions surrounding romantic love derive, in this sense, both directly and indirectly from Shakespeare's plays, and it is in movies that this phenomenon can be most clearly observed.

Influence

As I have intimated, this book is not a consistently sustained 'source study' arguing that all film genres ultimately derive from Shakespeare's precedents. 'Adaptation' alone is also not quite the right word to describe the relationship, even after taking into account Cartmell and Whelehan's ambit claim that 'At its best an adaptation on screen can re-envision a well-worn narrative for a new audience inhabiting a very different cultural environment, and their relationship to the "origin" may itself change enormously'.[10] Instead, I offer a two-way study of 'influence' concentrating on the plays' continuing, if unobtrusive, presence in film genres, and secondarily on ways in which our familiarity with these film genres can be used as an interpretive tool to shed light on Shakespeare. Just as his plays have the capacity to reveal new meanings to suit new times, so new times reveal new meanings in his old works, meanings that previous generations of readers and audiences were not attuned to noticing. One thread of the argument is that since Shakespeare's plays had for some centuries been consolidated in cultural and popular consciousness through theatrical practices, traditions of reading and critical analysis, and educational systems, the existence of his plots when organised into overarching generic types expressed a powerful but largely concealed influence on the burgeoning film industry during at least its first fifty or so years into the twentieth century. A second thread suggests that the development of independent cinematic genres such as romantic comedy, screwball comedy, musicals, movies based on disguise, and romantic tragedy created unique opportunities for recontextualising Shakespeare's plays, not only presenting but also distancing them in a fresh, defamiliarised light, revealing them as contemporary texts dealing with issues still alive in the modern world. Like the Ghost of the deceased King Hamlet who comes back to haunt and influence the actions of at least his son, influence can work underground and beyond conscious reach: 'Well said, old mole. Canst work i'th' earth so fast?' (*Hamlet*, 1.5.164). There is, as Jacques Derrida expresses in his own consideration of *Hamlet*, a 'spectral' quality in the nature of influence, as it works through processes of cultural transmission, leaving little material mark but a ghostly impression.[11] But the image of the old mole popping up its blind head every now and then might do just as well as images of ghosts and spectres.

Harold Bloom has reminded us that the word 'influence' comes with a 'matrix of relationships', percolating through a filter that he equates with a form of 'tyranny' and overlapping with other contentious terms like 'source' and 'analogue'.[12] A recent literary historian, Robert A. Logan, begins his study of Marlowe's influence on Shakespeare saying 'By "influence," I mean not simply the conscious or subconscious selection of elements in another writer's work but, more significantly, the use(s) to which they are put.'[13] Logan is happy to draw on 'new notions of boundless and heterogeneous intertextuality'[14] in approaching the subject with a wide remit, having regard to both 'specific and wide influences'[15] and their 'overlapping' relationship with 'sources' that are usually taken to be more fixed:

> Sources can be easy to talk about unless they are confused with influences. If sources have traditionally ranged from definite to probable, influences have ranged from definite to possible – in which case they have

been confused with analogues ... Whereas sources have knowingly created a sense of certainty, influences have often stood in the shadows of uncertainty.[16]

Influence can be even more subtly and broadly revealed than in relation simply to literary relationships. Porscha Fermanis, writing on the influence of eighteenth-century philosophy on Keats, refers in turn to the work of David Spadafora, who, as Fermanis points out,

> has reminded us, on the one hand, an influence can be significant without being overt or explicit; on the other, influence is by no means the only available intellectual tool to hand. Circulating ideas, intellectual currents and various kinds of political unconscious can mould epistemological structures and provide a series of critical foci or contexts for a writer's work.[17]

The reference reminds us that history of philosophy uses the notion of influence without the degree of 'anxiety' felt by writers and critics – John Locke's influence on later philosophers is accepted as a perfectly legitimate point of discussion – whereas literary historians are probably more comfortable with the certitude of 'sources', finding influence more difficult to discuss. As scholars we are trained (and as teachers we teach) that it is a duty to acknowledge sources, at least of a textual nature, but influences on the way we think and write are considerably more amorphous, difficult to locate with precision, and therefore less clearly subject to acknowledgement. The task of tracking Shakespearean influence through the centuries down to twentieth-century films is therefore more contentious than finding sources. A range of currents and conduits have carried and modified his plays' influence on succeeding generations and in different media, and I can hope to catch only a small part of the picture.

Jane Austen's novels serve as analogies in a more limited corpus, since they have been used as prototypes and models for some romantic movies, as well as informing the 'rom-com' genre as a whole. Just as Shakespeare took most of his plots from earlier works and forged them into his own, innovatively hybrid generic types like romantic comedy, romantic tragedy, and dramatic romance, so Austen built upon earlier romantic novels and courtesy books, most of them now largely forgotten except by specialist literary historians. Her own works look less original when viewed in the light of her precursors' practice, although still accomplished and perfect in their way.[18] Austen inflected with her own spirit of irony the situations she depicts and plots she constructs, to perfect formulas for a recognisable type of fiction, which has not only survived but grown in celebrity and has led to modern redactions. These novels are part of the scaffolding for the enormously popular genre of romance fictions in prose, and partly through them Austen's own influence as a much-loved novelist has extended into the genre of 'chick flick' films today. In some cases the influence is conscious and built into a marketing strategy for films. *Emma* and *Clueless*, *Pride and Prejudice* and the Anglo-Indian *Bride and Prejudice*, and even the fictional biography *Becoming Jane*, are films that, as Lisa Hopkins and others have shown, proudly trade on the 'brand' of Jane Austen's novels. In many other cases, however, the influence is almost certainly unconscious and mediated even when it is undeniably close, since the brand has become a recognisable 'Jane-Austen genre'.[19] It is beyond the scope of this book to argue the case of Austen in detail, but such a study would provide an example of the processes that include direct sources, indirect influences, and similarities of genre, linking her novels and later movies. Shakespeare's case is more complex because not just one literary type is involved but several, often leading back to individual plays that have created virtual genres in their own right. At least it seems obvious that screenwriters, and perhaps the film-making industry as a whole, have absorbed literary traditions and performance conditions that include the canonical plays of Shakespeare as shadowy but important cultural influences. This is true even when that influence is not explicitly acknowledged by or even necessarily known to the film-maker, or recognised by viewers, since it has inevitably been percolated through different paths of historical agencies in literature, theatre, music, opera, cinema, and others. It is undeniable that 'media' are 'mediated', and behind some lie prototypes derived from Shakespeare.

Nor is the degree of Shakespearean influence confined simply to Western forms. Japanese Noh dramatists have made similar claims of indebtedness, and Boris Pasternak detected in language at least 'the invisible presence of Shakespeare and his influence in a whole host of the most effective and typical devices and turns of phrase in English', an 'elusive foundation' that he tried to convey when translating Shakespeare into Russian.[20] This is not to claim that Shakespeare's works are 'universal', a critical term nowadays shunned, but instead to argue that, for various reasons of transmission of his texts, his pervasive *influence*, however localised, is as close to universal as it can get. At the same time, it will be an inevitable part (but only a part) of my theme that the undoubtedly modern technical and performance possibilities opened up by the mass medium of cinema influenced film versions of Shakespeare's plays, and that the availability of genres, which have been made popular and profitable by the medium, has naturally been exploited in adaptations globally.

Introduction 11

There are dangers, of course, in suggesting links between the present and the past and between literature and film, although the rewards may lie in realising the creative possibilities of renewed insight. Stephanie Trigg says as much in the journal *Screening the Past*, in speaking of the problematical nature of interdisciplinary work linking the past (in her case, medieval times) with modern cinema. Trigg warns that interpretation runs the risk of being

> too tolerant of loose, or flattening comparisons and analogies between different historical periods, different media, and different academic disciplines. On the other hand, it is only by exploring these possibilities that we can make those periods, those media, and those disciplines talk to each other, to explore the myriad ways we make sense of the past and the present.[21]

The attempt, Trigg suggests, offers 'a powerful capacity to articulate dynamic, changing relationships between the present and the past'. In the present instance, an extra contribution lies in an enhanced understanding of some ways in which literary and dramatic genres interpenetrate with the history of cinema, through complex avenues of cultural transmission and adaptation, mutually illuminating each other. Just as we find richer resonances in films by noticing a Shakespearean substructure of genre, so Shakespeare's plays reveal new meanings that emerge from the way they are recontextualised into a different medium and different times.

The concept of influence is not only more general than sources, it is also less fixed. It seems reasonable to distinguish a source as something copied from or consciously imitated, an immediate model, from influence as a process of mediation through other, more direct sources and cultural conduits. To quote Logan again, in exploring a writer-to-writer influence, he suggests:

> Only under the best of conditions can an originating text be identified as the cause and an influence as the effect. The originating text passes through the transforming chambers of the writer's psyche to emerge as a force whose inception can be difficult to recognize: in such a case, one can only guess at the origins of the influence.[22]

Logan goes on to argue that influences can range from the cultural to the personal, 'emotional to intellectual, superficial to deeply psychological, tangible to intangible', in ways that are 'not always easy to categorize'. In these senses, the initiating impetus of a Shakespearean play inevitably stands at many removes from a modern film, and there lies between them a set of intervening, intertextual contexts.

Anthony R. Guneratne, presents a more general and abstract model of adaptation, also focused on genre but using a different critical terminology. Guneratne uses the term 'intermediation' to describe Shakespeare's influence on the present:

> I use this term to signify the increasing symbiosis between different media, particularly digital media and older technologies such as nitrocellulose film stock. In *Shakespeare on Film* Judith Buchanan refers to John Dryden's tripartite idea that adaptation could be metaphrase (literal translation), paraphrase (a sense of the text with the author kept in mind), and imitation (wherein some aspect of the original finds reflection), as well as to Dudley Andrew's definition of transmediation as 'the systematic replacement of verbal signifiers by cinematic signifiers.'[23] Adhering to the frameworks Buchanan and Andrew invoke, one might observe that critics of filmed Shakespeare have either chosen to favor the idea that the best adaptations best preserve Shakespeare's dialogue metaphrastically, or gravitate to the other extreme of valuing those that depart as much as possible from the original transmedially. Yet the key idea that a Restoration dramatist and a film theorist share, in this instance, is that words such as those of Shakespeare can be rendered recognizably in another medium, although neither definition is conclusive. Dryden might have further refined his categories and Andrew, as Yuri Lotman and other semioticians might observe, discusses two separate, semiotic transactions (the translation of printed texts into verbal signifiers, and the translation of verbal signifiers into equivalent images), which is not to say that cinema has not been the beneficiary of translatibility.[24]

However inviting Guneratne's model is, I choose not to adopt its theoretical terms, partly because the genre he is analysing is particularly 'the Shakespeare movie', rather than Shakespeare's influence on cinema more broadly. Reflecting on his critical terms, however, I seem to be adopting the model of adaptation as 'imitation', which is the term commonly adopted by Renaissance theorists.

So far as I know, there is only one writer who pursues as relentlessly as I do an argument that Shakespeare has influenced the genres of modern movies, the philosopher-critic Stanley Cavell. In *Pursuits of Happiness: The Hollywood Comedy of Remarriage*,[25] Cavell explores the fact that between 1934 and 1949 a spate of films appeared dealing comically with a theme that he describes as 'remarriage'. His excavations unearth the influence of Shakespearean comedy and, more particularly, romance, and more particularly still, *The Winter's Tale*: 'the Shakespearean structure surfaced again, if not quite on the stage' in these films, partly, he argues, because of the new-found maturity of motion pictures soon after the advent of sound, and, second, because of a similarity between Shakespeare's heroines and post-war women:

> at the same date there was a group of women of an age and a temperament to make possible the definitive realization of the genre that answered the Shakespearean description, a date at which a phase of human history, namely, a phase of feminism, and requirements of a genre inheriting a remarriage structure from Shakespeare, and the nature of film's transformation of its human subjects, met together on the issue of the new creation of a woman.[26]

Cavell returns many times to the idea of 'the connection between Shakespearean comedy and a central genre of American comedies', and with other aspects of comparison in mind: 'in Shakespeare this is called the green world or the golden world; in four of the seven major Hollywood comedies of remarriage this world is called Connecticut'.[27] The seven films he refers to are, *It Happened One Night*, *The Awful Truth*, *Bringing Up Baby*, *His Girl Friday*, *The Philadelphia Story*, *The Lady Eve*, and *Adam's Rib*, some of which I consider from different points of view in later chapters. I am indebted to Cavell's book in ways that will be reflected in my account, not least because he attempted the speculative kinds of links I draw,[28] though I do resist what appears to me as an unnecessarily narrow concentration on remarriage, and on *The Winter's Tale*. Perhaps rashly, my argument will be broader, that Shakespeare was a significant presence behind movie genre history before and well after 1934, and that the influence was pervasive in films dealing with different kinds of love, covering courtship, marriage, and post-marriage. I will also suggest that recognition of the relationship between Shakespeare's romantic comedies, taken as a generically composite set of audience expectations, is mutually illuminating, shedding light first on an area of film indebtedness that has not been sufficiently recognised, and second on the potential for finding new meanings in Shakespeare's plays through fresh readings and performances. Cavell himself showed awareness that the approach has wider implications when he came later to write *Contesting Tears: The Hollywood Melodrama of the Unknown Woman*,[29] in which, although the Shakespearean influence is not so prominently presented, it is again seen to be an ingredient behind film melodrama or 'weepies'. Once again he attributes the cause to the emergence of a new female sensibility that invites comparison with some of Shakespeare's heroines.

The fact that there are few sustained accounts other than Cavell's books that employ this genre-based approach partly reflects the difficulty of tracing culturally mediated influences, let alone hypothesising sources that are not explicit or consciously adverted to by the makers of a film. Well aware of the danger, I try to address it by focusing on the issue of genre predominantly, rather than aspects of echoed language or familiar character types. One who seems willing to use the approach through genre is Harry Keyishian, in his essay 'Shakespeare and Movie Genre: The Case of *Hamlet*'.[30] He proposes a metaphor, suggesting that Shakespeare's plays have been adapted into movie genres (such as film noir) as though they are being poured into pre-existing moulds. In some instances at least, Shakespearean plots *were* poured into Hollywood genres like moulds, but it may be possible to go further and suggest that in some cases it was Shakespeare who created the moulds themselves, even before the medium of film was invented. Tony Howard, writing in the same volume as Keyishian, edges towards a similar kind of study of Shakespeare's influence, but his own contribution is limited to acknowledged 'offshoots':

> Just as 'Shakespeare' permeates our culture iconographically from cheque cards to cigars, so in mainstream film culture the plays have functioned as myths and sources; they materialise repeatedly and often unnoticed on cinema screens through allusions and variations, remakes, adaptations and parodies. In this broader, culturally important, sense 'Shakespeare film' is not only populated by Olivier, Welles, Branagh and company – Jean-Luc Godard, Jean-Paul Sartre and James T. Kirk are also there, alongside Cole Porter, Katharine Hepburn, Arnold Schwarzenegger, Mel Brooks and Sid James. Here we can only point to a vast terrain of cinematic appropriation, and suggest some historical implications of 'free' Shakespearean film.[31]

The title of Douglas Lanier's essay, 'William Shakespeare Filmmaker', indicates an approach that highlights the intrinsically cinematic techniques used by Shakespeare. He begins with reference to George Méliès's *La Mort de Jules César* (1907), a film lost but described by Robert Hamilton Ball in his indispensable account of Shakespeare in silent movies.[32] Shakespeare dreams the assassination of Julius Caesar, wakes up and stabs a loaf of bread, thus releasing his writer's block. Through crude allegory this shows a play not as a product of the stage but as springing from the author's imagination, '"fathering forth" the text as a cinematic entity' in the words of Carolyn Jess-Cooke, borrowing the term from Edward Said.[33] Other films reclaim Shakespeare as a popular artist, separating his works from the literary by showing him exercising an imagination that is 'fundamentally cinematic', not that of a 'theatrical wordsmith'. Lanier also suggests the corollary, that the process of film-making is in some ways 'fundamentally Shakespearean'. 'Linking Shakespeare to film becomes a means for articulating (or simply accepting) the cinema's considerable ambitions as a media form.'[34] In another essay, Lanier describes 'post-fidelity' adaptation of Shakespeare into different media as a form of 'rhizomatics' (borrowing the term from Deleuze and Guattari), the creation of new processes by yoking apparently very different rootstocks: In his 'arboreal conception of adaptation', Lanier suggests, 'A rhizomatic structure ... has no single or central root and no vertical structure. Instead, like the underground root system of a rhizomatic plant, it is a horizontal, decentred multiplicity of subterranean roots that cross each other, bifurcating and recombining, breaking off and restarting.'[35] It seems that we need metaphors – ghosts, moles, offshoots, rootstocks (and for Deleuze and Guattari, the activities of wasps) to describe the process of creative adaptation. In speaking of transhistorical genres we can add other metaphors such as 'family resemblances' (a focus of Altman's attention),[36] rivers, and indigenous songlines. Sometimes, as Samuel Crowl points out, it may be a stray detail in Shakespeare's play – 'an image, metaphor, character, or atmosphere' – that will 'evoke in the film director a resonance with a particular movie genre',[37] but in such cases it may be that the Shakespearean reference points to a distant source for the movie genre itself. In 'Shakespeare's imbrication with cultural processes of adaptation',[38] Shakespeare's texts are not reverently treated as privileged 'sources', but rather as 'collaborators' in a mutual act of re-creation and new creation. Cartelli and Rowe, who give close analytical attention to the 'cultural processes' involved in adaptation, also describe them in terms of 're-framing of earlier framings' that can be inserted into a variety of '*citational environments*'.[39] Among these are genres.

Genre

> There are always genres. There are always aesthetic forms. And they always possess their own logic. Even when films were new, they deployed generic and aesthetic conventions from photography, from the theatre, from popular stories, and from numerous other forms of art, entertainment and representation.[40]

Generally speaking, a basic theory of genres was established in classical times, mainly by Aristotle, and revived in the humanist recuperation of classical knowledge of the Renaissance.[41] Since then they have never gone away, although critical attention to the subject has periodically waxed and waned. Shakespeare worked knowledgeably with the ancient genres in mind, but he also consciously expanded the range by breaking the 'rules' in developing mixed and hybrid forms, such as in what later came to be described as tragi-comedy. History plays, adapting English chronicle and classical historical sources to the stage, were more or less invented by Shakespeare. In these, ignoring Sir Philip Sidney's critical admonitions against 'mongrel tragi-comedy' and 'mingling kings and clowns' on stage,[42] he included figures like Falstaff in company with Prince Hal. They could end almost randomly with marriage (*Henry V*) or death (*Richard II*). Another example of Shakespeare's generic experimentation is his staging of pastoral, a genre classically confined to poetry, in stage plays such as *As You Like It* and *The Winter's Tale*. He was also not above ridiculing his own practice of mixing genres, in the words of Polonius: 'The best actors in the world, either for tragedy, comedy, history, pastoral, pastoral-comical, historical-pastoral, tragical-historical, tragical-comical-historical-pastoral, scene individable or poem unlimited. Seneca cannot be too heavy, nor Plautus too light. For the law of writ and the liberty, these are the only men' (*Hamlet*, 2.2.398–403). Film-makers later inherited, at least tacitly through the intermediary of theatrical practice, the legacy of Shakespeare's experiments in genre, and far from creating new generic types in a vacuum, they built upon precedents from history. The ancients invented a dramatic category called comedy, presided over by the muse Thalia, which was mainly satirical in nature, inviting laughter at the behaviour of lower social classes. Shakespeare learned from his contemporary John Lyly in expanding the range to foreground love in aristocratic circles, creating romantic comedy (comedy derived from relationships between the sexes). Some modern literary historians have pinpointed even more particularised sub-genres within romantic comedy, such as 'epithalamic comedy', representing 'the moments between marriage and consumption'.[43] Movies accepted comedy of love as a dominant genre, but have continued to evolve into bifurcated sub-genres such as 'rom-coms', melodrama, musical comedy, screwball comedy (which I will characterise as 'odd-couple' romantic comedy), and others. Meanwhile, the more classical, satirical conception of comedy as ridiculing low life continued into films as sub-genres like satire, black comedy, farce, comedy thrillers, parody films, sex comedies, and so on. The reasons for such apparently endless splintering of dominant genres into niche categories has more to do with marketing the films to consumer expectations than with genre theory, a complication that Shakespeare's example had again anticipated. In the First Folio his plays are categorised as comedies, histories, and tragedies, while the title pages of Quarto plays made finer distinctions suggesting the mingling of these overall genres: *King Lear* was variously printed as a 'History' and a 'Tragedy', *Hamlet* was a 'Tragical History' on the 1603 Quarto title page, *The Merchant of Venice* was a 'Comedy' in the

Folio but a 'Comical History' on the Quarto, *Love's Labour's Lost* is given a finer discrimination as a 'Pleasant Conceited Comedy'. In the Induction to *The Taming of the Shrew* the action to follow is described to Christopher Sly as a 'pleasant comedy' designed to alleviate melancholy, but even he shows some awareness of different kinds of comedy available to Elizabethan audiences:

> SLY Marry, I will, let them play it. Is not a comondy a Christmas gambold or a tumbling-trick?
> PAGE No, my good lord; it is more pleasing stuff.
> SLY What, household stuff?
> PAGE It is a kind of history.

It would seem that Shakespeare anticipated the need for more descriptive sub-genres, to draw on his audience's experience and guide their expectations of what is to come.

A recent, brief, and convenient definition of 'genre movies' (a term subtly different from 'genre in movies', although this is not especially important in this context) is given by Barry Keith Grant:

> Put simply, genre movies are those commercial feature films which, through repetition and variation, tell familiar stories with familiar characters in familiar situations. Popular cinema is mostly composed of genre movies – the kind of films most of us see, whether we 'go to the movies' or 'to the cinema', or watch films on DVD or videotape at home. Throughout film history genre movies have comprised the bulk of filmmaking practice, both in Hollywood and other national countries, the films that are made, distributed and exhibited in commercial venues everywhere are overwhelmingly genre movies.[44]

'Repetition and variation' lies at the heart of classical and Renaissance conventions of genre too. Shakespeare and his First Folio editors were fully conversant with genres in drama of their time and, as students of a humanist education, they also generally drew on classical theory for the roots and sub-divisions of epic, poetry drama and tragedy, comedy, and pastoral. In the making of twentieth- and twenty-first-century films there is a similar relationship to Shakespeare's genres as there was between Shakespeare and the classical ones. In both cases the source genre is vestigially present as an historical survival, but treated over time as ripe for transforming, adapting, and hybridising.

For the most part the field covered in this book is mainly what is known as 'Hollywood movies', a term that denotes a meta-genre in its own right.[45] It includes box-office, commercial films, mainly emanating from the American industry based on a studio system such as

Hollywood (and some examples from Bollywood), rather than independent, privately financed works. The dominant time frame has emerged here (rather than being initially chosen) as covering films from the early history of the medium, especially the 1930s (when 'talking pictures' became a mass medium), through the 1940s and 1950s, though occasionally I have ranged forwards in time where it seemed relevant to show surviving influence. The reason for this focus on earlier films is mainly that it seemed increasingly clear to me, and has also been argued by some film historians, that in the first half of the twentieth century the mainstream, traditional Hollywood genres, viewed as relatively discrete categories, were in the process of developing their own micro-histories and repertoires of 'classic' filmic sources. Dominant movie genres were being established and consolidated by repetition, in a concentration of substantially similar, 'recycled script films', which formed the basic corpus for later developments.[46] A potent reason behind this was marketing, which was made easier when groups of films could be publicised as conforming to a basic 'formula' that is 'constructed or marked for commercial consumption', building upon 'those aspects of representation that entail the generation of expectations'.[47] After the 1950s, the drive for novelty led to hybridity and the self-conscious mixing of genres into an apparently endless proliferation of new sub-genres. The process no doubt reflected the increasingly experienced sophistication of movie-going audiences, as well as the industry's voracious appetite for changing well-worn, potentially exhaustible patterns. In the earlier period, then, we would expect to find a more conservative assimilation from theatrical traditions, and from the kind of tried and tested performance modes offered by the long, received history of Shakespeare production, rather than from the necessarily brief history of film itself. Indeed, some of the very earliest movies were filmed stage performances of Shakespearean plays. In time, these inherited conventions of genre became a 'sediment' in both senses of that word: matter that settles and remains at the bottom of a liquid, and the geological meaning of 'particulate matter that is carried by water or wind and deposited on the surface of the land or the bottom of a body of water, [which] may in time become consolidated into rock'.[48] The process of gradual sedimentation was occurring markedly in the first few decades of cinema history, and after the 1950s Shakespeare had become so deeply embedded in the medium that the influence is less immediately visible. It does seem an observable fact, confirmed by developments in film theory from the 1970s onwards, that after the mid-century movies become more intertextually entwined, as there grew a large enough corpus to provide cinema history and theory with its own landmarks and reference points within the medium. The periods equate roughly with the distinction often made between 'classic Hollywood' from the 1920s to the 1940s when major genres were clarified and developed in a relatively orderly way, and 'New Hollywood' (from the mid-1970s onwards) when genres multiplied, hybridised, and bifurcated into sub-genres, although there are enough exceptions to make this generalisation rather loose.[49] If the Shakespearean influence as a 'sediment' still remained, it had become so naturalised within films that it had become not direct 'source material' but a distantly visible, though still palpable presence. This process of a steady and partial submerging of the Shakespearean influence made it seem more necessary, by an act of critical hindsight and preservation, to enshrine obvious and often conservative adaptations of his own works in one genre all their own, the 'Shakespeare movie', as a sub-genre of the 'heritage' film.

Even in the earliest stage in the history of movies (though late in his own posthumous career), Shakespeare had a foothold.[50] From 1899 we have a precious few seconds that remain from an original four minutes, showing the death of King John, played by the great actor-manager Herbert Beerbohm Tree. It was shot on 68-mm film, not from the stage but in a movie studio with a painted background. This can be seen as among the first close-ups in moving pictures, as Kenneth Rothwell points out in *Early Shakespeare Movies: How the Spurned Spawned Art*.[51] It was shown at the same time as the opening of the stage production at Her Majesty's Theatre, London, no doubt as publicity.[52] The king dies in histrionic fashion on his throne, clutching his throat and arching his body in agony, as the film material itself threatens to disintegrate before our very eyes (which it does after less than a minute). In a strange and certainly unintended way, the flickering image mirrors the words being spoken by John in the written text at this point (though obviously only mouthed in the silent clip):

> I am a scribbled form, drawn with a pen
> Upon a parchment, and against this fire
> Do I shrink up. (*King John*, 5.7.32–4)

It seems like a statement applying to the medium itself, and those brought up in the 1950s will have amusing memories of this literally happening by accident before their very eyes, caused by the overheating of highly inflammable celluloid. Scenes from Shakespeare provided equally pioneering and auspicious moments for the new technical form. *A Midsummer Night's Dream*, made in the United States in 1909 by Vitagraph, was filmed outdoors in a literal forest (or at least woodlands) under natural light. Among other camera tricks, it shows the disappearance and reappearance of Puck, who also puts a girdle round the earth not in forty minutes but about four seconds. Illusionism in the play is matched by the technical capacity for ocular magic offered by the medium.

Shakespeare holds an equally honourable place in the movie history of those nations that experimented early with moving pictures, since there are snippets, scenes, and even longer versions of his plays during the first years of the century.[53] In France in 1900, a three-minute segment was shown of Hamlet duelling with Laertes, the hero being played by the famous Sarah Bernhardt, thus still today demonstrating another achievement shared with Shakespeare's plays, the ability to bring back the dead from their graves and change their gender. Ghostly voices came to emerge from Edison wax cylinders being played behind the screen simultaneously. The Paris Exposition, where this film first showed, was the basis for the Société Film d'Art, which was committed to 'rehabilitating film's unsavoury reputation',[54] bringing to middle-class audiences Shakespearean high culture in the medium whose roots lay in working-class entertainment.[55] The famous Méliès brothers produced a ten-minute slice of *Hamlet* with Georges sharing the role of the Prince. Scenes from *Richard III* appeared in America in 1908 and 1912, and the earliest surviving full feature film (1 hour 33 minutes) made in America was *Richard III*, which has only recently been rediscovered.[56] Meanwhile, other brief versions of Shakespeare appeared from Italy and Germany as well as France, the United States and Britain. Between 1908 and 1912, Vitagraph in Brooklyn produced 'one-reelers' of many Shakespeare plays, no doubt also designed to overcome a class stigma hanging over the new medium, thus introducing a fruitful and creative tension between the demotic roots of the filmed entertainment and the high-art cultural capital of Shakespeare's works.[57]

The foothold gained by Shakespeare in the first few years in the history of the film medium must also have contributed an influence towards the creation of movie genres, before these had clearly formed. There was nothing in the medium itself at that stage to make any particular genres intrinsically predictable, and they evolved through other channels. It was influences from other, established cultural areas that filtered into movies, and gradually coalesced around some recognisable genres: 'The genres of early cinema are mostly adapted unthinkingly from other sources, mainly popular ... music hall, the variety theatre and vaudeville, the circus, the fairground, itinerant theatre, the amusement arcade.'[58] Hilary Radner points out that 'Plays, novels, Biblical tales, and epic poems were all revisited in cinematic narratives',[59] and, a little higher on the social scale of culture, though still having roots in popular entertainment, came Shakespeare's plays. There gradually emerged the broadest possible understanding of genre, 'defined as an empirical category that serves to name, differentiate, and classify works on the basis of the recurring configurations of formal and thematic elements they share'.[60] John Frow describes a genre as a 'system', within which individual examples share some formal features, topics, thematic structure, 'implication' (background knowledges), rhetorical functions, and sometimes physical settings.[61] In the first twenty or so years, film genres were only emerging under the influence of established performing arts.

The title of an interesting contribution to film studies, Vera Dika's *Recycled Culture in Contemporary Art and Film: The Uses of Nostalgia*,[62] encapsulates aspects of my argument: Shakespeare is constantly present as 'recycled culture' in films, and a part of the effect of his presence is a kind of historical nostalgia. Indeed, at least two recent books attribute the surge of Shakespeare on screen and stage in the 1990s partly to a *fin de siècle* spirit.[63] However, in fact the content of Dika's book, which draws extensively on the works of Fredric Jameson, refers mainly to films quoting films or reflecting the eras in which they were made, and does not look back to influences from times before movies existed. Only very rarely does this book, and other works of literary theory, refer to earlier drama, literature, art, and culture. For example, Barry Langford's prime aim of presenting 'historical contexts' for film pertains exclusively to the history of cinema.[64] Meanwhile, 'the ghost in the machine' lies in surviving traces and memories of Shakespeare behind film genres. Plays like *A Midsummer Night's Dream* and *Romeo and Juliet*, for example, offered to the new medium fully fledged, familiar genres within viewers' experience, so they were well placed to generate countless imitations. Moreover, they already occupied the space towards which the medium of film was headed, 'at the intersection of high and mass culture'.[65] The relationship was both contestatory and symbiotic. In silent films, his name was invoked to give legitimacy and respectability to the new plebeian form of entertainment,[66] but the association in turn gradually rescued Shakespeare from Victorian notions that his plays were the preserve of an upper bourgeoisie who could afford to attend the theatre, returning him to his Elizabethan popular status. Much later, during the 1990s, filmed versions of plays such as those by Kenneth Branagh and Baz Luhrmann, decisively brought the plays to a young, mass audience. The set of paradoxes highlight the chameleon nature of these plays, capable of generating apparently infinite varieties of adaptation. A related paradox is the capacity of each play, on the one hand, to be 'globalised' by multinational Hollywood companies, as evidenced by Michael Hoffman's *A Midsummer Night's Dream* (1999), and yet, on the other, 'localised' in, for example, the Indian adaptation of *The Comedy of Errors*, *Angoor* (1988) or the Singaporean variation on *Romeo and Juliet*, *Chicken Rice War* (*Jiyuan qiaohe* (2000). Given all these unique qualities, and narratives familiar from endless performances, the Shakespeare corpus provided the new medium of cinema with a set of well-developed genres perfect for appropriation. We can begin to speak confidently in terms of the more famous of Shakespeare's plays creating the pattern of 'repetition and variation' based on familiarity and surprise that would qualify each as a major generic influence behind films, even when they make no explicit reference to Shakespeare.

There is another, and rather different, way of seeing Shakespeare as part of the history of genres in movies. It can briefly be proved that he has made his way into almost every conceivable film genre identified within the medium, and there are not many other cultural forces of which this can be said. So-called 'mega-genres' describe groups through technical and industrial aspects, and here we might list some with their Shakespearean significances. Defined in terms of length, the early adaptations were one-reelers of eight, twelve, or twenty minutes, and Shakespeare was immediately adapted, sometimes by condensing a play into a whole reel by relying on its familiarity, or presenting a well-known episode where the context in the play was already known. The same contextual knowledge could also be presupposed in silent films, where the image is dominant and could be presumed to invoke a narrative. Later, the plays also effortlessly found their way into audio-visual movies in the 1930s, because of their primacy of language. In terms of funding sources, over the history of cinema the plays have been sponsored by large Hollywood and Bollywood studios, small independent companies, and television stations, by teams or solitary auteurs, private companies, national arts councils, and self-financed by novices and amateurs. In black and white, Laurence Olivier's *Hamlet* won Academy Awards in 1948, while in colour *Shakespeare in Love* did the same in 1999. Virtually every language in the world is represented among the body of adaptations, since they had already been translated as plays. Below these mega-genres, more popular genres are encountered as soon as we walk inside a video rental library. We spot groupings and look around for the ones we know we enjoy. These categories owe little to taxonomical rigour, and the logic behind them depends on the librarian's wish to guide customers quickly to their favourite form of entertainment, but one thing they have in common is amenability to incorporating Shakespeare's plays, sometimes in parody. I set myself the challenge of finding examples in a conceptual video library, using as a basis the genres listed comprehensively on a detailed website written and edited by Tim Dirks, called 'Film Genres: Origins and Types'.[67] My version below is vulnerable in the obvious sense that it mixes up genres and sub-genres, but in itself the listing reflects the fact that genre creation is always in a state of flux, redefinition, and finessing.

Epic (*Julius Caesar* (1953))
War (*Henry V* (1944))
Murder (*Richard III* (1996))
Crime and Gangster (*Men of Respect* based on *Macbeth* (1991))
Thrillers, Psychological Thrillers (*A Double Life* referencing *Othello* (1947))
Film Noir (Orson Welles's *Macbeth* (1948) and *Othello* (1952))
Western (*Jubal* based on *Othello* (1956))
Science Fiction (*Forbidden Planet* based on *The Tempest* (1956))
Musicals (*Kiss Me Kate* (1953) and *West Side Story* (1961))
Horror (Polanski's *Macbeth* (1971))
Children's Animations (*The Animated Shakespeare* (1994) and *The Lion King* recalling *Hamlet* (1994))
Romantic Comedy (*Much Ado About Nothing* (1993))
Romantic Tragedy or Melodrama (*Romeo and Juliet*))
Grunge (*Tromeo and Juliet* (1996))
Disaster (*The King Is Alive* referencing *King Lear* (2000) and Jean-Luc Godard's *King Lear* (1987) set in Chernobyl)
Teen-Flick (*10 Things I Hate About You* based on *The Taming of the Shrew* and *Much Ado About Nothing* (1999) and *She's the Man* based on *Twelfth Night* (2006))
Samurai (*Throne of Blood* based on *Macbeth* (1957))
Supernatural (Any number of witches from *Macbeth*)
Zombies (*Warm Bodies* partly based on *Romeo and Juliet* (2013))
Road Movies (*My Own Private Idaho* (1991) based on *1 Henry IV* is sometimes grouped here)
Erotic and Pornographic (*The Secret Sex Lives of Romeo and Juliet* (1969))
Lesbian (*Macbeth: The Comedy* (2001); *Better than Chocolate* (1999) was marketed as 'a lesbian *Midsummer Night's Dream*')
Gay (*Were the World Mine* (2008) clearly referencing the *Dream*)
Cult (Jarman's *The Tempest* (1979) and his *Angelic Conversation* (1985), based on the Sonnets)
Avant-Garde (Coronados's *Hamlet* (1976) and his *A Midsummer Night's Dream* (1985))
Sports Films (arguably the most unlikely genre in Dirks's list, covered by *O*, the basketballing version of *Othello* (2001), and versions of *Twelfth Night* including *She's the Man* (2006) and its Indian remake set in the cricketing world, *Dil Bole Hadippa!* (2009))

There are of course any number grouped under family, drama, classics, biography, nostalgia, festival, specific national outputs (or just world), or some others that come to mind. Contemplating such a list, most critics who write on Shakespeare movies would conclude that the play is grafted on to a pre-existing movie genre (and probably this is how directors work in practice),[68] but I entertain the other possibility that the apparent ease with which Shakespeare can be adapted in this way is partly explained by the fact that his plays have had some part in the creation of these movie genres.

The list above reveals problems about genre theory itself. For example, the groupings are not all along the same line of abstraction. Some are derived from literature (comedy, drama, fantasy, romance), some refer to a setting (western, road) or subject matter (war, sports, disaster, supernatural), others are predicated on the recurrence of certain empirical elements (musicals), still others target an audience (children's, lesbian, gay), others refer to affectiveness and emotions aroused in audiences (melodrama sometimes known as 'weepies', erotic, thrillers, horror), and so on. Viewed from a distance, such lists begin to resemble the well-known, apparently arbitrary classificatory system of animals offered by Borges from 'a certain Chinese Encyclopedia', *The Celestial Emporium of Benevolent Knowledge*. Secondly, we immediately realise that many actual films can be grouped under two or more headings, and that potentially all films are hybrid in genre.[69] Bollywood is not alone in creating movies that consciously draw on many of the groups (though its eclecticism was inherited from Parsi popular entertainment rather than Western sources). This suits the Shakespeare industry, as Carolyn Jess-Cooke has suggested, since even apparently orthodox Shakespearean film adaptations do more than simply representing the original play. Instead they negotiate 'prior conceptions' of the play across 'historical periods and media' (and genres, we might add). They demonstrate that 'adaptation is both a collaborative and hybrid exercise, often involving the superimposition of a number of texts … Adaptation theory invariably visits the idea of textual transposition'.[70] However, the main point to note at this stage is not that the allusive frameworks offered by genres should be more self-consistent, nor that Shakespeare 'invented' such genres, but that his plays have been shaped to fit these diverse groups. Since there are so many of them, I feel licensed in quixotically adding more, based on the influence of individual plays by Shakespeare. The primary aim, though, is not to proliferate categories nor seriously suggest we need new ones, but rather to uncover a strand in the historical creation of genres that has escaped close attention – the Shakespearean precedents.

Writers for the screen

Other reasons help to account for the ubiquitous presence of Shakespeare in cinema history. The educational system in different countries favoured and created an iconic status for his texts and created definable audiences, before and during the period of the rise of the film industry. The Newbolt Report of 1921 is a cornerstone of postcolonial theory, used to explain the conspicuous dominance of Shakespeare's works (among other English classics) in schools and universities, not only in Britain but also in its current and former colonies like India and the United States, two countries that quickly established themselves as powerhouses in the development of cinema.[71] In the United States especially, one of the most numerous catchment areas for movies lies among college students, most of whom can be relied on to study Shakespeare and to recognise without prompting the dominant markers of his most celebrated plays.[72] In addition, and for different reasons dating further back in history and hinging on reception by national writers in different cultures, the Shakespearean presence entered countries that had never been under British rule. Germany's most famous literary figures in the Romantic period, Goethe and Schlegel, virtually appropriated him as part of their own national identity, the former through his translations and literary influence, the latter through his criticism and scholarship. Following their lead, Shakespeare's plays steadily became absorbed into the national theatrical repertoires. *Hamlet* was the flagship play – '*Deutschland ist Hamlet*' ('Germany is Hamlet') famously proclaimed the poet Ferdinand Freiligrath in 1844.[73] In the early twentieth century, *A Midsummer Night's Dream*, with its potential for surrealistic effects, influenced the Middle-European generation of Max Reinhardt who re-created the play on film in its tonal complexity, with effects of visual strangeness and magical realism.[74] In Japan, Shakespeare's drama infiltrated more local theatrical traditions such as *Noh* and *Kabuki*,[75] and fed into Japanese films through Akira Kurosawa's example. Reasons for this process of cultural appropriation have been called 'an excruciatingly complicated and yet exceptionally enticing question',[76] whose answer lies in the work of a series of distinguished scholar-translators, from Tsibouchi Shoyo (1859–1935), who was himself a novelist, playwright, and critic. Shoyo and others recognised that 'there are various technical respects in which Shakespearean poetic drama is closer to traditional Japanese drama like Noh or Kabuki than it is to modern western realism'.[77] In Russia the story may have been complicated by the hostility of Tolstoy and later Stalin,[78] but the translation of eight plays and the Sonnets by Boris Pasternak cemented the presence there, to the extent that the most prominent film-maker, Grigori Kotsintsev, after his early and radical saturation of these plays in his theatrical training, felt confident enough to make magnificent Russian versions of *Hamlet* and *King Lear*. Poland, another great film-making nation, had accepted Hamlet as politically 'the Polish Prince' in the nineteenth century, and the broader appreciation of Shakespeare persisted through communist and democratic regimes alike, down to the publication of Jan Kott's book, *Shakespeare Our Contemporary*, which was enormously influential in its own right beyond Poland.[79] In the light of processes such as these, and related national assimilations of Shakespeare into colonial and non-colonial countries, it is not at all surprising to detect his presence at every level of the increasingly international and popular industry of film-making. Shakespeare became a recurrent reference point for plots, themes, and character types, and his plays also deeply influenced the national film styles. His plays provided a set of globally recognised generic patterns. The one country that to some extent resisted was France, under the influence of its own centuries-old antagonism to its island neighbour across the Channel, and also enshrining the generally negative views of Shakespeare held by some of its own revered writers. Voltaire, for example, regarded *Hamlet* as 'monstrous', and Molière preferred to represent French contemporary society and issues, rather than looking to the past or to England for his sources and material. Besides, he thought he could do better than the English master of comedy. As a result, it might be argued, the whole ethos of French cinema is distinctively different from that of other major film-making nations, partly because it developed without the central influence of Shakespeare's plays.

More subtly than educational, literary, and theatrical processes, there may be an extra and all-important reason for a sometimes stealthy and indirect infiltration of Shakespeare into box-office films, especially in Hollywood. The mediators between the old and the new are the endless ranks of professional screenwriters, who unobtrusively underpin all aspects of the industry, and to them Shakespeare as a writer is their great antecedent and mentor, self-evidently the most successful writer for popular entertainment who has ever lived. Journeymen screenwriters rarely achieve the fame of their literary equivalents whose books appear under their own names, and they usually come to public attention only when something goes wrong, such as the anti-communist witch-hunts in 1950s Hollywood. The strike of the Writers Guild of America in 2007–8 crippled the whole movie industry in the United States and made their importance plain to all. More often, they are simply ignored or neglected as individuals, and their contributions to film-making are taken for granted, both by the industry and by film theorists, whose main concentration is upon the image rather than the word. Confirmation came from a screenwriter who gave Groucho Marx many of his best lines. The obituary of Irving Brecher reports:

> During the Writers Guild of America strike of 2007, he made a video in which he urged the writers not to settle. 'Since 1938, when I joined what was then the Radio Writers Guild, I have been waiting for the writers to get a fair deal. I'm still waiting. As Chester A Riley would have said, "What a revoltin' development this is!" But he only said it because I wrote it.'[80]

Another who puts the case is John Logan in his BAFTA and BFI Screenwriters' Lecture in 2011: 'There is a notion that what cinema is, is pictures, sweet and nuanced visual storytelling, it certainly is that. But it is also language, it is also characters expressing themselves through dialogue, and dialogue has become so devalued in movies. I want speeches, I want language, tripping language, I want nuance.'[81] The one area that might be an exception, the auteur movie, seems, on the contrary, to prove the rule, since in this case it is the directorial role that is considered that of an author, and the writing is once again subsumed beneath the filmic concerns of creating visual illusions and effects. It is significant that one of the greatest auteurs of all, Orson Welles, was steeped in Shakespeare and his films show their deep influence in all aspects of genre, language, and imagery.

In terms of the unsung, backroom screenwriters, times may not have changed all that much in four hundred years of performance practice. One of the most learned scholars of Elizabethan drama, G. K. Hunter, has pointed this out in a rare foray into film studies:

> What about the role of the writers, those inborn élitists? The Elizabethan system, like the Hollywood one, put them at the bottom of the status pile, for if the actors were dependent on the owner, the writers in their turn were dependent on the actors, who approved the flat fee for a script written to their standards. In consequence the writer had no share in the ballooning success of a great hit, and so had no great investment in team loyalty ... At the beginning of mature drama in the 1580s and 1590s we find an inevitable clash between the humanist dream of eloquence as a passport into the élite and the reality that the money extracted from an undifferentiated public was the only money available. These writers started by supposing that the artisans of acting would be bowled over by the condescension of their betters, and were disgusted to discover that this was not the case.[82]

Shakespeare himself became an exception since he was not only a writer but an actor and sharer in the companies he worked for, but, as Hunter points out, other journeymen writers like Robert Greene were more representative of the unsung scriptwriters and more equivalent to

Hollywood's, sometimes resentful at their lack of recognition when, as Robert Greene complained, players were seen to 'get by scholars their whole living'.[83] Indigent Cambridge scholars in particular offered their services to write plays for the Elizabethan stage, in some desperation to earn meagre wages. Hunter concludes:

> when we look at the accounts of Faulkner's, Fitzgerald's, or Nathaniel West's film-writing careers, we see the same sense of self-betrayal as Greene displays. From their point of view, Hollywood is run by 'uncultured' persons who cannot appreciate good writing when they see it, who hire mere hacks to rewrite the master's prose in a form more suitable for their vulgar purposes.[84]

Books have been written about the process of adapting novels into movies, but invariably the centre of attention is the textual source (whether from 'classics' like Dickens, Austen, Tolstoy or 'popular' texts by Chandler, Spillane, Fleming), and not the screenwriter's contribution. Even the most thorough study, *The Encyclopedia of Novels into Movies*, gives little or no information about the latter, leaping from source text to finished movie without considering in any depth the intermediary role of screenwriting.[85] My interest here is fleeting rather than systematic, since it is their general involvement in the process of making a movie to fit a popular genre that matters to my argument, not their individual quirks, output, and styles.

Most screenwriters, as professionals, bring to their jobs a knowledge of earlier literature, and aspirations to match it. They usually have some training in an appropriate field of writing and experience of reading, often as journalists, dramatists, budding creative writers, students, or occasionally as teachers of literature. Although it is difficult to ascertain through statistics, scriptwriters can all be assumed to be reasonably well-read and and to have tertiary experience of classical drama and literature. Writers for films understandably use their literary knowledge whenever they can get away with it, often 'smuggling' it into the scripts they write, and with incongruous results. *Body and Soul* (1947), a film noir about a boxer, is an unexpected place to find William Blake's poem beginning 'Tiger, Tiger, burning bright' quoted and requoted as a leitmotif. It was unlikely to have been the choice of either the director or the producing company (Enterprise, later MGM), given the lowly status of such B-movies, but that of the writer alone. In this case it was Abraham Lincoln Polonsky, and his background is instructive. Polonsky also wrote and directed *Force of Evil* (1948) (not to be confused with Welles's *Touch of Evil*), but when he came to write in the 1950s he had to use a pseudonym, since as a self-confessed Marxist and member

Introduction 29

of the Communist Party he was targeted and blacklisted by the House Un-American Activities Committee. Polonsky had studied English at the City College of New York, and after a brief time in the merchant navy he graduated from Columbia Law School and practised as an attorney, before writing for movies. Later still he was a union organiser. He also wrote several novels. When MGM took over stock from the bankrupt Enterprise Studios, Louis B. Mayer dropped *Body and Soul* from their list, no doubt because of its overt criticism of capitalism but also perhaps partly because Polonsky's Blakean references (if they were consciously noticed) may have been regarded as a little highbrow for the vehicle. To this day, the University of California Riverside offers a prize for fiction named after Polonsky. His career may not have been so inconspicuous as those of many thousands who have written for movies, but it is probably not untypical in its close connection with literature.

Watching *The Simpsons*, with its dense network of literary, political, and cultural references, convinces one that nowadays the large fleet of backroom writers are likely to be literature graduates from universities, hoping to augment their income or even earn a living. Nobody *but* such a person could have added this, for example, to episode 15 of series 15, *Co-Dependants' Day*. Moe the barman serves the newly alcoholic Marge and her more frequently bibulous husband Homer with wine rather than the more expected Duff beer:

> MOE All I got's this old stuff here. Chateau Latour 1886. Ah I should just throw this out.
> MARGE No, it'll have to do. [*He pours, they drink from wine glasses*]
> MOE That'll be four bucks. Now in a step I perhaps should have taken initially, let me look up the value of that bottle in this wine collectors' guide here [*reads*] ... Oh what have I done? Oh, let me dry my tears on this lost Shakespeare play [*sobs and crunches volume clearly named The Two Noble Kinsmen by William Shakespeare*]

The Two Noble Kinsmen is not entirely by Shakespeare since he collaborated with John Fletcher, and it may not be 'lost', but it is certainly one of Shakespeare's least well-known plays, and the reference suggests a student of literature wrote the lines in *The Simpsons*. More evidence of journeymen screenwriters' saturation at least in *Hamlet* comes from the cult science fiction television series *Star Trek*, where we find among titles of episodes Shakespearean quotations such as *The Undiscovered Country*, *The Conscience of the King*, *Thine Own Self*, *Remember Me*, and *Mortal Coil*. More accidentally, we find *Measure for Measure* as the title of a film in a series about 'Guns of the Civil War'. And even *Star Wars* is full of quotations. *Doctor Who* in 2007 built an episode called

'The Shakespeare Code' around the Doctor returning to Shakespeare's England and exercising a decisive influence on the plays to come. Not only is this another example where many of the allusions, and the general temporal enigmas explored, could not have occurred without the input of an informed writer, but it also shows the deep imbrication of Shakespeare in popular culture of the twentieth century and beyond.

Of course Shakespeare is not the only reference point for these sometimes gratuitous writers' intrusions. In the film noir *The Big Sleep* (1946), we find this rather extraneous piece of 'comic relief' when the hero emerges from the bedroom:

> BACALL So you do get up. I was beginning to think perhaps you worked in bed like Marcel Proust.
> BOGART Who's he?
> BACALL You wouldn't know him. A French writer.
> BOGART Come into my boudoir.

Writers can mischievously insert pointed references to their own enforced effacement, and even sly jokes at their own expense. Whether or not philistine movie moguls controlling the industry know or care, the writers at the bottom are often keen to display their erudition in scripts. This exchange comes in *Eyes in the Night* (1942), again a minor B-movie in the noir genre, depicting a blind detective, 'Mac', who has a guide dog called Friday:

> BUTLER Are you blind?
> MAC Blind as a bat.
> BUTLER Oh I'm sorry.
> MAC Why? Milton and Homer were blind, weren't they?
> BUTLER Yes sir, but they complained about it.
> MAC Oh, they did?
> BUTLER Yes sir. 'Oh loss of sight of thee I most complain. Blind among enemies. Oh worse than chains, dungeons, beggary or decrepit age.'
> MAC [*chuckles*] Milton, eh? ... Don't stand around spouting poetry ...

The digressive quotation from Milton's *Samson Agonistes* in this dialogue between a 'hard-boiled' detective and a butler draws attention to the writer's role within films, while obliquely suggesting viewers are 'blind' to their contribution. Other Hollywood writers conspicuously lament their 'invisibility' in the system. Billy Wilder in particular, when he came to be a director, did not forget the writer's plight:

> Billy Wilder's characters are frequently trapped in language, creatures of words ... Many work with words for a living: the writers (or in two cases songwriters and a film producer) of *The Lost Weekend*, *Sunset Boulevard*,

Ace in the Hole, *Kiss Me Stupid*, *The Front Page* and *Fedora* all struggle to complete just one more project.[86]

Sunset Boulevard (1945) shows the screenwriter as a professional with lofty literary judgement and aspirations, trapped in a system that requires slavish mediocrity to fashion and obeisance to 'stars',[87] while *The Lost Weekend* (1950) focuses on an alcoholic and bankrupt writer experiencing the professional hazard of writer's block. Both films use Shakespearean quotations in contexts of nostalgic envy, quietly bemoaning or celebrating the position of creative writers in an intertextual tradition lying behind movies. The frustrations of writers in the film-making process are revealed in the number of movies that place such a self-referential or orphic character at the centre of the plot – *Paris When It Sizzles* (1964) and *Breakfast at Tiffany's* (1961) being a couple of the obvious examples, while in *The Last Time I Saw Paris* (1954), significantly based on a short story by F. Scott Fitzgerald, the central character is yet another frustrated, alcoholic novelist. Within the Hollywood system, Paul Dehn, who wrote several of the James Bond films and also *Planet of the Apes*, adapted both *The Taming of the Shrew* and *Macbeth*, demonstrating original insights especially into the latter. Ever since Merchant Ivory's *Shakespeare Wallah* (1965), many films from the Indian subcontinent have liberally quoted from Shakespeare in the oddest places: the apparent decline of his cultural influence is lamented in Deepa Mehta's *Bollywood/Hollywood* (2002) by the elderly grandmother.

Few cinema commentators even mention, let alone analyse, the position of the writer or that person's educational background, and invariably the concentration lies on directors, who often deliberately obscure the writer's contribution in order to aggrandise their own role. The writers sometimes hit back. In the middle of an inadvertently comic film from 1936, *Murder with Pictures*, where a murder is detected through press photographers taking 'pictures', we hear the startling lines,

– Shakespeare's wearing your hat.
– If you'd been wearing it, you'd be dead.

The camera pans to reveal a bust of Shakespeare on which a casually placed hat now has a bullet hole through it. Once again, there is a sardonic, almost coded writer's comment here, suggesting that if Shakespeare were a contemporary screenwriter, he would be just as neglected and his words as mangled as any of the others. Exactly this point is made in the very weird *Witch Hunt*, made in 1993 but set in 1953, satirising McCarthy's Hollywood 'witch-hunts' from the point of view of film noir writers. Shakespeare in person is resurrected from the grave as a sycophantic screenwriter, his words from *Macbeth* are shamelessly plagiarised. Among other things, it is a reference to the adversities suffered through history of writers for the screen, linking them up with their great exemplar, Shakespeare. Similar sentiments were expressed by the German/Danish Douglas Sirk, a director rather than a writer, but a man highly educated in three different universities. He directed *Magnificent Obsession* (1954) and *All That Heaven Allows* (1955) for Universal-International Pictures, and his comments indicate not only the same kinds of partially concealed conflict between the studios and the actual makers of films, but also between a literary education and popular art:

> As a theater man, I had to deal with high art. I would play farces and comedy to make money, and classics for the elite. But we were trying to escape the *elitaire*. So slowly in my mind formed the idea of melodrama, a form I found to perfection in American pictures. They were naive, they were that something completely different. They were completely Art-less. This tied in with my studies of the Elizabethan period, where you had both *l'art pour l'art* and you had Shakespeare. He was a melodramatist, infusing all those silly melodramas with style, with signs and meanings. There is a tremendous similarity between this and the Hollywood system – which then I knew from only far away. Shakespeare had to be a commercial producer. Probably his company or his producer came to him and said, 'Now, look, Bill, there's this crazy story – ghosts, murder, tearing the hair, what-do-I-know. Completely crazy. It's called Magnificent Ob... no, *Hamlet* it was called. The audiences love this story, Bill, and you have to rewrite it. You've got two weeks, and you've got to hold the costs down. They'll love it again.' So, my God! A director in Hollywood in my time couldn't do what he wanted to do. But certainly, Shakespeare was even less free than we were.[88]

The suggestion behind Sirk's comments is that such tensions between art and commerce can be creative and can also lead to novel uses of the material garnered from studying Shakespeare, in this case connections made between Shakespeare's works and cinematic melodrama.

Finally, in focusing specifically on works dealing with love, I have in mind a broader aim than simply establishing a scholarly line of influence leading from an early modern dramatist to modern movies. For over a century, cinema, as the most internationally popular and accessible art form dealing with emotions, has shaped our attitudes to love, our ways of conceptualising and possibly even of 'feeling' its many-splendoured powers. Meanwhile, in the three hundred years before the invention of cinema, this kind of psychological and cultural power had been exerted by Shakespeare as the dominant popular writer of all time and in virtually every country in the world. His unique brand of romantic comedy, allied with the genre of romantic tragedy in *Romeo and Juliet*, have provided the Western world (and beyond) with a set of dominant assumptions about what love is and how it operates. Linking up the two forces, Shakespeare and movies, reveals an irresistible influence over our own emotional lives and the ways in which we construct our narratives of love. It will be a refrain I shall repeat with differences in this book that Shakespeare rarely, if ever, uses characteristics of genre as 'mere' conventions, but rather he constantly invests them with the kinds of emotional significances and justifications that give them a human dimension, shedding light and providing a language through which to understand and articulate our own experiences. Nowhere is this more evident than in the most conspicuously artificial and superficially fictional genre attributes of romantic comedy and romantic tragedy, such as expectations of happiness or disaster, the proximity of music and love, ways in which love is a negotiation between strong characters in initial conflict, disguise and mistaken identity as ways to explore love relationships, and so on. The genres he more or less created, by fusing elements of different kinds such as romance, comedy, and tragedy, have found their way into our own tacitly held narratives of love that we use to shape our emotional expectations and interpretations. Shakespeare helped to prioritise some paradigms of love in his comedies, tragedies, and romances, each of which was, at some times brazenly and at others surreptitiously, absorbed into movies, which in their turn have contributed to our own convenient fictions and living attitudes to love.

Notes

1 Deborah Cartmell and Imelda Whelehan, *Screen Adaptation: Impure Cinema* (London: Palgrave Macmillan, 2010), 86.
2 Sergei Eisenstein, 'Dickens, Griffith, and Ourselves' (alternatively titled 'Dickens, Griffith, and Film Today'), in *Film Form* (1942). There are various different translations of this passage available, and here I use the words in Leo Braudy and Marshall Cohen (eds), *Film Theory and Criticism* (New York: Oxford University Press, 2004 [1974]), 444.
3 Allardyce Nicoll, *Film and Theatre* (London: George G. Harrap, 1936), 18.
4 Cartmell and Whelehan, *Screen Adaptation*, 86.
5 Douglas Lanier, '"I'll Teach You Differences": Genre, Literacy, Critical Pedagogy, and Screen Shakespeare', in Anthony R. Guneratne (ed.), *Shakespeare and Genre: From Early Modern Inheritances to Postmodern Legacies* (London: Palgrave Macmillan, 2012), 257–70.
6 Richard Burt (ed.), *Shakespeares after Shakespeare: An Encyclopedia of the Bard in Mass Media and Popular Culture*, 2 vols (Westport, CT and London: Greenwood Press, 2007).

7 Timothy Corrigan, *Film and Literature: An Introduction and Reader* (Upper Saddle River, NJ: Prentice Hall, 1989), 93.
8 The critic most interested in this process is H. R. Coursen: see, in particular, *Shakespeare Translated: Derivatives on Film and TV* (New York: Peter Lang, 2005).
9 The word is used by Anthony R. Guneratne in *Shakespeare, Film Studies, and the Visual Cultures of Modernity* (London: Palgrave Macmillan, 2008). See also the essays by diverse writers in Guneratne's edited collection, *Shakespeare and Genre: From Early Modern Inheritances to Postmodern Legacies* (London: Palgrave Macmillan, 2012).
10 Cartmell and Whelehan, *Screen Adaptation*, 23.
11 Jacques Derrida, *Specters of Marx: The State of the Debt, the Work of Mourning, and the New International*, transl. Peggy Kamuf (London: Routledge, 1994).
12 Harold Bloom, *The Anxiety of Influence: A Theory of Poetry* (New York: Oxford University Press, 1973).
13 Robert A. Logan, *The Influence of Christopher Marlowe on Shakespeare's Artistry* (Aldershot: Ashgate, 2006), 9.
14 Logan quotes this phrase in turn from Stephen J. Lynch, *Shakespearean Intertextuality: Studies in Selected Plays and Sources* (Westport, CT: Greenwood Press, 1998), 1.
15 Logan, *The Influence of Christopher Marlowe on Shakespeare's Artistry*, 17.
16 Logan, *The Influence of Christopher Marlowe on Shakespeare's Artistry*, 13.
17 Porscha Fermanis, *John Keats and the Ideas of the Enlightenment* (Edinburgh: Edinburgh University Press, 2009), 12. See also David Spadafora, *The Idea of Progress in Eighteenth-Century Britain* (New Haven, CT: Yale University Press, 1990), 388.
18 See, for example, Penelope Joan Fritzer, *Jane Austen and Eighteenth-Century Courtesy Books* (Westport, CT: Greenwood Press, 1997).
19 The argument is followed up by Lisa Hopkins in *Relocating Shakespeare and Austen on Screen* (London: Palgrave Macmillan, 2009); and see Linda Troost and Sayre Greenfield (eds), *Jane Austen in Hollywood*, 2nd edn (Lexington: University of Kentucky Press, 2001). See also Cartmell and Whelehan, *Screen Adaptation*, ch. 6.
20 Boris Pasternak, 'From "Notes of a Translator"', in Carl J. Proffer (ed.), *Modern Russian Poets on Poetry* (Ann Arbor, MI: Ardis, 1976).
21 Stephanie Trigg, 'Transparent Walls: Stained Glass and Cinematic Medievalism', *Screening the Past*, 26 (2009). Online: www.latrobe.edu.au/screeningthepast/26/early-europe/stained-glass-cinematic-medievalism.html.
22 Logan, *The Influence of Christopher Marlowe on Shakespeare's Artistry*, 12.
23 Judith Buchanan, *Shakespeare on Film* (Harlow: Pearson Longman, 2005), 3–5.
24 Guneratne, *Shakespeare, Film Studies*, 43–4.
25 Stanley Cavell, *Pursuits of Happiness: The Hollywood Comedy of Remarriage* (Cambridge, MA: Harvard University Press, 1981).

26 Cavell, *Pursuits of Happiness*, 20.
27 Stanley Cavell, *Cavell on Film*, ed. by William Rothman (New York: State University of New York Press, 2005), 306, 96.
28 See also another critic who takes similar confidence from Cavell's approach, Leland Poague, 'Cavell and the Fantasy of Criticism: Shakespearean Comedy and *Ball of Fire*', *CineAction*, 9 (Summer 1987), 47–55.
29 Stanley Cavell, *Contesting Tears: The Hollywood Melodrama of the Unknown Woman* (Chicago: University of Chicago Press, 1996).
30 Harry Keyishian, 'Shakespeare and Movie Genre: The Case of *Hamlet*', in Russell Jackson (ed.), *The Cambridge Companion to Shakespeare on Film* (Cambridge: Cambridge University Press, 2000), 72–84.
31 Tony Howard, 'Shakespeare's Cinematic Offshoots', in Russell Jackson (ed.), *The Cambridge Companion to Shakespeare on Film* (Cambridge: Cambridge University Press, 2000), 295–313, 295.
32 Robert Hamilton Ball, *Shakespeare on Silent Film: A Strange Eventful History* (London: Allen & Unwin, 1968), 36–7.
33 Carolyn Jess-Cooke, *Shakespeare on Film: Such Things as Dreams Are Made of* (London: Wallflower Press, 2007), 33, quoting from Edward Said, 'On Originality', in *The World, the Text, and the Critic* (Cambridge, MA: Harvard University Press, 1983), 135.
34 Douglas Lanier, 'William Shakespeare, Filmmaker' in Deborah Cartmell and Imelda Whelehan (eds), *The Cambridge Companion to Literature on Screen* (Cambridge: Cambridge University Press, 2007), 61–74, 63.
35 Douglas Lanier, 'Shakespearean Rhizomatics', in Alexa Huang and Elizabeth Rivlin (eds), *Adaptation, Ethics, Value* (London: Palgrave Macmillan, 2014), 21–40, 28.
36 Rick Altman, *Film/Genre* (London: British Film Institute), ch. 6.
37 Samuel Crowl, *Shakespeare and Film: A Norton Guide* (New York: W. W. Norton & Co., 2008), 155.
38 Lanier, 'Shakespearean Rhizomatics', 23.
39 Thomas Cartelli and Katherine Rowe, *New Wave Shakespeare on Screen* (Cambridge: Polity Press, 2007), 26, 29.
40 Steve Neale, *Genre and Hollywood* (London and New York: Routledge, 2000), 213.
41 For a general account, see Rosalie Colie, *The Resources of Kind: Genre-Theory in the Renaissance* (Berkeley: University of California Press, 1973).
42 Sir Philip Sidney, *A Defence of Poetry*, in Katherine Duncan-Jones and Jan van Dorsten (eds), *Miscellaneous Prose of Sir Philip Sidney* (Oxford: Oxford University Press, 1973), 114.
43 Adrienne L. Eastwood, 'Between Wedding and Bedding: The Epithalamic Sub-Genre in Shakespeare's Comedies', *Exemplaria*, 22 (2010), 240–62.
44 Barry Keith Grant, *Film Genre: From Iconography to Ideology* (London: Wallflower Press, 2007), 1.
45 See Neale, *Genre and Hollywood*, 255.
46 See Neale, *Genre and Hollywood*, 246 ff.

47 Neale, *Genre and Hollywood*, 252.
48 www.encyclopedia.com/topic/sediment.aspx.
49 See Cartmell and Whelehan, *Screen Adaptation*, 89–90.
50 The most recent account of silent Shakespeare films is by Judith Buchanan, *Shakespeare on Silent Film: An Excellent Dumb Discourse* (Cambridge: Cambridge University Press, 2009).
51 Kenneth S. Rothwell, *Early Shakespeare Movies: How the Spurned Spawned Art* (Chipping Campden: International Shakespeare Association, Occasional paper no. 8, 2000).
52 See Eddie Sammons, *Shakespeare: A Hundred Years on Film* (London: Shepheard-Walwyn, 2000), 62. The extract can be viewed on the videotape *Silent Shakespeare* (British Film Institute).
53 See Ball, *Shakespeare on Silent Film*.
54 See Prakash Younger, 'Film as Art', in William Guyon (ed.), *The Routledge Companion to Film History* (London: Routledge, 2011), ch. 3.
55 Rothwell, *Early Shakespeare Movies*, referring to David A. Cook, *A History of Narrative Film* (New York: Norton, 1996), 51.
56 Issued on videotape by Kino Video (New York, 2001), restored by the American Film Institute.
57 See Hilary Radner, 'Film as Popular Culture', in William Guyon (ed.), *The Routledge Companion to Film History* (London: Routledge, 2011), 16. On the larger issues of the culture debates in film history, see Patrick Brantlinger, *Bread and Circuses: Theories of Mass Culture as Social Decay* (Ithaca, NY: Cornell University Press, 1983); and, of course, the classic essay by Walter Benjamin, 'The Work of Art in the Age of Mechanical Reproduction' (1936), in *Illuminations: Essays and Reflections*, ed. Hannah Arendt, transl. Harry Zohn (New York: Schocken Books, 1968).
58 Michael Channan, *The Dream That Kicks: The Prehistory and Early Years of Cinema in Britain* (London and New York: Routledge, 1996), 34–5.
59 Radner, 'Film as Popular Culture', 17.
60 Raphaëlle Moine, *Cinema Genre*, transl. Alistair Fox and Hilary Radner (Oxford: Blackwell Publishing, 2008), 2.
61 John Frow, *Genre* (London: Routledge, 2006).
62 Vera Dika, *Recycled Culture in Contemporary Art and Film: The Uses of Nostalgia* (Cambridge: Cambridge University Press, 2003).
63 Mark Thornton Burnett and Ramona Wray (ed.), *Shakespeare, Film, Fin de Siècle* (London: Palgrave, 2000); Susan Bennett, *Performing Shakespeare: Shifting Shakespeare and the Contemporary Past* (London: Routledge, 1996).
64 Barry Langford, *Film Genre: Hollywood and Beyond* (Edinburgh: Edinburgh University Press, 2005).
65 Paul Coates, *Film at the Intersection of High and Mass Culture* (Cambridge: Cambridge University Press, 1994).
66 Kenneth S. Rothwell, *A History of Shakespeare on Screen: A Century of Film and Television* (Cambridge: Cambridge University Press, 1999), ch. 1 *passim*.

67 Tim Dirks, 'Film Genres: Origins and Types'. Online: www.filmsite.org (accessed 5 March 2009).
68 See, for example, Maurice Hindle, *Studying Shakespeare on Film* (London: Palgrave Macmillan, 2007), 88–90.
69 Ira Jaffe, *Hollywood Hybrids: Mixing Genres in Contemporary Films* (Lanham, MD: Rowman & Littlefield, 2008).
70 Jess-Cooke, *Shakespeare on Film*, 53.
71 See, for example, Ania Loomba, *Shakespeare, Race, and Colonialism* (Oxford: Oxford University Press, 2002); Barrie Wade and John Shepherd, 'Shakespeare in the Curriculum: Direction by Content' (dealing with the Newbolt Report), *Educational Studies*, 19 (1993), 267–74.
72 For the many and ambiguous factors lying behind the saturation reception of Shakespeare in the United States, see Michael D. Bristol, *Shakespeare's America, America's Shakespeare* (London: Routledge, 1990), although Bristol's argument is perhaps lacking in not taking into account the cinematic contribution from Hollywood.
73 See Manfred Pfister, 'Germany Is Hamlet: The History of a Political Interpretation', *New Comparison: A Journal of Comparative and General Literary Studies*, 2 (Autumn 1986), 106–26.
74 See Jack J. Jorgens's analysis of Reinhardt's *Dream* in *Shakespeare on Film* (Lanham, MD: University Press of America, 1991), ch. 2.
75 See Kuniyoshi Munakata, *'Hamlet' Noh Style: Collected Versions 1982–1990* (Tokyo: Kenkyusha, 1991).
76 See Tetsuo Kishi, *Shakespeare in Japan* (London: Continuum, 2005), preface.
77 Kishi, *Shakespeare in Japan*, ch. 1.
78 See Leo Tolstoy, *On Shakespeare and on Drama*, transl. V. Tchertkoff (New York: Funk & Wagnalls Company, 1906 [1903]); Eleanor Rowe, *Hamlet: A Window on Russia* (New York: New York University Press, 1976).
79 Jan Kott, *Shakespeare Our Contemporary* (London: Methuen, 1965); Krystyna Kujawińska-Courtney, 'From Kott to Commerce: Shakespeare in Communist and Post-Communist Poland', in Krystyna Kujawińska-Courtney and R. S. White (eds), *Shakespeare's Local Habitations* (Łódź: Łódź University Press, 2007), 13–33.
80 Ronald Bergan, 'Obituary: Irving Brecher', *Guardian*, 12 March 2009.
81 Available to British viewers through the British Film Institute website, and otherwise there are some excerpts (including the section quoted) on YouTube: www.youtube.com/watch?v=jm0TN2fqTMs (accessed 7 June 2015).
82 G. K. Hunter, 'The Making of a Popular Repertory: Hollywood and the Elizabethans', in John Batchelor, Tom Cain, and Claire Lamont (eds), *Shakespearean Continuities: Essays in Honour of E. A. J. Honigmann* (Basingstoke: Macmillan Press, 1997), 247–58, 249–50.
83 Robert Greene, *Greene's Groatsworth of Wit* (1592), quoted in Hunter, 'The Making of a Popular Repertory', 250.
84 Hunter, 'The Making of a Popular Repertory', 250.

85 John C. Tibbetts and James M. Welsh (eds), *The Encyclopedia of Novels into Movies* (New York: Facts on File Inc., 1998).
86 Gregg Rickman (ed.), *The Film Comedy Reader* (New York: Limelight Editions, 2001), 237.
87 See Daniel Brown, 'Wilde and Wilder', *PMLA*, 119.5 (2004), 1216–30.
88 'Two Weeks in Another Town', Interview with Douglas Sirk, *Bright Lights Film Journal*, 6 (1977), now available online: www.brightlightsfilm.com/48/sirkinterview.php.

1

'Madly mated': *The Taming of the Shrew* and odd-couple comedy

There are enough movie versions of *The Taming of the Shrew* to show that its plot played a vigorous role in film history from the early days, and therefore it is not debatable as a Shakespearean contribution to cinema genres. One way or another, in immediately recognisable versions or forcibly adapted, in English or another language, *The Taming of the Shrew* has in its own right been filmed anew in virtually every year of the medium's history.[1] This is actually quite odd, since it is one play that appears to be unredeemably Elizabethan, its reliance on patriarchy and domestic violence apparently beyond the pale even to earlier decades in the twentieth century. It seems to come from an earlier, less enlightened tradition than the kind of romantic comedy perfected by Shakespeare under Elizabeth I in the 1590s. As Diana E. Henderson writes, 'Of all Shakespeare's comedies, *The Taming of the Shrew* most overtly reinforces the social hierarchies of its day', having 'an anachronistic plot premised on the sale of women' that would seem to disqualify it from modern consumption.[2] And yet the play has been constantly played on the stage and filmed, for different social purposes, which even include revealing progressive possibilities. At times it is used to reinforce sexist views, while at others the film versions have sought to present the conflict between Petruccio and Katherina as a battle of the sexes with no winner, and occasionally they even turn it into a feminist statement of equality.[3] Films always reflect the concerns of the decade and culture in which they are made, and *Shrew* revivals can, for example, focus on issues of domesticity when this becomes a national priority (as in the 1950s), or on the more unruly and subversive nature of 'gender wars' in libertarian generations. In her chapter, Henderson summarises the cultural agendas that lie behind particular versions, and we shall see some of them at work in this chapter.

Right from the silent days, Shakespeare's play with its own name has been filmed: in 1908, 1923, 1929, 1966 (restored version of the 1929 one), 1967, and 1999. Non-English versions have appeared in Italy

(1908, 1913, 1942, 1980, 2004 in animation), France (1911), Germany (1919/20, 1930, 1943, 1955, 1962), India (1932, 1955), Hungary (1943), Mexico (1946, 1947, 1949, 1953), Spain (1955), Russia (1960), and no doubt many others, while the United States has kept pace with Britain for the play in English. The number of television versions (1939, 1956, 1973, 1975, 1976, 1980, 1983, 1988, 1993, 2003 (as *The Shrew in the Park*)) reflects the underlying closeness of Shakespeare's plot to television family 'sitcoms', where husbands and wives are conventionally expected to fight each other as much as they make up. A single adaptation could have a significant afterlife. Cole Porter's musical *Kiss Me, Kate* first played on Broadway in 1948 and ran in different theatres for over 1,000 performances from the 1970s until the twenty-first century. The original 1948 Broadway stage version was filmed in 1953 and later in television adaptations. Picking up the pun used in a nineteenth-century stage performance by J. A. Sterry, *Katherine and Petruccio, or The Shaming of the True*, various twists on the acknowledged plot reveal themselves in titles such as *The Cowboy and the Shrew* (1911), where the woman is presumably likened to a horse to be lassoed into submission, *The Framing of the Shrew* (1929, with a black cast), and *He Flew the Shrew* (1951). Several other Westerns based on Shakespeare's play have recently been traced and closely analysed by Elinor Parsons, alongside other 'reframings'.[4] *10 Things I Hate About You* appeared in 1999 and was rapidly parodied in 2001 as *Not Another Teen Movie*, whose working title in the United States was *Ten Things I Hate About Clueless Road Trips When I Can't Hardly Wait to Be Kissed*. There are other examples completely unrecognisable from their titles, such as *The Iron Strain* (1915) in which a spoilt heiress is kidnapped, tamed, and married by a 'wild man' from Alaska, and more recently *Deliver Us from Eva* (2003), set unpromisingly in the Los Angeles Health Department.

It does appear to be the case that at any one time, somewhere in the world, under some title or other, *The Taming of the Shrew* is being re-adapted. At the very least, then, it is clear that this play has been a continuing and prominent cultural presence in film history, and it begins to look less like a hypothesis and more like a certainty that, for better or worse, it has had a continuing significance for film genres. Given the extraordinary exposure in the modern world of a play that many might regard as objectionable, some feminists have claimed the play is used as blatant propaganda for misogynistic social practices. However, the fact that invariably a strong female lead is chosen, and represented as equally spirited and dominant as the male, indicates that the effect of the play is usually more complex than a straight underwriting of patriarchy, particularly since Shakespeare has painted Petruccio as far from an admirable hero but rather a bizarrely dressed and disruptive fortune-hunter. Moreover, there is an argument that, whatever Shakespeare's intentions (and we can never truly know them), *The Shrew* has the potential to be performed to support married love as companionate, if mutually abrasive, since it provides in its sub-plot a parodic critique of a more conventional, decorous, but dubious courtship. Marriage itself is the event that changes Katherina into a cooperative partner but puts her sister Bianca into a questionable light as the new 'shrew'. In this sense the play can be placed instead in a genre more generally renamed 'the battle of the sexes'. The Internet Movie Database has enshrined a genre called 'Shakespeare's-Taming-of-the-Shrew genre', just as I will later propose a 'Shakespeare's-Romeo-and-Juliet genre', alongside other, more composite comic genres innovated by Shakespeare that have entered the history of film. My own choice here is 'odd-couple comedy'.

Furthermore, as was his custom when he found a plot strand that worked, Shakespeare himself was the first to adapt it. In *Much Ado About Nothing* the abrasive 'battle of the sexes' is played out between Beatrice and Benedick alongside the more conventionally romantic yet insecure wooing of Claudio and Hero. This time, as if foreseeing that audiences might in the future object to the brutal metaphor of 'taming' a woman or at least training her into the role of an attack falcon for the man (4.1.174–95), Shakespeare strengthens the woman and makes her genuinely an equal to the man and an agent for emotional independence. She is a template for Congreve's Millamant, who will negotiate to marry only on her own terms, after testing more stringently a man who is less bluff and manipulative than Petruccio. In this sense films based on *Much Ado* might be added as rather less ideologically fraught versions of the same genre, as can *Antony and Cleopatra* where the 'shrew' is once again depicted alongside a man who, like Benedick, is seen as less effective in his 'taming' than Petruccio. Although it is clear that Shakespeare, in revising the formula, strengthened the woman and weakened the man, yet his 'repeats' are contributions to a 'Taming-of-the-Shrew genre' in movies. As some feminist critics like Kathleen Rowe can argue, the formula, apparently paradoxically, can allow the opposite of the play's misogyny and patriarchalism, and denote instead 'the transgressive woman' shown in 'female resistance to masculine authority … through what might be called the *topos* of the unruly woman or the "woman on top"'.[5] The teen movie *10 Things I Hate About You* (1999) was hailed by publicists and reviewers as a remake of *The Shrew* but, apart from the recognisable names – Padua High School, Kat, Patrick, and Bianca – and the initial situation in which Bianca cannot 'date' until her apparently man-hating older sister does, in fact the way the plot unfolds is actually more comparable to *Much Ado*. Like Beatrice, Kat is tricked into thinking Patrick is genuinely interested in her, while Patrick, initially as antisocial as Kat and a fortune-hunter like Petruccio, comes to resemble Benedick in falling in love with Kat against his inclinations. The writers of this film may have come to Shakespeare's conclusion, that the 'taming' metaphor to describe courtship and marriage is less appealing to audiences than a romantic comedy genre, where the expectations are more directed towards the creation of a loving couple and a spirit of social harmony stemming mainly from a rebellion against the *senex*, a repressive father. Shakespeare helps at other times in the movie, providing romantic quotations and a sub-plot involving a girl smitten with his works, and overall it is not exclusively an adaptation of *The Shrew* so much as an example of the time-honoured strategy of using Shakespeare to give respectability to a movie that is aimed at college students studying his plays.

No matter how popular *The Taming of the Shrew* is in the theatre and in movies, it has rarely been a favourite with critics. This is partly because it lacks the wit and lyrical poetry of the romantic comedies, owing more to the stereotypical characters of Italian *commedia dell'arte* and the broad, farcical effects of native English comedy than to the conventions of romance, but it is also due to an innate reservation many hold about the subject matter. Even before feminists raised consciousness to the extent of objecting to the brutal treatment of Katherina and the play's apparently unquestioning endorsement of male supremacy, its basic premises of radical inequality between men and women and of the unrestrained right of a father to dispose of his daughters in arranged or coerced marriages were so immediately and powerfully negated by Shakespeare himself in other plays. His 'strong' romantic heroines like Portia, Beatrice, and Rosalind, by contrast, give *The Shrew* the air of a much older tradition. Noah's wife, who is not in the Bible but in the morality cycle plays of Shakespeare's boyhood, was portrayed as a shrew who did not take seriously her husband's prediction of the devastation to be dealt to the earth in the Flood. Also more or less contemporary was the Italian *commedia dell'arte* 'Punch and Judy' (or at that time in England, Joan) in which Punch is dressed in the motley of a jester rather like Petruccio – even his name may be an echo of the original Pulcinella – and spends a lot of his time beating his wife. In Protestant England at the time when Shakespeare was writing, on the other hand, marriage based on companionship above all was historically becoming the norm.[6] For all these reasons critics have been embarrassed by the play, sometimes apologetic about what they see as its distasteful sexual morality and crude comedy. But the fact remains that the play is embedded firmly in the popular repertory and in countless film adaptations, always reflecting some attitudes to equality and inequality current at the time of performance.

There are various possible explanations for the popularity. The politics of the medium of film vis-à-vis 'legitimate theatre' is one. Film-makers have always had an ambiguous love-hatred for Shakespeare since, on the one hand, he can stand as a conservative figure from high culture, confirming the plebeian roots of the new medium and casting doubt on its artistic legitimacy. On the other hand, adaptations into film of Shakespeare's plays could lend the respectability of 'classics' in theatrical tradition to the new, popular form. Furthermore, if a play itself can be represented as still having popular appeal, then this power struggle has a different dimension again, showing Shakespearean drama as having an abiding popularity that is equal to the movies' contemporary appeal. Paradoxically, not only can films claim serious cultural capital by invoking Shakespeare, but, equally, early practitioners could claim that Shakespeare really 'belongs' as comfortably in the popular medium as in the Victorian theatres with their wealthier patrons. In this rather complicated dynamic between different cultural forms, *The Taming of the Shrew* was particularly useful, because it adds legitimacy to the film industry while underwriting an ideology of sexual politics that has in the past generally been associated, however wrongly, with working-class rather than middle-class communities. In short, *The Shrew* at one stroke opens up many possibilities, making acceptable the new technology as a vehicle for a conservative ideology of marriage, or a polemical representation of relations between men and women more generally at times when issues such as equality and 'the new woman' were becoming openly discussed in society. As an over-simplification of a complex history of reception, one response from benighted male movie-goers might have been: 'Look, not only is Shakespeare entertaining but he allows us to treat our wives badly.' However, correlatively some readings redeem the play from condemnation by turning 'Kate the curst' into a strong, modern, and independent woman with a mind of her own, and in regarding more critically the contrasting wooing behaviour of her sister, Bianca. In this sense, films based on the 'Shrew genre' have been vehicles for such powerful and individual movie actresses as Carole Lombard, Irene Dunne, Jean Arthur, and Katharine Hepburn, who could hold their own with male stars of their time.

If the film history of *The Taming of the Shrew* exemplifies in the film industry tensions between social conservatism, populism, and egalitarian attitudes, so also does it contain its own potential contradictions as a play. Shakespeare's mingling of different forms of source material creates three plot structures that in many ways contrast with each other – Petruccio and Kate, the Bianca sub-plot, and the trick played in the 'Induction' by a nobleman on the drunken pedlar Christopher Sly, who perhaps surprisingly does not reappear at the end of Shakespeare's *The Shrew*. He does come back at the end of the play that may or may not have been its source published in quarto, *The Taming of a Shrew*, and here he claims to have been taught in a dream how to tame his own shrewish wife. The actor playing Sly in *The Shrew* either sleeps onstage through the duration or, more likely, is forgotten and doubles as Petruccio. Shakespeare may have adjudged this interlude to be a useful device to ease the audience into the play, to set up the generic expectations as those of a 'pleasant comedy' to cure melancholy, and even to distance and critically frame the play itself as merely 'household stuff', a wish-fulfilment dream of a comic but distasteful character. It shows Shakespeare anticipating his own practice in *A Midsummer Night's Dream* in depicting Bottom waking up to find himself the love object of the fairy queen, and Puck's final challenge to audiences to dismiss the play as 'but a dream'. The action of the films to be canvassed here suggest it is digressive and largely irrelevant to their purposes, and that the function of establishing expectations of a comedy can be fulfilled by the conventions of the medium itself in its opening credits with their musical accompaniment, a device unavailable to Shakespeare.

Although the Bianca plot in some ways anticipates with a critical edge Shakespeare's more familiar mode of romantic comedy, the 'shrew-taming' on the other hand is highly *un*romantic and quite different, in some ways the opposite. Although all three plot strands involve versions of courtship, only the parallel amatory history of Bianca draws to any great degree upon literary romance, the genre that was to become Shakespeare's source for romantic comedy. The other two plots owe nothing at all to this tradition, and their dominant presence in the play in fact has the effect of satirising and critiquing the sub-plot involving the conventional heroine Bianca and her equally conventional romance lovers, who are the characters who adopt the romance device of disguise. The anti-romantic material predominates and, as a recent editor of the play has pointed out, that material has its origins not so much in literary works but in a quarry treated with notorious reluctance by literary scholars, 'folktale and oral tradition'.[7] It is the juxtaposing of Petruccio's rough wooing (if it can be called that) and Katherina's unconventional resistance, with the overt artifice of Bianca's plot, that give the air of the former being more 'real' and of the latter as being dependent on disguise and crafty trickery. As G. K. Hunter proposed in dealing with the Christopher Sly sub-plot, the play is constructed by Shakespeare into 'a series of planes of reality', demonstrating 'that all reality is relative', a principle inducted with Sly's waking dream.[8] In terms of the play's treatment of love, *The Shrew* is the only comedy in which Shakespeare moves beyond courtship into marriage, fulfilling in the Bianca section Rosalind's prophecy in *As You Like It* that 'Maids are May when they are maids, but the sky changes when they are wives' (4.1.140–1), while in the resolution of the Petruccio/Katherina plot there is at least a suggestion that marriage between honest, independent people, no matter how adversarial, can have more promise as the basis for companionate marriage. The main, 'taming' plot, in this sense, provides films with a clear, formulaic narrative line built around two powerful, antagonistic actors whose presence reduces those around them to vapid hypocrites. The fact that the play ends up endorsing patriarchy and even domestic violence is a consequential and major problem that is dealt with in different ways in different productions, and depending on the specific aura of the chosen stars and the social mores in the time when the film was made. If Shakespeare found this plot in oral and folktale traditions, as seems likely, it is his play that once again has assimilated and superseded his sources so completely that it has passed into cultural history as our own, modern equivalent of the 'oral and folktale', since so often his example is not explicitly tagged in its modern derivatives.

Filmed versions of Shakespeare's Shrew

The various 'orthodox' film adaptations of *The Taming of the Shrew* reveal all these historical ambivalences, solving – or failing to solve – the perceived problems in different ways. The most important decision has always been choosing which film stars to cast in the central roles, often husband and wife teams who had a composite and preferably notorious image in gossip columns. The extra-diegetic factors have been prominent in filming *The Shrew*. Mary Pickford was Katherina in the famous 1929 version, and her image was far from that of a docile wife. She had acted since the age of six as a child star ('The little girl made me. I wasn't waiting for the little girl to kill me'), and became the most famous female artist on the silent screen in a variety of roles: 'I'm sick of Cinderella parts, of wearing rags and tatters. I want to wear smart clothes and play the love.' She was one who successfully moved from silent movies into 'talkies', making several hundred films before she retired in 1936 at the young age of forty-four. Personally, Pickford became wealthy enough to be professionally independent, one of only thirty-six founders of the Academy of Motion Picture Arts and Sciences. She named her home by an anagram of her own and her then husband's name, 'Pickfair', regarding her husband (1920–36 before divorce) as 'a little boy who never grew up', a man whom she regarded as marked by 'purposeless motion' and 'always faced a situation in the only way he knew, by running away from it'. That feckless real-life husband, Douglas Fairbanks, was her Petruccio in the film. He had also been a child star, was professionally associated through a business venture with Pickford since 1910, and was also a founding member of the Academy. He was certainly not known for the qualities Pickford seemed to detect in him, his fame resting on roles in silent films as a comedy heart-throb and then an athletically inclined swashbuckler, such as in his lead roles in *The Thief of Baghdad*, *Robin Hood*, and *Zorro*. Since childhood he had been prey to depression and pathological jealousy, which became more crippling in middle age, despite his continuing image as a fun-loving Peter Pan. Pickford and Fairbanks were seen as 'the king and queen of Hollywood', the first glamorous, celebrity pair in movies, being greeted by a crowd of 300,000 when they visited London and Paris. Divorcing Pickford after a well-reported affair, he immediately married a chorus girl but died prematurely in 1939, reportedly uttering as his last words, 'Never felt better'. Despite the commercial success of *The Taming of the Shrew*, directed by Sam Taylor, Pickford was to regard it as an unmitigated disaster for her, refusing to allow it to be re-released until after Franco Zeffirelli's version in 1966, while for Fairbanks it became his swansong before falling into public neglect as an ageing roué.[9]

Although the Pickford–Fairbanks *Shrew* is unsubtle and rough-edged, in some ways it unexpectedly declines to patronise the audience as much as the later version by Zeffirelli, which seems to fall back on the reading that modern audiences, presumptively like Elizabethans, remain incapable of seeing sexual politics in terms other than assumptions of male supremacy and misogyny. Various stratagems are used in the 1929 film at least to qualify such an interpretation. Petruccio, true to Fairbanks's popular roles, is good-humoured and dashing (in every sense), and his stance is summed up in repeated laughs inherited from broad stage performances. These become irritating, but suggest that the character is mocking and enjoying the dilemmas rather than motivated by sadism. This becomes relatively convincing because the film represents the couple as deserving each other, not only because they are both perverse but also because they are both dynamic and powerful presences. The power is distributed equally, since all the physical domination is on the side of Katherina, wielding her whip and striking the man, while all the psychological abuse is on his side and generally speaking he refrains from repeated physical violence. The key has been struck in the opening scene, where Christopher Sly has been replaced by puppets of Punch and

Judy in their caricatured roles. Meanwhile, in the contentious final scene where Kate must deliver an out-of-character homily on wifely obedience, a surprise is sprung. In a famous moment that utilises the resources of film in a way that could not easily be replicated on a stage, Pickford is shown in close-up delivering a broad wink, presumably either to Bianca as an encouragement to play the game in order to get what she wants, or to the audience to indicate that she speaks only in irony to allow her husband to win the wager. The distancing wink has been anticipated several times earlier in the film, most obviously when Kate overhears her husband explaining to his dog (or in soliloquy in the play) how he will extend his 'taming' tactics into the marital bed, after which she regains the upper hand in the power struggle by ignoring his perverse conduct and even clapping with mockery at his antics. As she begins to enjoy the badinage as a game, Petruccio's irritation mounts, preparing the way for her final, conspiratorial wink. The strategy used in this film to avoid some ideological problems in the twentieth century is to enhance the element of play.

The next 'royal couple' in entertainment circles who played the parts, this time under Zeffirelli's direction in 1967, was a liaison made in heaven for those who wished to make Shakespeare a box-office success, since Richard Burton was one of the best-known Shakespearean actors of his time while his wife Elizabeth Taylor was the screen goddess of the era. The two had prophetically met while acting together as Antony and Cleopatra in Joseph Mankiewicz's follow-up to *Julius Caesar*, the film *Cleopatra* (1963), and they were to marry twice consecutively (1964–74 and 1975–76). Zeffirelli initially acknowledges 'William Shakespeare without whom they would have been at a loss for words', and like Olivier's *Henry V*, the opening and costuming take us into the period of Elizabethan times, as though the film will be showing us not modern mores but Elizabethan ones. Although this film is technically far more sophisticated and visually sumptuous than the 1929 version, and already Zeffirelli has discovered the haunting music composed by Nino Rota, yet in terms of theme it is arguably more simplistic. It relies overtly on the actors' reputations and personalities, and on the extra-diegetic knowledge of the marriage between Burton and Taylor. The assumption is that, despite appearances, they must be compatible in some way, and that their marriage must be based on a powerful sexual attraction reflected in the energetic physicality of their interactions. The personae played by the actors in *Cleopatra* would still have been in audiences' minds, as well as pointing to a connection between Shakespeare's use of a similar adversarial relationship – sex as power struggle in which the female is at least an equal for the male – in two apparently very different plays. Ironically, the classically trained

Burton was to say in his own person that the most important thing in life is not love but language, and in this film the emphasis that may be used to excuse the misogyny is that the wooing is not a matter of feelings but of language. The text gives some authority for this, since at the crucial moment of Kate's capitulation, her line is 'What you will have it named, even that it is' (4.6.22), so that an old man, in fact Lucentio's rich father, Vincentio, becomes in a word a young woman and the sun becomes the moon. In terms of the play's design this is not so perverse or eccentric as it seems, since there are at least three characters who have disguised themselves, while in the Induction Christopher Sly is persuaded that he is in fact a lord rather than a drunken commoner. In the situation, Kate's way of avoiding conflict is not to continue manifesting 'the spirit to resist' (3.3.93) that Pickford maintains in her own way, but to avoid conflict by simply agreeing with Petruccio's forms of words. This may be the film's way of avoiding its own discomfort with the play, and of explaining the final speech, which Taylor delivers without any trace of Pickford's irony, since the implication is that, like the wooing itself, it is merely language used to sustain a convenient fiction. 'For 'tis the mind that makes the body rich' (4.3.170), even when garments are 'poor' or incongruous, is one way of justifying such a courtship, 'So honour peereth in the meanest habit' (4.3.172). It is all a triumph of persuasive rhetoric over reality and even feelings, with an implication that this is how Elizabethans seriously regarded marriage. However, such an intellectual approach seems to be at odds with the manifestly visual, slapstick comedy that is the film's main strategy, as well as the exploitation of the well-known marital relationship and mutual but tempestuous physical appeal between Burton and Taylor at the time.

A *musical* Shrew

The reception of Shakespearean comedy into musical films as a genre will be the subject of Chapter 3, but those relating to *The Shrew* belong here. *Kiss Me Kate* (1953, based on the stage version of 1948) is perhaps best seen in its historical context of post-war revision of the role of women, as Diana Henderson mentions. After being liberated and even coerced into the workforce during wartime, women in most countries then had to be inveigled back into domesticity through restrictive public policy, advertising, and more subtly and affectively through movies, in order to clear the employment situation for males returning from war-related activities. As Henderson sums up, 'Rosie the Riveter was supplanted by Kate the Happy Housewife'.[10] As if to draw attention to this context, a photograph of the central male character as a soldier in his younger days appears on the wall and he momentarily contemplates it as a backdrop to his poignant song, 'Where Is the Life That Late I Led?'. The overt attempt to base the plot on *The Shrew* is evidenced by the fact that words from Shakespeare's play begin not only this Cole Porter song but also others, such as the jaunty, fortune-hunting 'I've Come to Wive It Wealthily in Padua' and 'Were Thine That Special Face'. The penultimate song, 'Brush up Your Shakespeare', sung with exaggerated amateurishness by the comic and philistine pair of 'enforcer' hoodlums, turns this movie into an unashamed homage to bardolatry, where Shakespeare's own populism is celebrated over elitism.

However, my emphasis here falls on the internal dynamics of the relationship between 'tamer' and 'shrew', who this time are represented as having been formerly married, now divorced, but still bickering. As a 'backstage' musical, the offstage behaviour of Fred (Howard Keel) and Lilli (Kathryn Grayson) spills into the actual stage performance of a musical version of *The Taming of the Shrew*. As indicated by the woman's name-calling ('louse') and her antagonism (her memorable song is 'I Hate Men', delivered with angry, physical forcefulness), this Kate is no pushover. Mutual physical violence breaks out and threatens to destroy the performance, culminating in the on-stage episode where, provoked by her slaps, Fred/Petruccio beats Lilli/Kate on the posterior. Such a gesture of domestic violence would not be tolerated either on- or offstage these days, although at the time the image was used on all publicity material for the film and arouses raucous laughter from the stage audience. As the fictional characters of Petruccio and Kate wrangle, the fickle 'other woman', Lois (Ann Miller), playing a Bianca figure, whose theme tune is 'Too Darn Hot' in a scene that fell foul of the 1950s censors, flirts not only with Fred but also later Lilli's new love, Tex. She woos her own real-life Lucentio, who is not only an actor and 'hoofer' (tap dancer) but also a compulsive gambler. Naturally, since the whole tone is comic, the ending of the offstage plot also mimics that on stage, the knots of complications are gradually loosened with the help of comic 'enforcers', and Fred and Lilli are finally reconciled, while Lois commits herself to 'settling down' with Bill, announced in her song 'Always True to You in My Fashion'. The equivalent of Katherina's celebration of wifely obedience is Lilli's 'I Am Ashamed That Women Are So Simple'. What is perhaps distinctive about the relationships in the film is the final sense that the denouement is not such a surprise as in Shakespeare's version, since Lilli's emotional dependence on Fred, and Lois's need for stability despite her flightiness, are strongly signalled from the very start of the movie. Thus prepared, the ending marks an equilibrium that has always been an implicit destination for the plot, whereas Shakespeare problematises anything that smacks of such complacency or sentimentality. Even allowing for the gradual watering down of the production in its path from a Broadway musical to a film (and even before, its descent from a predecessor, the 1935 production mounted by Alfred Lunt and Lynn Fontanne), one can still see the kind of material that Irene Dash has analysed in the stage versions. She stresses that the women depicted are professionals and all 'strong women ... who are torn between their roles as wives and as independent professionals who have a clear sense of self', reflecting the new realities confronting women in the twentieth century. Dash points out that Kate is not so much submissive to Petruccio but given support by him at crucial moments, and that there is a 'clear rapport' between the two that underpins their relationship.[11] Despite the unequal power relations depicted, there is an underlying compatibility imputed.

Several conclusions can be drawn about this difference, pertaining to Shakespearean adaptation into modern musical comedy. First, the 'happy ending' based on the emotional appeal of marriage itself, as a normative and even natural institution for human beings, is even stronger in films of the 1950s than in Shakespeare's representation. In the 1590s play, neither of the marriages seems necessarily based on such values, since there have been socially defined motivations: fathers arranging marriages, avaricious young men seeking young women who come with a large dowry, emotional conflict and physical violence, and a substantial element of simple trickery. Shakespeare's version is considerably more uncomfortable than *Kiss Me Kate*, since in the film we are aware that, despite their divorce and desire for individual independence, Fred and Lilli are indissolubly connected through their love for each other and that they 'deserve' to be married. In Shakespeare's play we cannot be so certain at all, and it seems important that the various characters are initially *mis*matched and any potential compatibility is forcibly repressed from the representation. This differs from the underlying expectations in Shakespeare's depictions of Beatrice and Benedick, and certainly Antony and Cleopatra, where conflict is presented as a sign of such preoccupation with each other that the relationship is justified. This difference between *The Shrew* and *Kiss Me Kate* in itself suggests that modern musicals find their more fertile origin in Shakespeare's romantic comedy, a different genre based on lovers facing some external threat to their wooing, as we shall see in Chapter 3.

'Odd-couple' comedy

The most successful adaptations of *The Shrew* in modern times are works that rarely advert to Shakespeare directly but which do see a new human potential in the 'Taming-of-the-Shrew genre'. Shakespeare himself rarely uses conventions inertly, but rather infuses them with some plausible human significance, and it is in these movies that we see psychologically penetrating explorations of the genre based on conflict between initially mismatched characters.

Stanley Cavell in *Pursuits of Happiness* draws attention to the Shakespearean influence on modern films of a certain type, which he calls 'the Hollywood Comedy of Remarriage' and film theorists classify as 'screwball comedies'. As I have intimated, while I am grateful for his pioneering effort, I disagree with his analysis at some points, in particular his tracing of the films back to *The Winter's Tale*. Despite Leontes being given a second chance with his wife Hermione, this seems marginal to the films' concerns, especially because so few of their protagonists have been married. Sometimes they have known each other previously (like Benedick and Beatrice in *Much Ado*), but this seems to imply not a state of 're-marriage' but of maturity, suggesting a post-romantic phase in the movement towards relationship. Instead, I would propose that several of the films nominated by Cavell do indeed have a Shakespearean prototype but that it is *The Taming of the Shrew*, and that in the reception of a genre this play is par excellence Shakespeare's play of marriage as a battle of the sexes. It depicts a power struggle that at least potentially can raise issues of equality, pitting a strong woman against a strong man. Rather than *re*-marriage, power relations in the journey towards marriage, and underlying marriage itself, constitute the central issue in these films, as well as in *The Shrew* (despite the fact that Petruccio and Kate are formally married fairly early in the play, their relationship can hardly be said to be resolved by the ceremony itself). The courtship paving the way towards marriage is conflictual rather than romantic, threatened by mutual antagonism rather than parental opposition, and certainly not harmonious. At its core, the play shows a man attempting to condition his wife, or initially his future wife, into a subservient role, to 'tame' her, with degrees of success that can vary depending on the way the play is presented in the theatre. However, the man and woman are presented not only as in conflict with each other, but also as equals in terms of energy and animal spirits, and as equally determined not to forfeit independence by being subsumed into coupledom. Far from being indifferent, they positively resist each other in their spirited temperamental differences, suggesting that an apt description of the genre may be 'odd-couple comedy'.[12]

Tina Olsin Lent describes the main characteristics of screwball comedy, without mentioning Shakespeare at all, in this way:

The films' plots characteristically involved a sexual confrontation between an initially antagonistic couple whose ideological differences heightened their animosity. Their courtship entailed the verbal and physical sparring referred to as the battle of the sexes, and their recognition of mutual love and decision to marry (or remarry) ultimately reconciled the sexual and ideological tensions.[13]

Some clear similarities with *The Shrew* immediately come into view. Lent's main aim is to link up the genre with changing contemporary events: for example, the 'flapper' image of emergent women's freedom:

In three significant areas, the screwball women protagonists perpetuated the attributes of the flapper: her personality and behavior, her participation in the paid labor force, and her more egalitarian relationship with men. Although they lacked the flapper's overt sexuality, the screwball heroines shared her vitality, physical freedom, spontaneity and vivaciousness.[14]

Further contextualisation reveals an emphasis on changing marital norms in the 1920s, during which divorce rates increased markedly, while courtship as represented in popular women's magazines emphasised friendship, play, and independence of the 'new woman' paradigm: 'the screwball comedy also used role-playing to show how the companionable relationship emerged from separate, often hostile, identities' presented as 'two complementary opposites'.[15] The genre came to its maturity in the 1940s, although it had antecedents such as *Theodora Goes Wild* (1936), in which an eccentric extrovert from out of town (Melvyn Douglas) draws out and liberates Theodora (Irene Dunne), who is inhibited by her censorious and restrictive family and community, but has revealed her 'wild' side by publishing a scandalous novel under a pseudonym. The man's self-conscious use of a phrase from *As You Like It*, 'a poor thing but mine own', glances at least at some Shakespearean substratum, and although the couple are not always abrasive to each other, they do complement each other's different styles of behavioural 'wildness' and discrepant 'ideologies'. Others are *Love Before Breakfast* (1936), which overtly references *The Taming of the Shrew*, and the British *Second Best Bed* (1938), whose title draws on the wording of Shakespeare's famous will. Both of these are analysed perceptively in Elinor Parson's account.[16] Lent argues that sexual antagonism, even to the point of violence and presented as comedy and farce, together with eccentric qualities in both protagonists and anarchic individualism are motivating forces behind screwball comedy. It is not difficult to see the potential for this genre to be found in *The Taming of the Shrew* as it has been adapted to historical attitudes and circumstances.

Of all genre terminology from Hollywood, the most opaque to non-Americans must be 'screwball comedy'. 'Screwball' suggests synonyms like wacky, idiotic, farcical, and so on, but in fact the meaning is much more precise and counter-intuitive, as Richard Maltby describes:

> The term 'screwball' has its origins in baseball, and was coined around 1930 by New York Giants pitcher Carl Hubbell, who made baseball history in the Major League All-Star game in July 1934 by striking out six opponents with his screwball pitch. Propelled into wider public usage, 'screwball' came to mean unbalanced, eccentric, unpredictable, unconventional, or lunatic.[17]

The screwball in baseball is a pitch whose spin causes it to swing and dip unexpectedly, and an analogy in cricketing parlance is the 'googly' or 'wrong-un', a ball that would be expected to turn one direction while in reality it does the opposite. Such aerodynamic and pitch movements became attached to a particular kind of female comic lead, a 'screwball dame', and 'as a style, screwball combined a verbally witty high comedy of manners and a low comedy of pratfalls, slapstick, and physical violence'.[18] The 'heroines' might not invite the same vocabulary of menace as Kate, who is described as 'intolerable curst, / And shrewd and froward so beyond all measure' (1.2.88–9), but as 'screwy dames' regarded as so perverse and refractory ('froward') as to be unmarriageable. However, closer inspection of the films reveals that the male equivalent may be just as eccentric, that the abrasiveness builds upon a deeper, intuited compatibility as between Beatrice and Benedick, and that versions of freedom, play, and mutual preoccupation underlying their apparent bickering give audiences the promise of a companionate future for such a 'madly mated' couple (3.3.116).

At the heart of screwball comedy are a man and a woman initially in opposition but eventually 'mated'. They are equally animated but often divided by class or experience, and even if the audience expects eventual rapprochement, each spends the action resisting their underlying compatibility, maintaining hostility, indifference, and sometimes violent behaviour towards each other. The genre differs from romantic comedy in several ways analysed by Wes D. Gehring in *Romantic vs. Screwball Comedy: Charting the Difference*, especially in filmic style linked with subject matter: 'the screwball variety places its emphasis on "funny", while the more traditional romantic comedy accents "love"'.[19] In terms of the overall field of Shakespearean comedy, whereas romantic comedy is centrally about courtship while *The Taming of the Shrew* is predominantly about marital relations, these can be quite different in practice, as Rosalind points out:

ROSALIND Now tell me how long you would have her after you have possessed her?
ORLANDO For ever and a day.
ROSALIND Say a day without the ever. No, no, Orlando; men are April when they woo, December when they wed. Maids are May when they are maids, but the sky changes when they are wives. I will be more jealous of thee than a Barbary cock-pigeon over his hen, more clamorous than a parrot against rain, more new-fangled than an ape, more giddy in my desires than a monkey. I will weep for nothing, like Diana in the fountain, and I will do that when you are disposed to be merry. I will laugh like a hyena, and that when thou art inclined to sleep. (*As You Like It*, 4.1.135–48)

In *The Shrew* it is Bianca who plays out the expected convention of premarital agreeableness followed by uncooperativeness in marriage, while Kate evidences the alternative. The basic pattern of the sexual career of the main characters in screwball movies, as described by Maltby, bears other marks of comparison with the depiction in *The Shrew*:

> What differentiated screwball comedy from other versions of romantic comedy was that the obstacle to the couple's successful romance was provided not by an external agent but by their own mutual hostility. The characteristic screwball-comedy plot was constructed around the clash of incompatible personalities and values, and much of screwball's energy comes from the escalating and apparently irresolvable conflict between its incompatible romantic couples. This conflict, however, takes place within the conventions of romance, of comedy, of classical Hollywood cinema's profound commitment to the creation of the couple.[20]

The pattern therefore is one where 'an initially antagonistic couple discover or rediscover romance through a sequence of combative verbal and physical exchanges, until they reconcile the sexual and ideological tensions that separate them'.[21] Although Maltby relates the genre to Shakespearean comedy as analysed by Northrop Frye, the quite specific source, which is in fact rather different from Shakespeare's romantic comedies, is not mentioned. It is clearly *The Taming of the Shrew*. Wheeler Winston Dixon, writer of *American Cinema of the 1940s*, notes the connection in an *obiter dictum* without following it up: 'many of the romantic comedies of the thirties and forties present a variation of *The Taming of the Shrew*, with the unruly, upper-class, willful woman brought to heel by the moral superiority of her socially inferior, virile lover.'[22] In a famous scene in Ernst Lubitsch's film *Bluebeard's Eighth Wife* (1938), the hero is seen actually reading *The Taming of the Shrew* with great attentiveness, after which he storms down the corridor into the bedroom and slaps his eighth wife on the face. When she simply slaps him back he retreats in some confusion back to the text to find where he had gone wrong. He then tries again, this time smiling at his wife first, before placing her on his knee and spanking her, uttering only the word 'Shakespeare'. The female 'double crossing animal' is still not cowed and the twist in the tale is that she 'tames' him.[23] In this case the reference to Shakespeare's play is unusually direct, and its difference from the conventional pattern described by Rosalind is implied:

> NICOLE Here's to our agreement. No love-making, no quarrels.
> MICHAEL Just like an ordinary married couple.
> NICOLE I said no quarrels.

Shakespeare himself seems to have used and re-used the 'Shrew genre' in quite unexpected plays. The perverse, graveside wooing by Richard Gloucester of Lady Anne, daughter-in-law of Henry VI and widow of Prince Edward whom Richard has murdered, is a cameo example: 'Was ever woman in this humour wooed? / Was ever woman in this humour won?' (*Richard III*, 1.2.215–16), while Henry V's wooing of Catherine of France is a brief, muted, but structurally complete comedy of this kind, reconciling national differences with marriage through Henry's aggressive and unromantic expressions backed up by implied threats based on his military victory. In a more structurally central way, apart from *The Shrew*, Shakespeare used the pattern in depicting the relationship between Beatrice and Benedick in *Much Ado About Nothing* and to some extent also, with tragic-comic effect, in *Antony and Cleopatra*, and in *Venus and Adonis* where the gender roles are reversed and the man is the resistant one. It seems to have been one of his recurrent paradigms of love, but it should be distinguished from the romantic form, in which lovers resist impediments external to the relationship to pursue their love. Shakespeare's own form of 'screwball comedy', as most completely played out in *The Shrew*, has a quite different origin in 'the battle of the sexes'. Perhaps a neutral term to use is 'odd-couple comedy', where mutual antagonism is a prelude to mutual collaboration. The defining passages belong to Petruccio:

> I am as peremptory as she proud-minded,
> And where two raging fires meet together
> They do consume the thing that feeds their fury. (2.1.131–3)

And:

> For I am he am born to tame you, Kate,
> And bring you from a wild Kate to a Kate
> Conformable as other household Kates. (2.1.270–3)

The film credited with initiating the rather short-lived genre of screwball comedy is *It Happened One Night* (1934). Despite Cavell's suggestion that it is a 'comedy of remarriage' standing in a line of inheritance from Shakespearean romance and in particular *The Winter's Tale*, its provenance, I argue, lies more squarely in the anti-romantic comedy of marriage, *The Taming of the Shrew*. The precedent is mentioned by the director. Frank Capra in his autobiography described the two characters as a spoiled heiress (Ellie Andrews played by Claudette Colbert) and 'a guy we all know and like' (Peter Warne played by Clark Gable): 'And when he meets the spoiled heiress – well, it's *The Taming of the Shrew*. But the shrew must be worth taming, and the guy that tames her must be one of us.'[24] When we meet Ellie on her rich father's boat she is on hunger strike because her father is attempting to annul her marriage to a man he disapproves of. She upsets a tray of food and terrifies the servants in exactly the way Katherina does in all the *Shrew* films. 'I'll scream if I want to', she shouts, and dives off the boat, intending to elope to New York to join her frivolous aristocratic 'aeroglider', King Westley. The 'taming' process occurs on her picaresque journey when she is appropriated by Peter, a reporter wanting to scoop the story of the eloping heiress with a $10,000 reward offered for returning her to her father. Peter uses the same strategy of depriving her of creature comforts, not simply to break her spirit as Petruccio does but more to force her to face up to the material necessities of her condition without relying on buying her way out of problems. He immediately types her as an 'ungrateful brat' and a 'spoiled brat of a rich father', refusing to allow her to buy chocolates on the train:

> ELLIE Here boy, box of chocolates, please.
> PETER Never mind, son, she doesn't want it.
> BOY The lady said …
> ELLIE Of course I do …
> PETER Beat it.
> ELLIE Well, you've got a nerve.
> PETER You're on a budget from now on.

They trade insults: 'Your ego is absolutely colossal … Yeah?, how's yours?' When their impecuniousness forces them to share a motel room, Peter strings a blanket between their single beds, providing not only a central metaphor of 'the walls of Jericho' but also a thematic reference to the threat of his sexuality to her inexperience: 'the walls of Jericho will protect you from the big bad wolf'. Despite her continuing to 'cross' him, Ellie gradually learns Peter's lessons in thrift and streetwise adaptability, sleeping in a haystack, eating a 'starvation diet' of carrots freshly pulled from the ground, learning how to eat a doughnut in working-class fashion ('40 millions and you don't know how to dunk'), and colluding in petty theft, and she even begins to enjoy her new life of deprivation: 'Oh, I'd change places with a plumber's daughter any day.' To evade detection, she even effectively role-plays the 'plumber's daughter' when they pretend to have a domestic quarrel in front of detectives who are looking for her, and she responds warmly to the bonhomie of their impoverished and working-class fellow travellers. At this stage their public status is comparable with that of Petruccio and Kate, since, although not married, they are pretending to be so in order to get cheaper accommodation. Ellie enters into the spirit by turning her emotional opposition into a stereotypical marital squabble. Eventually she discovers she is in love with Peter rather than 'King', and at the (re-)wedding ceremony she elopes again, this time with Peter. The final mood suggests that life chooses life as Ellie allows herself to become firmly the property of Peter rather than of her father or spurned fiancé. In the words of another 1930s film title, they are 'Made for Each Other'. (Made in 1939 and starring one of the most frequent screwball heroines, Carole Lombard, *Made for Each Other* is not, in fact, a 'shrew-taming' narrative but a melodrama.) After the constant acrimony, resistance, and bullying, Ellie and Peter significantly become aware of their love only after they have left each other's company. Peter's earlier description of the (impossible) lover he seeks – 'somebody that's real, somebody that's alive. They don't come that way no more' – indicates that their equal feistiness and aggression link them with each other emotionally, if not in class interests until Ellie chooses to change ranks. By the end, her father observes, 'you've changed, Ellie', and even Peter changes to some extent. Whereas at first he is mystified as to 'what makes dames like you so dizzy', by the end he must admit 'I'm a little screwy myself'.

What is interesting about the cross-references between *It Happened One Night* and *The Taming of the Shrew* is not just the matters of influence or genre in themselves, but the way in which the movie provides a revealing gloss on the play. Capra gives explanations where Shakespeare gives problems, and it is as if the experience of the Depression and a modicum of Freudianism popular in the 1930s have given the director a material and psychological insight into *why* Shakespeare's characters behave as they do. Ellie's emotional difficulties stem from her material circumstances as the single daughter of a single father who is wealthy and possessive of her. Ellie is running away from her background in order to find some form of independence, but at the same time her very background has incapacitated her from the kind of survival in ordinary circumstances that Peter must teach her. Adult love is represented as the final prize that gives her independence from her father, but simply replaces him with an equally controlling but less wealthy husband. Significantly, Ellie's declaration of love is no less abject than Katherina's wifely homily. In Shakespeare, we know little of the character of the father, Baptista Minola, except that he is a rich citizen of Padua who has no wife but one spoiled daughter whose unruly elder sibling resents the situation. Petruccio comes as an unashamed fortune-hunter like Peter (whose name links him), who claims no more than 'You're just a headline for me ... What I want is your story.' Peter's loveless 'taming' involves forcing the woman to accept conditions of living that have no relation to her wealth but instead to survival, while Petruccio's taming is equally to distance Kate from her rich but emotionally unsatisfactory family background, and accept physical discomfort and social embarrassment in return for future happiness (we must assume). It would have been a socially useful fable in the Depression years in America. There is another moral Peter suggests, that Ellie is the product of bad and indulgent parenting, and his lesson is directed as much at the father as the daughter: 'She needs a guy that'll take a sock at her once a day whether it's coming to her or not. If you had any brains you'd have done it yourself.' In short, where Shakespeare uses character stereotypes to fuel his story, the film gives these characters plausible motivations stemming from their class roots, and these motivations can potentially and fruitfully be read back into *The Shrew* as the basis for a possible stage production. *It Happened One Night*, in following the generic pattern given by *The Taming of the Shrew*, also offers a critical interpretation of the play, opening up new ways of accepting and remodelling the motivational lacunae in Shakespeare's version. Although the events are no less improbable, the motivations are given some plausibility, at least for 1930s audiences.

Carole Lombard shows her lively aptitude as a 'screwball' heroine in playing Kay Colby in *Love Before Breakfast* (1936). In character, she does make explicit reference to Shakespeare's *Shrew* in speaking of future marriage with leading man Preston Foster (Scott Miller): 'But this wouldn't be any *The Taming of the Shrew* you know. I'm not gonna come crawling after you've broken my spirit.' Scott replies sardonically, 'I'll take my chance.' Despite her disavowal, however, the situation is problematical from the point of view of twenty-first-century sexual politics, and does bear some resemblances to the more unpleasant side of Shakespeare's plot. Although Scott does not succeed in fully 'taming' Kay, it is not for want of trying, and he exudes the same kind of ruthless, masculine complacency and emotional cruelty as Petruccio, presented by the film in an uncritical light. He will not for an instant entertain the possibility that Kay is happily in love with her fiancé Bill, exercising his power as Bill's boss to transfer him to Japan, to Kay's grief. Wealth and power are Scott's weapons, which he uses in a merciless pursuit of Kay that would now be classified as stalking in its most menacing and coercive light. Worse, he is abetted by Kay's mother, who wants such a handsome and rich executive as her son-in-law, and the film does little to challenge the apparent rightness of this. Several times he forces or tricks her into compromising situations in which reliance upon his worldly power is her only means of survival. We are manipulated to collude in Scott's pursuit, seeing the woman as literally 'dizzy' at one stage, and increasingly to see the hapless Bill as so boring and passive in contrast to the glamorous Scott as to be unworthy of such a vital lover as Kay. There is only one way in which the woman's claim not to have her will broken operates, and that is the final shot in which they are married but continue to bicker and quarrel. The implication is that the conflict is essential to the 'odd-couple' relationship and that it will continue to be the glue that holds them together into the future. Two other prevailing assumptions running throughout the film, equally questionable but tacitly imposed on audiences, are first that Scott's relentless pursuit is a badge of a trustworthiness, security, and consistency of purpose that is more appealing than the domestic boredom offered by Bill, and second that a beautiful and spirited woman must inevitably fall in love with a commercially successful multimillionaire with matinee-idol looks. The 1930s was not a decade in which film-makers could predict the gender wars of later years, so the presentation is in tune with norms of the time, but after the Second World War it would become difficult to sustain such unreconstructed views. The next movie to be examined, made after the war, presents a more equal struggle.

Adam's Rib (1949) draws on the potential of *The Shrew* to represent an underlying power struggle between husband and wife, the potential mutuality of which is enhanced by the casting of Katherine Hepburn as a mature and powerful lawyer fighting explicitly for principles of equality before the law, for men and women alike. Her husband is the Assistant District Attorney, played by an equally forceful Spencer Tracey, who fights for the rule of law as it actually is, 'whether right or wrong', prejudiced or unprejudiced. Each attempts to 'tame' the other into submission, and words like 'unreasonable' and 'overbearing' are used by each to tarnish the other. It is a moot point which character deserves the adjectives more, or whether either succeeds in 'taming' the other. In the lawsuit they contest, Adam prosecutes a woman who has shot at her husband whom she has found in a compromising position with his mistress, while Amanda defends the woman. The wife in the trial is accused of 'frequent fits of violent temper', but it emerges that there is a reason for her behaviour, stemming from her husband's failure to listen to her point of view and his shameless adultery. Amanda's point in defending the woman is that if she were a man, provocation would be accepted as a defence and, therefore, if the law treated men and women equally the wife should be exonerated – an argument that the jury accepts. Amanda points out that, while male violence is commonly seen as justifiable in self-defence or as a response to provocation, 'nobody looks at [the woman's] violence as justified'. The naturalness of provoked violence is accepted for both men and women equally:

> AMANDA Every living being is capable of attack, if sufficiently provoked. Assault lies dormant within us all. It requires only circumstances to set it in violent motion.

The opposition in the courtroom between husband and wife, although comically handled, leads to divorce proceedings, and as in the 'inset' case the husband claims provocation and disparagingly acknowledges arguments for gender equality: 'I'm old-fashioned, I like two sexes ... I don't want to be married to a new woman, a competitor, competitor, competitor. If you want to, go and be a real he-woman, but not with me.' He angrily says that if his wife fights him professionally in court it is turning the law into a 'Punch and Judy show', and he explicitly accuses not only the female defendant but also his wife of 'shrewishness'. Amanda's point, voiced with equal vehemence, is that Adam has not listened to her point of view, and that it is he who has set up the confrontational situation and provoked her. The end of the film shows both in more non-belligerent and negotiated roles in order to avoid divorce. The wife, having made her point in court on behalf of all women, accepts for herself a continuing domestic role, while the husband learns to listen and even to cry, the very thing he had accused women of doing only to get their way, although it is not clear that either advance will be consistently maintained. Adam hears that he is to be promoted to a judge, but this does not necessarily mean Amanda is finally 'tamed' into an inferior role since she strongly hints she will now run for Congress to pursue her political aim to achieve equality for women in public life.

Adam's Rib can, then, be seen as an example of the 'Taming-of-the-Shrew genre', with some indirect influence also from *Othello* since jealousy in two sets of 'love triangles' is a strong theme. The result in this case, expressed in the repeated metaphor of competitiveness raised in the film, is a nil–nil draw between husband and wife. Amanda says to Adam of the court case, 'I wish it could have been a tie, Adam', and in their own personal power struggle, it is. The new cultural influence evident by

1949 is surely the increasingly expressed arguments that women encouraged to enter the workforce in the Second World War should not have to accept passively a return to 'domestic duties' afterwards. The argument for equality and against male dominance has entered a new phase by this time, and, as in other periods, Shakespeare's play could be used to reflect different sides of the argument and conflicts. The 'Taming-of-the-Shrew genre' within the 'battle of the sexes' still survives in cinema, evident in more recent films such as *The Ugly Truth* (2009), in which the female producer of a television interview programme clashes with her male supervisor on the nature of relationships. But although vestiges of Shakespeare are evident, as I have observed of other patterns after the 1950s, the intertextual echoes tend to refer mainly to other films rather than to *The Taming of the Shrew* itself, which had long before been assimilated into Hollywood genres.

All about Bianca

If there is an equivalent updating of *The Shrew* for a 1950s audience, it might come not from a highlighting of the taming of Kate but analysis of the more insidious presence of the ambiguously drawn Bianca. She is the younger sister who, favouritised by their father, cannot contemplate marriage until her older, 'shrewish' sister is paired off. The plot datum occurs also in a movie like *You Were Never Lovelier* (1942), starring Rita Hayworth. Here, the 'difficult' daughter must be married off before options are opened for the more compliant and conventionally beautiful one. This requires stratagem and disguised identity, creating first a fictional lover and allowing her, like Beatrice and Kate in different ways, to accommodate herself to the make believe. Given the deliberate intricacies of the sub-plot concerning Bianca's three suitors, who are all cunning and to varying degrees confusingly disguised, it is not surprising that most productions of the play simplify or even drastically shorten this part of the plot, so as to focus attention on Petruccio and Kate. However, in Shakespeare's design, the sub-plot is important for various reasons. It enhances the straightforwardness of the 'shrew-taming' narrative since, however behaviourally perverse they are, both Petruccio and Kate are 'plain speakers', in contrast to Lucentio, Gremio (who hires and disguises Lucentio as a Latin tutor), Hortensio, who disguises himself as a music teacher, and even Bianca herself, who colludes in the disguises because she loves Lucentio and marries him in secrecy. By contrast, the 'shrew' plot, with its basis in traditional folktale, is simpler to comprehend. Bianca's story, stemming from classical Italian 'intrigue' plots as well as romantic comedy, is meant to be complicated and based on deception, whereas Petruccio asserts of his wedding to Kate that his wooing is not based on material disguise – 'to me she's married, not unto my clothes':

> Well, come, my Kate. We will unto your father's
> Even in these honest, mean habiliments.
> Our purses shall be proud, our garments poor,
> For 'tis the mind that makes the body rich,
> And as the sun breaks through the darkest clouds,
> So honour peereth in the meanest habit. (4.3.167–72)

In fact Kate, and apparently also Petruccio, are very wealthy, so 'mean habiliments' are a form of disguise (as is Petruccio's conscious role playing), but they are designed not to obscure the truth but to clarify it. If there is a benign side to Petruccio's lesson, it is that despite his brutal strategy he is seeking to base the relationship on inner qualities, on seeing the worst side of each other, and some version of eventual cooperation rather than on deceptions created by outer trappings. Zeffirelli's production suggests that in the outcome this is a marriage of equally forceful personalities operating within a patriarchal framework, though he does nothing to make the ending ironic. This prepares the way for the surprise reversal of the ending, where Bianca proves herself to be recalcitrant in her expected marital relationship, while Katherina accepts its limitations and compromise. Shakespeare himself may have been more interested in the convoluted plot strand, since he had used it in *The Two Gentlemen of Verona* (probably the earlier play) by contrasting the relationships of Proteus and Julia on the one hand and Valentine and Silvia on the other, and was to repeat the 'disguised suitor' plot with significant variations in the Hero–Claudio sub-plot in *Much Ado* and the Viola–Orsino plot in *Twelfth Night*. In fact, so much stage time is taken up in *The Shrew* with the wooing for Bianca that in the text itself it qualifies as an equal plot rather than a sub-plot. Both are commercially motivated, but while one is conducted by coercion, the other is pursued by crafty manipulation, dissimulation, and jealousy, not only on the part of the male suitors but also by the more prized woman who emerges as an emblem of 'unconstant womankind' (4.2.14).

The only filmed version of *The Taming of the Shrew* to pay full attention to Bianca's wooing is the one made in 1980 for television by the BBC, in the series whose brief was, perhaps misguidedly, to remain 'loyal to Shakespeare's texts' (although rather inexplicably this production omits the Christopher Sly Induction and adds at the end an irrelevant and completely extraneous madrigal). Apart from such lapses, even the obscure and riddling by-play using Latin and technical musical terminology are faithfully played out, at the risk of alienating modern audiences. However, this was one of the better productions in the often moribund BBC series, partly because of the choice of a genuine comic as Petruccio, John Cleese, a casting that in part gains extraneous, meretricious meaning from the character's willingness to marry Kate were she 'as old as Sibyl' (1.2.69), since Cleese's 'Basil Fawlty' was married to 'Sybil' in the wildly popular British TV series, *Fawlty Towers*. By allowing Cleese to play the familiar character of Fawlty while giving full rein to Shakespearean language, and with the BBC series' necessary austerity of a small budget and constraints of filming in a small studio, the production highlights facets missing from the other, more glamorous, colourful, and farcical versions. As Michael Anderegg notes, in this production 'Jonathan Miller chooses to naturalize the play and downplay its farcical elements and flamboyance as much as possible',[25] which is so unusual in comparison with other versions that the tone is significantly sombre. For example, the verbally powerful analogy to training a hound or taming a 'haggard' or bird of prey, and the language of the Galenic doctrine of 'humours' (a word repeated with full force seven times) that prescribed abstinence for a 'choleric' temperament, point to an uncomfortable Elizabethan strain that cannot be easily made acceptable to modern sensibilities, and which highlights the cruelty of the process depicted. It also paradoxically makes almost believable the possibility that by the end Kate has in fact been 'tamed' not into abject submission but into something like a mutually sustained and genuine affection – though the actress Sarah Badel must take credit for this 'wonder, if you talk of wonders' (5.2.111). On the other hand, by also giving full emphasis to the 'counterfeit supposes' in the Bianca plot, the BBC production allows us paradoxically to find in the play a different seam that feeds into some movies where we may not at first sight expect to find material from *The Taming of the Shrew*.

I would argue (with some trepidation) that Mankiewicz's classic film *All About Eve* (1950) is one such unexpected and unacknowledged beneficiary of Shakespeare's comedy. Set in the world of American theatre, this film is drenched from first to last with Shakespearean references. It begins at the end of the story, in the awards ceremony for the 'Sarah Siddons Society' (fictional, but the film led to the creation of such a society), and in one famous scene the universally recognisable painting of Siddons as Lady Macbeth stands between Bette Davis and a youthful Marilyn Monroe. The ruthlessness of Lady Macbeth is one of the characteristics demonstrated by the ambitious young actress, Eve Harrington, who is involved in a professional 'murder' and usurpation. Meanwhile, the character played by Bette Davis is recalled as a child star who made her debut as a fairy in *A Midsummer Night's Dream*, demonstrating even at that age a characteristic individualism by appearing in the role 'stark naked' – presumably a reference to Reinhardt's version made fifteen years before *All About Eve*. The surprising, underlying similarities of genre between *All About Eve* and *The Taming of the Shrew* emerge if we respect Shakespeare's design, which places more weight than productions usually afford on the plot concerning Bianca. To rename *The Shrew* as 'All About Bianca' conveys the nuance. At the beginning of each work, Bianca and Eve respectively are presented as quiet victims living in the shadow of a more dominant woman, Kate/Margo, who is played in the film with unforgettable shrewishness by Bette Davis. Bianca cannot marry until her apparently unmarriageable sister finds a husband, while Eve as an aspiring actress shines only the dimmest of lights beside her famous and charismatic idol, whom she must replace before she can claim her own theatrical fame. However, by the end the roles are to some extent reversed. Just as Kate has accepted a more docile social role, Margo has accepted that her career and her independence are now curtailed, and she is upstaged decisively by her 'understudy' who now receives the Sarah Siddons award and can do what she likes in relationships, having temporarily even stolen the loyal lover of Eve. Bianca and Eve both emerge from under their respective shadows to prove themselves adroit plotters, moving towards their goals by cunningly manipulating various men who are either guileless (Gremio and Hortensio/Bill and Lloyd) or crafty (Lucentio/Addison DeWitt), generally being involved in subtle betrayals, and 'stealing' men from other women. There is even a subdued but telling parallel between the respective fates of Kate and Margo, since the latter, after being 'shrewish' and persecutorial towards her most ardent suitor, Bill Sampson, has a closely comparable scene of mutual tenderness at a meal in a restaurant, when she accepts in turn marriage, ageing, and semi-retirement, or at least a decision to curtail her desire to play women characters younger than herself. In the scene Eve is sitting at a different table with her Machiavellian patron, the critic DeWitt, after arguing in the ladies' room with her so-called friend, Karen. The quietly achieved moment of resolution between Margo and Bill has the same emotional frisson as the final kiss between Petruccio and Katherina. Margo announces to the table that she will not be playing the diva's role expected of her, either in the new play or in her own life:

> BILL I shall propose the toast, without wit, with all my heart. To Margo. To my bride-to-be.
> MARGO Glory hallelujah.

KAREN Margo! – when are you going to do it?
BILL Tomorrow we'll meet at City Hall at ten and [to Margot] you're going to be on time.
MARGOT Yes.
LLOYD City Hall – that's for prize fighters and reporters. I see a bishop, a cathedral, banks of flowers ...

They discuss what Margo is going to wear and, recalling the parsimonious Petruccio rather than Kate, she jokingly promises 'something simple over a night-gown'. Bill toasts the continuing friendship of all of them: 'There are very few moments in life like this. Let's remember it.' Such good-humoured openness and vulnerability, like the marriage itself, would have been unthinkable for Margo before this moment, and signals her chastening if not taming. Bill's behaviour towards her, while not as outrageous and physically demeaning as Petruccio's towards Katherina, has always been similar to the general approach of Petruccio, a combination of plain-speaking, even to the point of humiliating Margo with bluntness, of honest encouragement, and of occasional high praise. Petruccio's various speeches may be disingenuous but they open a new, possible way for Kate to see or construct herself:

> I find you passing gentle.
> 'Twas told me you were rough, and coy, and sullen,
> And now I find report a very liar,
> For thou art pleasant, gamesome, passing courteous,
> But slow in speech, yet sweet as springtime flowers.
> Thou canst not frown. Thou canst not look askance,
> Nor bite the lip, as angry wenches will,
> Nor hast thou pleasure to be cross in talk,
> But thou with mildness entertain'st thy wooers,
> With gentle conference, soft, and affable. (2.1.237–46)

Petruccio's praise is based on a disingenuous strategy, and Bill's moments of praising Margo have a more clearly genuine basis but similarly resist the world's fêting of Eve:

BILL The so-called art of acting is not one for which I have a particularly high regard.
MARGO Here, here.
BILL But you may quote me as follows. Tonight Miss Margo Channing gave a performance in your cockamamie play, the like of which I have never seen before and expect rarely to see again, unquote.
MARGOT He does not exaggerate, I was good.
BILL You were great.

In a rather strange way, we have in this strand of the plot a 'taming-of-the-shrew' narrative acceptable to modern times, revealing the process of bringing the recalcitrant Margo into line with social pleasantries and subtle emotional manipulation rather than physical taming. The end result, however, is no less remarkable, and persuades me to believe that Bette Davis, who was so willing to play 'shrewish' older women from Mildred in *Of Human Bondage* (1934) to Jane Hudson in *What Ever Happened to Baby Jane*, may be the best shrew who never actually played Katherina, at least on film.

Meanwhile, Margo's shrewishness, which has been indiscriminatingly directed at all her friends, comes gradually to be focused on Eve Harrington, with a purposeful misquotation of Shakespeare in the play that Mankiewicz was going on to film, *Julius Caesar*: 'Eve, evil, Little miss evil. How does that go? Something about the good they leave behind. I played it once in rep …'. Kate's words contemptuously dismissing the women at the end of *The Shrew*, 'Come, come you froward and unable worms' (5.2.174), are coincidentally echoed with equal ferocity when Karen calls Eve a 'contemptible little worm'.

Who's afraid of shrews?

The screwball or battle-of-the-sexes genre had a brief, little-noticed revival in the 1960s, and to observe it we return to Burton and Taylor. Their much-publicised marriage – or, indeed, marriages – were notorious for being based on conflict between strong and equally demanding, independent personalities, and in some ways the true film they made together that exhibits the battle of the sexes in the 'Taming-of-the-Shrew genre' came in 1966 with *Who's Afraid of Virginia Woolf?*, which in early drafts was called *The Exorcism*. Edward Albee's tortured, black satire on marriage has several references to Shakespeare.[26] Most relevant here is an argument between the married couple about whether the moon is up or down, recalling the most famous interchange in *The Shrew*, followed by George's 'Truth or illusion? Who knows the difference…?', which has been seen as a central point for analysis by scholars of Shakespeare's play.[27] Moreover and fundamentally, despite its topical context in deconstructing the American dream of the perfect marriage, Albee's play in its filmed adaptation turns on the same kind of brutal power struggle as *The Shrew*, though without Shakespeare's good-humoured, if problematical ending. Martha calls it a 'boxing match'. Over a disturbing, alcohol-fuelled evening, George and Martha argue viciously with each other in front of the young, newly wed Nick and Honey, and the emotional cruelty on both sides has no bounds with taunts over their sterile childlessness obscured by fantasies of an imaginary child, broken dreams, and infantilism. The younger character's line, 'Hell, I don't know when you people are lying, or what', could just as easily be Shakespeare's bewildered old man, Vincentio, whom Petruccio and Katherina end up agreeing is a young maiden, and in front of whom they argue whether the sun or moon is shining: 'But is this true, or is it else your pleasure?' (4.6.72):

MARTHA [*Passing on information*] There is no moon now. I saw it go down from the bedroom.
GEORGE [*Feigned glee*] From the bedroom! [*Normal tone*] Well, there was a moon.
MARTHA [*Too patient; laughing a little*] There couldn't have been a moon.
GEORGE Well there was. There is.
MARTHA There is no moon; the moon went down.
GEORGE There is a moon; the moon is up.

…

MARTHA [*Between her teeth*] There is no goddamn moon.

…

MARTHA [*With finality*] There is no moon; the moon went down.
GEORGE [*With great logic*] That may very well be, Chastity; the moon may very well have gone down … but it came back up.

…

MARTHA That is not true! That is such a lie!
GEORGE You must not call everything a lie, Martha. [*To Nick*]
NICK Hell, I don't know when you people are lying, or what.

…

GEORGE [*To Nick*] Truth and illusion. Who knows the difference, eh, toots? Eh?
MARTHA You were never in the Mediterranean … truth or illusion … either way.
GEORGE If I wasn't in the Mediterranean, how did I get to the Aegean? Hunh?
MARTHA OVERLAND!
NICK Yeah!
GEORGE Don't you side with her, houseboy.
NICK I am not a houseboy.
GEORGE Look! I know the game … Someone's lying around here; somebody ain't playing the game straight …
MARTHA [*Pleading*] Truth and illusion, George; you don't know the difference.
GEORGE No; but we must carry on as though we did.[28]

The 'game' includes both characters lecturing the younger couple, Nick and Honey, about the realities of marriage life, and it includes Martha echoing Petruccio with the public 'Give me a kiss'. The play ends, like *All About Eve*, with a woman chastened if not 'tamed', in fear not of her husband but of an existential loneliness:

GEORGE   Are you all right?
MARTHA   Yes. No.
GEORGE   [*puts his hand gently on her shoulder; she puts her head back and he sings to her, very softly*]:
Who's afraid of Virginia Woolf,
        Virginia Woolf,
        Virginia Woolf,
MARTHA   I ... am ... George ...
GEORGE   Who's afraid of Virginia Woolf ...
MARTHA   I ... am ... George ... I ... am ...
    [GEORGE *nods, slowly.*]
    [*Silence; tableau.*]

There are signs that in just this one exhausting evening, the initially more idealistic younger guests are gradually turning into the brawling older couple, and that in both couples the nasty bickering represents attempts to 'tame' the partner into submission as part of a repetitive behaviour based on co-dependent needs. As a vision of marriage the play offers a bleak view that is at least comparable with, and arguably influenced by, Shakespeare's in *The Shrew*. There may seem a long distance between the earlier, rough farce of disagreements in the path towards marriage and the twentieth-century black comedy of marriage (despite Albee's disclaimer, 'but it's not a funny play'[29]), but even such an inconsequential matter as the casting of Burton and Taylor in both indicates deeper similarities in genre. Both works are about power struggles or 'battles of the sexes' within marriage, and the latter is in essence an unacknowledged adaptation of the former into the frank and progressive idiom of the 1960s.

The example of films like *It Happened One Night*, *All About Eve*, *Who's Afraid of Virginia Woolf?* through to *10 Things*, all historically located in their own times and aimed at different audiences, can shame the more orthodox productions of *The Taming of the Shrew*, by at least realising the need to supply a set of character motivations that are comprehensible in modern contexts. While building upon Shakespeare's structure of a 'shrew-taming' genre, they make an effort to provide a plausible, contemporary sense to the fable. This is in contrast to the prevailing assumption of Shakespearean infallibility behind 'heritage' films of the play and many stage productions, tacitly underwriting elements of violence and reprehensible patriarchy as either hilariously funny to presumed 'groundlings' or ideologically unproblematic. This is what gives 'Shakespeare' a bad name, and misses the point that his plays can be adapted and rethought in relation to different social mores as social attitudes change. It is a mark of Shakespeare's writing itself, which is stressed in this book, that he rarely if ever uses a convention simply as an unchallenged datum, but rather he seeks to suggest some plausible motivation or human significance behind the convention, which can make it come alive in quite different historical times and local contexts. It is a commercial imperative for modern film-makers who use Shakespeare's generic structures, often without using his name, to make these structures emotionally and psychologically relevant and even compelling to their own audiences. In many ways, such unattributed adaptations may be more 'faithful' to the generic sources than antiquarian productions that do use Shakespeare's name yet make little attempt to provide a contemporary significance to his stories.

Notes

1 See Sammons, *Shakespeare: A Hundred Years on Film*, 133–41.
2 Diana E. Henderson, 'A Shrew for the Times', in Lynda E. Boose and Richard Burt (eds), *Shakespeare the Movie: Popularizing the Plays on Film, TV, and Video* (London and New York: Routledge, 1997), 148–68, 148.
3 For descriptions of different stage versions and their attempts to avoid or reinforce sexist attitudes, see Penny Gay, *As She Likes It: Shakespeare's Unruly Women* (London: Routledge, 1994).
4 Elinor Parsons, 'The Framing of the "Shrew": Screen Versions of "The Taming of the Shrew"', unpublished PhD thesis, Royal Holloway, University of London (2008).
5 Kathleen Rowe, 'Comedy, Melodrama and Gender: Theorizing the Genres of Laughter', in Kristina Brunovska Karnick and Henry Jenkins (eds), *Classical Hollywood Comedy* (New York: Routledge, 1995), 39–59, 41.
6 See, for example, Edmund Tilney's *Briefe and Pleasant Discourse of Duties in Marriage, Called the Flower of Friendshippe* (1568), repr. *The Flower of Friendship: A Renaissance Dialogue Contesting Marriage* (Ithaca, NY: Cornell University Press, 1992); Lisa Jardine, *Reading Shakespeare Historically* (Hoboken, NJ: Taylor & Francis, 1996), ch. 7.
7 Ann Thompson (ed.), *The Taming of the Shrew* (Cambridge: The New Cambridge Shakespeare, 1984), 9.
8 G. K. Hunter, *John Lyly: The Humanist as Courtier* (London: Routledge & Kegan Paul, 1962), 309–10.
9 See Rothwell, *A History of Shakespeare on Screen*, 28–34, for an affectionate and detailed account of the film.
10 Henderson, 'A Shrew for the Times', 149.
11 Irene G. Dash, *Shakespeare and the American Musical* (Bloomington, IN: Indiana University Press, 2010), ch. 2.
12 Cavell, *Pursuits of Happiness*, 123 and elsewhere.

13 Tina Olsin Lent, 'Romantic Love and Friendship: The Redefinition of Gender Relations in Screwball Comedy', in Kristina Brunovska Karnick and Henry Jenkins (eds), *Classical Hollywood Comedy* (New York: Routledge, 1995), 314–31, 315.
14 Lent, 'Romantic Love and Friendship', 317.
15 Lent, 'Romantic Love and Friendship', 325.
16 Parsons, 'The Framing of the "Shrew"', ch. 8.
17 Richard Maltby, 'Comedy and the Restoration of Order', in Jeffrey Geiger and R. L. Rutsky (eds), *Film Analysis: A Norton Reader* (New York: W. W. Norton & Co., 2005), 216–37, 219.
18 Maltby, 'Comedy and the Restoration of Order', 220.
19 Wes D. Gehring, *Romantic vs. Screwball Comedy: Charting the Difference* (Lanham, MD: The Scarecrow Press, Inc., 2002), 1.
20 Maltby, 'Comedy and the Restoration of Order', 221.
21 Maltby, 'Comedy and the Restoration of Order', 221.
22 Wheeler Winston Dixon (ed.), *American Cinema of the 1940s: Themes and Variations* (New Brunswick, NJ: Rutgers University Press, 2006), 52.
23 See analysis of the film in Bruce Babington and Peter William Evans, *Affairs to Remember: The Hollywood Comedy of the Sexes* (Manchester: Manchester University Press, 1989), 72–83.
24 Frank Capra, *The Name Above the Title* (New York: Macmillan, 1971), 164, quoted in Maltby, 'Comedy and the Restoration of Order', 231.
25 Michael Anderegg, *Cinematic Shakespeare* (Lanham, MD: Rowman & Littlefield, 2004), 163.
26 Qualified confirmation comes from admittedly dubious sources: see, for example, Michael Adams, *'Who's Afraid of Virginia Woolf?': Barron's Book Notes* (New York: Barron's Educational Series, 1985), 30 and 74. The 'imaginary baby' and related imagery seems to me to have some reference to *Macbeth*. It is also quite telling that in many Internet discussions of the play and productions there are unscholarly references to a connection between the plays, and often Martha is described, perhaps unkindly, as a 'shrewish wife' or simply a 'shrew', which may be significant since the word is no longer current except in relation to Shakespeare's play. For what it is worth, I have even found online in 'Essay Wizards' (and for sale, though I have not been tempted) an essay clearly intended for purposes of student plagiarism, titled 'Comparing and Contrasting "Who's Afraid of Virginia Woolf" and "The Taming of the Shrew"', so a teacher somewhere has thought of setting such a topic!
27 For example, by Hunter in *John Lyly*, 309–11.
28 Edward Albee, *Who's Afraid of Virginia Woolf?* (Harmondsworth: Penguin Plays, 1962), 117–19.
29 Quoted by Stephen J. Bottoms, *Albee: Who's Afraid of Virginia Woolf?* (Cambridge: Cambridge University Press, 2000), 16.

2
Dreams in the forest: romantic comedy

A film genre, as the term is being used in this book, has three dominant components that make up what Rick Altman calls its 'genetic blueprint':[1] a recognisable plot, a basic structure, and a recurrent ideology or set of assumptions about its subject matter. In romantic comedy the plot invariably centres on a love affair that is presented in ways that highlight comic incidents leading to a 'happy ending', which is most often betrothal. The structure can be encapsulated in Shakespeare's phrase 'the course of true love never did run smooth', since the main source of comedy lies in misunderstandings, 'misprisions', and adversities that impede the romance and create surprise and suspense, though the comic tone and presentation give comfort to the audience that love will be fulfilled. The pattern, running through adversity or chaos to harmony, is broadly the same in each case except *Love's Labour's Lost*, whose surprise ending is a kind of exception that proves the rule that audiences expect marriages. The underlying ideology of romantic comedy most often asserts the 'naturalness' of shared desire of lovers, and they have a literary motto in Virgil's 'Love conquers all things: let us too surrender to love' (parodied by Mae West in 'Love conquers all things except poverty and toothache', which adds an almost certainly unconscious parallel to Benedick's claimed toothache in *Much Ado*). Alongside these broad generic similarities there can be variations in sub-groups, which are examined in other chapters: musical comedy (Chapter 3) and 'screwball' or 'odd-couple' comedy (Chapter 1). Disguise and mistaken identity are considered separately (Chapter 5). In this chapter we look at some structural components of romantic comedy in general, insofar as they entered modern culture through Shakespeare's plays.

Shakespearean comedy as composite form

One thing that emerges from this book is that in the particular area of romantic comedy, Hollywood films often do not necessarily draw from a specific play by Shakespeare, but instead take elements from different plays within the dominant genre. The plays most generally alluded to, for obvious commercial reasons, are ones that are popular in school and college syllabuses. Shakespearean romantic comedy, for example, is generally understood to be a fusing of conventions and structures from *A Midsummer Night's Dream*, *Twelfth Night*, *As You Like It*, and *The Merchant of Venice*. In particular instances one play might be most obvious as a patterned influence, but more often films are built on elements that are common to this group of Shakespearean precedents. Many comedies and musicals actually quote Shakespeare or in some way explicitly identify a connection that suggests a genre. At the same time, if 'repetition with variation' is our shorthand description of genre, then 'variations' are inevitably explained partly by historical differences. Not only must we make a large allowance for the fact that Shakespeare's romantic comedies were written in the 1590s, exactly three hundred years before movies were even invented, but also the history of film spans not just a decade but a century and more, during which many historical changes occurred within each period: the Depression years of the 1930s, the Second World War, the consolidation of 'family life' in the 1950s, the dominance of youth culture in the 1960s and 1970s, and so on. With each change, movie styles change. Like fashions in dress, courtship rituals are constantly changing in subtle or ostentatious ways, and they vary geographically despite the increasing reach of globalism. However, the argument of this chapter is that despite the economic, political, cultural, and historical changes, some central, underlying motifs and patterns link Shakespeare's romantic comedies and Hollywood romantic comedies in ways that are not entirely coincidental but rather a matter of influence, in some cases direct but more often indirect, and which are primary and enduring through the different examples. Admittedly, many of the sources I suggest are not only unconscious but also tangential, allusive, or at times conjectural, and the relationship between movies and Shakespeare, as known within the film industry and as part of a ubiquitous but largely unacknowledged legacy for modern popular culture, could be amusingly encapsulated in an exchange from *Stage Door* (1937):

– Hamlet? Never heard of him.
– Certainly you must have heard of Hamlet?
– Well, I meet so many people ...[2]

Even to those who think they know little or nothing about Shakespeare, the name Hamlet rings bells as a real person, and they can be exposed to Shakespearean themes and genres without realising it.

The fact that movies may emerge not from a specific play but from a kind of 'composite' Shakespearean plot that fuses structural elements from several comedies reflects an educational system in the English-speaking world and beyond that takes as its repertoire well-known plays like *Twelfth Night* and *A Midsummer Night's Dream*. These are melded into a single cultural commodity called 'Shakespearean comedy'. But it is also a result of the dramatist's own flexible and hybrid linking of genres into something unique, which marks especially those he more or less invented himself, such as dramatised history, tragi-comedy, and romantic comedy. As G. K. Hunter puts it, 'Shakespeare's plays are built on a schematic framework ... but it is Shakespeare's way to avoid committing himself too far, and to allow diverse significances to burgeon round the framework of his materials'.[3] The merging of framework genres into something capacious is just as typical of movies as of Shakespeare's plays, as Richard Maltby points out: 'Hollywood movies are best understood as aggregations of familiar parts; their individuality is to be found in their particular combination of standardized, interchangeable elements. Romance and comedy, both staple ingredients of Hollywood's output, have been combined in a variety of ways throughout Hollywood's history.'[4] We may add, the combination of romance and comedy is true not only in 'Hollywood's history' but in Shakespeare's plays, since romances such as Thomas Lodge's *Rosalynde* and Sir Philip Sidney's *Arcadia* are among the sources for his comedies, spliced into an essentially new genre in his own time, romantic comedy. Classical and Italian comic traditions played their part in Shakespeare's apprenticeship as well,[5] but the shaping mode that he returned to from first to last is romance.

Some of the common and essential ingredients for a composite form emerging from Shakespeare's romantic comedies would include several shared structural assumptions, expectations, and motifs, and mere summary will anticipate some of these that emerge in cinematic romantic comedy. First, here are some salient characteristics of Shakespearean romantic comedy, many of them identified especially by the more general, theoretical works of Northrop Frye and C. L. Barber.[6] Frye especially claimed a genealogy for these plays that he traced back to classical New Comedy by Menander, but this seems a distraction and it is simpler to argue that Shakespeare created from disparate sources romantic comedy, at least for the modern world.

1. Sexual desire felt by at least two couples: up to five in *Love's Labour's Lost* and six in *A Midsummer Night's Dream* (if we count

Helena/Lysander and Titania/Bottom). Lovers eventually 'come to the ark' in marriage, two-by-two, by the end of their plays.
2. Resistance to desire, either through parental opposition, societal pressure, or preliminary, internal barriers within either man or woman or both (Kate and Petruccio, Beatrice and Benedick, and at least three of the four courtiers who initially vow to abjure the company of women in *Love's Labour's Lost*).
3. Misunderstandings, 'misprisions', and 'errors' that complicate the path of love.
4. Disguised or changed identity and/or cross-dressing, at least in some comedies.
5. Eventual acceptance of desire as a legitimate experience for young people (in all Shakespeare's comedies to some extent, but most explicitly in *Love's Labour's Lost*). This usually comes through a transformative or metamorphic set of experiences.
6. Emphasis on groups of characters rather than individuals, and usually presented formally as a double or triple plot structure (not necessarily with the subordination of plot and sub-plots).[7] The ensemble is expected to come together as an integrated community at the end, celebrating marriage.
7. More generally, following the findings of Bakhtin, a 'carnivalesque' enactment of social harmony in community rituals of holiday provides the destination of Shakespearean romantic comedy.
8. Resolution of conflicts, contradictions, and oppositions through the unravelling of problems or passing of time: 'thus the whirligig of time brings in his revenges' (*Twelfth Night*, 5.1.373).
9. Audience expectation that marriage will resolve problems and end the play, even if in Shakespeare's examples there are often troubling or problematical elements in the closure.
10. Expectation of community harmony achieved by the end, indicating a defeat of older, conservative values and a passing of power to the young.
11. Contrasting locations, one repressive and restrictive, the other emotionally liberating (courts and the Forest of Arden or Athens, Venice and Belmont, and so on). The latter settings have been categorised by Shakespearean critics since the work of Northrop Frye as 'green world' locations suggesting a more natural environment, as in the respective forests, or a faraway place where love is the predominant emotion and can flourish in due course, such as Illyria and Belmont. The contrast will become relevant in cinematic terms as one between a 'workaday' environment or even specifically a workplace where power relations are exercised, and a 'holiday' world where again love can be the centre of attention.

12. Songs and music punctuate the action, and in some cases plays end with the play's community witnessing or participating in a shared event, where singing and dancing represent communal integration, as it invariably does in musicals,[8] for example at the end of *The Merry Wives of Windsor* at the cost of the excluded, scapegoated figure, Falstaff.
13. Such scapegoats (Northrop Frye's word) or 'strangers' (Leslie A. Fiedler's term) or outsiders are conspicuously left out of the final festivities because they have opposed the comic drive – Shylock and Malvolio, for example – or abused hospitality, like Falstaff in *The Merry Wives*.[9]
14. Sub-plots involving different social levels of lovers: William and Audrey as 'country copulatives' (5.4.55–6), Touchstone the discontented courtier, Silvius and Phoebe as conventional figures from poetry, all in *As You Like It*; the incongruously matched Jaquenetta and Armado or Costard in *Love's Labour's Lost*.
15. Sometimes a rehearsed 'play within a play' (*Love's Labour's Lost*, *A Midsummer Night's Dream*).[10]
16. Metatheatre – acknowledgement of artifice and 'play', which simultaneously and paradoxically asserts a level of reality by drawing attention to fictiveness.
17. A general assumption that women will constitute a significant element – perhaps a majority – in the audience (Queen Elizabeth in particular as a targeted member of the audience), mirrored in the plays by a sense that the fictional women are guiding consciousnesses and committed to the autonomy of their emotions.
18. In each comedy there is a stock character of a fool, played by an actor who specialised in such roles (Feste, Touchstone, Lancelot Gobbo, and others). However, each is characterised more particularly, for example as a 'wise fool' or self-conscious jester, who comments on, sees through, and punctures the follies of others, or as a 'natural' who is himself foolish (Bottom, Dogberrry, Costard).[11]

The works of Frye and Barber in particular were very influential in academic approaches and college teaching in the mid twentieth century and they are often cited with approval in studies of cinematic romantic comedy: 'Frye [and Barber] can be credited with finding profundity in romantic comedy, and in comedy itself, that had eluded earlier generations of critics.'[12] Each argues in different ways that art gives expression to collective experiences repeated over time and equating to social rituals of 'festivity'. Their historical period, the 1940s and 1950s, comprised the decades that are generally regarded as a period of consolidation and development of cinematic genres such as romantic comedy, melodrama, and the musical, both on Broadway and in Hollywood. In fact it was not until their generation of critics, students, and theatrical practitioners that Shakespearean comedy was taken seriously as worthy of systematic analysis, rather than simply being praised as delightful, lightweight diversions, too delicate for the full weight of serious analysis, or else to be treated as ahistorical examples of poetic style to be analysed out of their historical context in a New Critical spirit. Frye in particular, Samuel Crowl reminds us, by switching attention to genre, provided a more challenging approach based on then topical approaches in archetypes and anthropology.[13] As I have suggested, Hollywood writers at least, and sometimes producers and directors, were inevitably products of educational fashions in their time, and certainly romantic comedy was at the forefront of teaching and criticism of Shakespeare from the 1950s onwards. However, the evolution of filmed romantic comedy from its arguably Shakespearean roots started much earlier, and was guided not primarily by theorists but by theatre practitioners, especially one like Harley Granville-Barker, who wrote at length about his directorial aims.

The repetitions, shared aspects, and influences emerge by comparing the template above from Shakespearean comedy beside significant elements encountered in many cinematic romantic comedies and musicals. Here I cannot be categorical in saying that *all* the relevant films share the same elements (if only because there are potentially hundreds of examples), and my list should more insistently include words like 'sometimes', 'often', 'frequently', or just 'occasionally'. I also repeat the point that I am not presenting the plays (except in some examples) as actual sources for the films, but rather as generic influences, and the repetitions will inevitably have something to do with coincidence and filmic intertextuality. But even with these qualifications, the shared territory is, I believe, clear and comprehensive, and all we need to do to show this is to reproduce the same summary with only a few refinements. Repetition is tiresome, but here it is used to prove the point.

1. Sexual desire is a fundamental driving force and a datum in film romantic comedies and perhaps even more clearly in musical comedies.[14] While in romantic comedy the focus is on one couple especially, in musicals the sexes hunt in packs – at least two men pursue one or two women, three men meet three women, while *Seven Brides for Seven Brothers* (1954) is an extreme example. As a result, and as in Shakespeare's comedies, there is little more than superficial individuation between characters who make up the courting patterns, each of whom is given a dominant trait.
2. Resistance to desire, through parental or societal opposition, institutional and bureaucratic indifference, internal barriers within either

man or woman, or all of these. In the context of film genres this drive has been equated by Kathleen Rowe with 'anti-authoritarianism' of a peculiarly feminine kind, with 'its attack on the Law of the Father and drive to level, disrupt and destroy hierarchy',[15] overturning or at least confusing male intentions in the process, but moving unobtrusively towards distinctively feminine commitments such as 'family bondings like marriage ... always moving dramatically towards conclusions in which people are united and conflict dissipated'.[16]

3. Misunderstandings, initial conflict, 'misprisions', and 'errors' (both words used repeatedly as significant concepts by Shakespeare) – these are elements just as central to romantic comedy on stage and in films.
4. Disguise, cross-dressing: while not often the implausible Elizabethan convention of physical disguise, there is frequently a strong issue of mistaken identity based on class, wealth, or professional grounds, amounting to disguise. So recurrent is this that Chapter 5 will be devoted to it.
5. Eventual acceptance of fulfilled desire as a legitimate goal for young people: again, as central a narrative event in cinematic romantic comedy as in Shakespeare.
6. Emphasis on social harmony rather than individual gratification, and the ensemble is expected to be integrated into a community at the end.
7. Following Bakhtin, a 'carnivalesque' enactment of social harmony in community rituals of holiday provides the destination of cinematic romantic comedy, as, for example, and most spectacularly, at the end of musical comedies like *Meet Me in St. Louis* and *Carousel*, but equally evident in most romantic comedies.
6. Resolution of conflicts, contradictions, and oppositions through the unravelling of problems or passing of time.
6. Audience expectation that marriage will resolve problems and end the film, as it ends the Shakespearean play – unless it is deferred as in *Love's Labour's Lost* and some films from the war experience, when the future could not be securely predicted.
7. Often, the expectation of community harmony achieved by the end indicates defeat of older, conservative values, overturning institutional blockages, and passing power to the young.
8. Contrasting locales figure in some musical comedies, and at the very least an exotic, 'faraway' setting is frequently chosen. There can be a figurative equivalent in, for example, a workplace contrasted with a 'holiday' environment, an artificial place like the disciplined, 'legitimate theatre' contrasted with a relatively 'real' and informal backstage environment for indulgence of emotional entanglements and expression, or depicting characters 'on holiday' from their usual living spaces.

9. Music (in romantic comedy) and songs (in musicals) punctuating the action as an attempt to direct and manipulate the audience's emotional participation in the narrative flow. Invariably such films end with the onstage community witnessing or participating in an ensemble event indicated by a musical crescendo or universal singing and dancing. Bollywood films provide the most joyous examples of this dimension.
10. There can be equivalents to Shakespeare's scapegoats, figures deliberately left out of the final harmony because they have represented some kind of opposition to the comic drive. For example, in *Bringing Up Baby*, Alice Swallow, as David Huxley's fiancée, had asserted a joyless creed that 'Our marriage must entail no domestic entanglements of any kind', and her primary commitment to 'work' and a merely functional marriage mean she loses 'her man' to the anarchically scatty and unpredictable Susan Vance.
11. Sub-plots involving different social levels of lovers seem not particularly significant in movies, but equally are not unprecedented.
12. The play within a play is typically reversed in those musicals categorised as 'backstage musicals' – the emotional imbroglios of the self-conscious performers are resolved, which heralds the occasion of the 'stage' performance to end the film.
13. Metatheatre – acknowledgement of artifice and 'play': we are rarely in any doubt that the movies in this genre represent an artificial and 'tinsel town' context, since so many of the characters are aspiring actors or involved in actual staged performances, and they draw attention to the fact.
14. A general assumption that women will constitute a significant element, again perhaps a majority, in the audience, mirrored in the films by a sense that the women are guiding consciousnesses in many of the movies and are primarily following their emotions in ways the men sometimes find difficult. This need not render irrelevant accusations of 'the male gaze' at work behind the camera, nor the commodification or fetishisation of females – far from it – but compared with other genres the musical tends to give equality or even empowerment to women in their search for a sexual mate even when (as in Shakespeare) the power structure favours the man. A sub-genre of romantic comedy (and tragedy) in films is known as 'chick flicks' in recognition of some essentially feminine attributes.
15. In many romantic comedies and more especially musical comedies, we find a character who fulfils one of the two possible roles ('wise' or 'natural') of the Shakespearean fool. Often the function is to act as a foil for the male hero as a naive and incompetent rival in love

(a 'fall guy'), or to comment on the developing complexities of emotions from an innocent, immature, or child-like perspective, but none the less offering a perceptive point of view, representing a pre-sexual perspective to emphasise or comment upon the changes being undergone in lovers.

Over the course of this and the following chapters, a selection of these aspects from 'composite' Shakespearean comedy will be analysed, insofar as they are reflected in some films.

...

There are some movie pioneers and innovators whose names are most regularly associated with classics up to the 1950s in the genres I am discussing. Director Ernst Lubitsch had worked with the Austrian Max Reinhardt's Deutsches Theater, and the acting style he encourages in his films is intrinsically theatrical, as Dan Sallitt mentions.[17] He evidently admired the repertoire of classical dramatic plots, filming early in his career a comic version of *Romeo and Juliet* (*Romeo und Julia im Schnee* (1920)), Oscar Wilde's *Lady Windermere's Fan* (1925), and *Carmen*, titled *Gipsy Blood in America* (1918), all in Germany. His *To Be or Not to Be* (1942), although predominantly a satirical rather than romantic comedy, is full of obvious references to Shakespeare, not least in the title.[18] Lubitsch's name is always linked with the phrase 'sophisticated comedy' and his hallmarks are the kind of moral ambivalence and mingling of poignancy with comedy that underline Shakespeare's comedies ('The web of our life is of a mingled yarn, good and ill together', in the phrase from *All's Well That Ends Well*, 4.3.74–5), and the frank admission that romantic idealism is always underpinned by sexual desire and seduction, which equally characterise Shakespeare's romantic comedies. The other director, Billy Wilder, was another émigré from Hitler's Europe, and he worked with Lubitsch on *Ninotchka* (1939) and other films. He is a director who often puts writers in the central role, as in *Double Indemnity* (1944), *The Lost Weekend* (1945), which has several Shakespearean allusions, and *Sunset Boulevard* (1950). Wilder's form of romantic comedy sometimes shows affinity with the character types initiated by Shakespeare where 'unsuspecting men are beguiled by beautiful and intelligent women',[19] and he recurrently uses disguise as a plot motif. Among actors who most notably star in romantic comedy is Cary Grant, whose strange accent and mannered demeanour, parodied by Tony Curtis in *Some Like It Hot* (1959), lends to his roles an air of old-fashioned American aristocracy and gallantry. We see the same male naivety and dim-wittedness that one finds in Orsino (*Twelfth Night*), Orlando (*As You Like It*), and the King of Navarre (*Love's Labour's Lost*). One of the great actresses of the period, Audrey Hepburn, who appears in another film that deals with the tribulations of a screenwriter, *Breakfast at Tiffany's* (1961), with her gamine appearance, verbal poise, and sophisticated, sprightly intelligence, also seems to epitomise aspects of Shakespeare's heroines, in plots that draw from his romantic comedy. The film is only loosely based on Truman Capote's novella (1958), which seems more than coincidentally close to Christopher Isherwood's novel *Goodbye to Berlin* (1939), which was adapted into the film *I Am a Camera* (1955) before the writing of *Breakfast at Tiffany's*, and later into the musical film *Cabaret* (1972). Like Isherwood's Sally Bowles, Holly Golightly is an anarchic muse to the narrator as writer, and an image of the twentieth-century liberated 'new woman'. The prototype of Shakespeare's Rosalind is a dramatic source for both in her sexual frankness, role playing, vitality, and androgynous appearance: in Capote's story Holly is described as having 'ragbag colors of her boy's hair' and she sings 'in the hoarse, breaking tones of a boy's adolescent voice'. However, the roles they play in their respective narratives are very different.

Of course, Shakespeare himself borrowed from earlier drama, literature, and classical literary theory, a heritage that he himself developed and passed on in his own refashionings to later generations. His adaptations are so effective, memorable, and influential because he rarely relies on a convention without infusing it with some human significance that can operate even when the artifice of the convention is acknowledged. The capacity to remain true to a generic source such as romance while also implying a psychological explanation for the genre's existence is a recognisable and unique emotional dimension of the plays, and it is intrinsic to Shakespeare's continuing currency in theatrical repertoires and popularity with contemporary readers. It is one of the qualities that lift his plays above the ruck of other innovative but less conceptually sophisticated works from his time, such as the plays of Lyly and Greene. It is also one secret to the apparently endless adaptability of his plays to new circumstances and times. The most obvious example is the use of disguise, which will be more fully considered in Chapter 5. The idea that a woman can trick her own lover by adopting a disguise still works in the case of Shakespeare, despite its patent absurdity today. No doubt it was more acceptable to Elizabethans as a convention, not only because of a conditioned willing suspension of disbelief in encountering a familiar comic trope, but also because audiences knew the actor was initially a disguised male anyway, but it seems on the face of it unlikely to deceive modern audiences. However, on stage and screen, the examples of Rosalind, Viola, Portia, and others continue to intrigue and convince us, because Shakespeare makes the convention comment on some much larger issue of identity, and he makes this function different in every case. Their disguises are not simply external, physical, and relating to gender, but based on distinctive modes of thinking about human beings in social and amatory relationships, playing out issues of recognition, role playing, and desire, in ways that transcend convention and take on significance for lives beyond the play. In Shakespeare's plays, disguise can function as metaphor, denoting sometimes the porousness and fluidity of gender definitions, or the wish to identify with a beloved person, the ability to change under the internal pressure of desire, and other forms of behaviour, states of mind, and emotional lability. In such ways some of the apparently most creaky, outdated, and blatantly artificial conventions from Shakespeare's theatre of comedy can be 'made new' in the medium of cinema, which is so adaptively sensitive to changing concepts and social norms. But the impetus for such adaptations comes from the variety of examples of what Shakespeare himself made of disguise, recognising the psychological resources and human potential of a visual conceit.

Romantic comedy is different in its origins, direct sources, and effects from 'odd-couple' comedy stemming from *The Taming of the Shrew*. It comes primarily from prose romance sources, while the latter is a form of comedy more familiar in earlier theatrical traditions, though with romance conventions in the Bianca plot. A description given by a film theorist to distinguish 'screwball' from 'romantic' comedy in movies will ring immediate bells in differentiating *Shrew* from 'romantic' comedy in Shakespeare's works: 'the accenting of sentiment over silly, a propensity for serious and/or melodramatic overtones, more realistic characters (often employed), traditional dating ritual (less controlling woman), and slower pacing (especially near the end of the picture).'[20] Each of these aspects can be adapted to fit Shakespeare's influential version of romantic comedy, although it is debatable whether the woman is 'less controlling' in all cases, except insofar as she arguably loses some freedom when slotted into the role of wife by the end of the work. Women in romantic comedy do guide the action, but more subtly and less robustly than the forceful women in screwball films. In the Shakespearean prototypes, sentiment as the celebration of love, represented as 'one's life is not complete without finding that significant other person',[21] dominates over farce. 'Serious overtones' and sombre plot developments emerge in events like the 'death' of Hero in *Much Ado*, the trial of flesh and the fate of Shylock in *The Merchant of Venice*, and the humiliation of Malvolio in *Twelfth Night*. The characters are more emotionally complex than the one-note, Punch-and-Judy figures in *The Shrew*, and there is often a backdrop of artisanal and working characters ('rude mechanicals', constables, stewards, lawyers) to expand the social canvas and imply diverse points of view coming to bear on situations. The plots develop not primarily in terms of a battle of the sexes as in *The Shrew* and *Much Ado About Nothing* (a unique fusing of romance and 'odd-couple comedy'), but through young lovers discovering their feelings early and resisting problems placed in the way of the match. The pacing does noticeably slow down in the final acts of the romantic comedies, where plays within plays are sometimes presented (as in the *Dream* and *Love's Labour's Lost*), where revelations emerge with a sense of suspended time generating wonder (*Twelfth Night*), or lovers muse poetically about their fortune (*The Merchant of Venice*). A part of the resulting impression is that love is hard-won but can reach a point of fulfilled stasis, and mutual love is an abiding rather than a fleeting emotion. However, earlier in films 'love cannot come easily', in Gehring's words, just as 'the course of true love never did run smooth' in Shakespearean comedy. Gehring later adds to the cinematic formula 'an older, experienced figure of practical wisdom', and even without looking at the Friar and the Nurse in *Romeo and Juliet* we find older characters in comedies, such as the Countess in *All's Well That Ends Well* and Duke Senior in *As You Like It*. The figure need not be conspicuously older, as the example of Berowne in *Love's Labour's Lost* shows. A writer on Hollywood, Nora Ephron, is quoted with a statement that could just as aptly refer to Shakespeare's lovers: 'talk was the sex of the romantic movie. People fell in love from what they said to one another', without the need for enacted or physical love-making.[22] Gehring adds to the mix 'occasional revengeful moments',[23] just as we can point to Malvolio's resolve to be revenged on his tormenters, or Shylock's final moments in *The Merchant*. There is in romantic comedy, despite its conventions, a 'believability factor' allowing audiences to empathise with characters and to feel 'this could happen to me'.[24] It is pointed out by film theorist Steve Neale that even the apparent unpredictability of plots in romantic comedy, as compared to westerns and war films, might be explained not in terms of an intrinsically more or less complex genre (as Neale himself tends to argue), but because romantic comedy draws on the considerably richer and more diverse pool of precedents in Shakespeare.[25] To all these characteristics shared by cinematic and Shakespearean romantic comedies, we can add more formal ones. In musicals, for example, the propensity for lovers to burst into song under the influence of emotion is comparable to the practice of Shakespeare, who in turn took the motif from prose romances such as Sidney's *Arcadia* as well as dramatic models, in which characters break into song or poetry under the emotional pressure of the moment.

Turning now to the filmed romantic comedies as a broader field, the list of similarities summarised above still applies, but with emphasis on 'green world' settings and juxtaposed locations, on misunderstandings in the process of courtship, the use of disguise (whether by cross-dressing or some other form of identity concealment and role playing), magic, whether literal or metaphorical, and the final endorsement of marriage as a form of achieved community harmony. As elsewhere in this book, many of the examples in this chapter are taken from the first fifty years of movie history, since this is the period in which, arguably, the Shakespearean influence is more direct than it came to be later, when the immediate sources for films are likely to be earlier films rather than the more distant influence from drama. Many musicals and romantic comedies take elements from different Shakespearean comedies as a common pool of related plot structures and themes.

The charming film *You Were Never Lovelier* (1942), starring Fred Astaire and Rita Hayworth, is a romantic comedy with musical elements, and although far from Shakespearean in quality, the influence is so insistently close to the surface that one could even argue it could hardly have been conceived and written in the way it was without the precedent of Shakespeare's comedies as a group. It gently draws from an array of influences. From *The Shrew* comes the initial situation that prevents younger daughters from marrying before the older (this time the second daughter), who in this case 'has a heart like an ice cube' and who 'freezes off' potential suitors. As in the case of Beatrice and Benedick in *Much Ado*, the heroine Maria Acunas (Hayworth) is tricked into thinking she has a lover, Robert Davis (Astaire), who turns out to be equally the victim of a trick, in this case played by her father in sending flowers anonymously. Showing a character type now more like Beatrice of Messina than Katherina of Padua, Maria is warned by her sisters, 'Don't frighten him with your intellect'. A muted version of Viola's poignant 'she never told her love' speech from *Twelfth Night* is reversed in gender terms:

> MARIA Am I the first girl you ever kissed?
> ROBERT I knew a fella once who came to a lull like this with a girl ...
> MARIA Yes?
> ROBERT He didn't know what to say.
> MARIA Oh, I heard of a man once who was in love with a girl and afraid to say so ...

They are, of course, speaking of themselves, as Viola is describing her fate in third-person narration. As in *Much Ado* and *Romeo and Juliet*, there is a masked or fancy-dress ball where emotions come to a head. Meanwhile, there is a mounting impression that Maria's father's secretary, Fernando, is a kind of generalised Shakespearean fool, and this role is finally clinched at the ball when he appears in motley and is called a 'jester'. Meanwhile, throughout the story, the impediment to love is not the father (who, as in *The Shrew*, wants his daughter married off) but a more internal one that stems from one Shakespearean theme par excellence – the differences between illusion and reality. This is constantly asserted by the father, whose stated intention from early in the movie is to make his daughter 'fall in love with an illusion' by creating an imaginary lover. He is convinced that if she meets a real-life lover 'she'll be disillusioned'. Later he tells Robert, 'Maria isn't really in love with you. She merely thinks she is'. To the young man's reply 'It's good enough for me', Acunas responds, 'There'll come a day when the illusion I created vanished. She'd see you as you really are', and Davis later says, 'I just want her to remember me as she thinks I am'. The danger that both have been led to 'make love under false pretences' also hangs over Beatrice and Benedick, who are tricked into expressing love, Claudius, whose wooing of Hero is conducted by the masked Don Pedro at the ball and who is persuaded later to marry Hero's 'sister', and Helena and Demetrius (still under the influence of magic juice from the flower love-in-idleness) at the end of the *Dream*, and even Olivia in *Twelfth Night*, who accepts Sebastian as a lover simply because he looks like Viola. Such a recurrent emphasis on illusions in love led to a common approach in criticism of Shakespeare in the early twentieth century, through well-known books by, for example, John Dover Wilson, H. B. Charlton, Harley Granville-Barker, and Muriel Bradbrook.[26] The implication that the father in the film is a kind of surrogate for his daughter's lover reminds us perhaps of theories popularised in the 1930s and 1940s by Sigmund Freud, who generated some of his ideas from *The Merchant of Venice*, *Hamlet*, and *Macbeth*. In the film, Maria is said to have been in love with the fictional knight Lochinvar as a fifteen-year-old, and Davis reprises her lapsed love by appearing as a knight in her garden, literally on a horse and in shining armour. The whole plot, while not attributable to one single play by Shakespeare as a source, is awash with elements of Shakespearean romantic comedy as a composite form, based on a conscious and explicit metatheatrical reliance that illusion asserted strongly enough may become reality. If one believes strongly enough in an illusion, it can come true, a sentiment that may tacitly underpin Shakespeare's practice in romantic comedy, as well as running through the appealing but less immortal *You Were Never Lovelier*.

Dreams in a green world

Shakespeare repeats scenes, sequences, and structures that he realises work effectively in the theatre, replaying them with fertile variations. In an unending process of source, influence, and intertextuality, his own practice has been taken as licence and encouragement by film-makers to continue drawing upon and varying some generically familiar elements. One of the strongest structural devices Shakespeare found in older, pastoral romance, and turned to his own use, was moving his characters into a destabilising environment in which they are transformed emotionally. Already in his earliest attempt at romantic comedy, *The Two Gentlemen of Verona*, the forest is a place where people are lost and lovers find themselves and each other, to be repeated in an orchard in Messina, forests outside Athens and Arden (or rather, Ardennes), and eventually a Bohemian sheep farm in *The Winter's Tale*, rustic Milford Haven in *Cymbeline*, different sea ports in *Pericles*, and an island where magic may flourish in *The Tempest*. Later we shall observe examples of such transformative environments in some Hollywood musicals. Of Shakespeare's, the most familiar to play-goers and movie-makers is the Wood of Athens, in which a frightening overnight stay transforms people's minds, feelings, and, in Bottom's case, body in magical ways. At the heart of the bewildering changes is the drive that is so much a staple in Hollywood movies, the human libido. The agency of change in *A Midsummer Night's Dream* – juice from the flower love-in-idleness – can take different forms in movies. In *I Married a Witch* (1942), it is a potion used by a witch who uses it to try to reverse a curse put on her family by an ancient patriarch that the sons will always marry the wrong woman – only to create the kinds of multiple problems that bedevil Puck in his attempts to match up the right couples. More recently, the equally farcical *A Midsummer Night's Rave* (2002), a conscious pastiche of Shakespeare's play, shows the irrational events being caused by consciousness-altering drugs and the air of psychedelic fantasy created by a musical rave party. There are many others to which we can turn.

The Philadelphia Story (1940) ranks among the greatest romantic comedies from Hollywood, and is among those included by Stanley Cavell in the sub-genre he suggests, comedy of remarriage, with links to Shakespearean romance. However, also like Cavell, in this case I find enough bells ringing in the film to lead us back more specifically to *A Midsummer Night's Dream*, in terms of a dominant ethos shared between film and play: 'it is very much to the point that Shakespeare's faery realm is the realm of the erotic', states Cavell suggestively.[27] The connection with the *Dream* illustrates one of the facets – or problems – of locating

Shakespearean adaptation that we encounter elsewhere in this book. Even if we do not find between play and film a set of easily recognised, one-to-one equivalents in either the plot or character roles, yet we can notice echoes of quotations, situations, and allusions, detecting through them some common themes and similar predicaments faced by characters who play various roles reminiscent of Shakespeare's. The ingredients are mingled together as if the elements of the play have been shaken up and rearranged into a pattern aligned with the shape of a generic forebear, in this case the *Dream*. Among the many qualities of *The Philadelphia Story* that make it a sparkling film, including the performances of Katherine Hepburn, Cary Grant, and James Stewart, it is arguable that part of its make-up reflects a memory of George Cukor's *A Midsummer Night's Dream* made four years before. An early signal comes in the exchange of truncated clichés as Tracy Lord's mother begins, 'The course of true love …', to be completed by Connor's misquoting, '… Never gathers moss'. The full exchange in *A Midsummer Night's Dream* has resonance for the triangle of male lovers around Tracy in the film:

> LYSANDER Ay me, for aught that I could ever read,
> Could ever hear by tale or history,
> The course of true love never did run smooth,
> But either it was different in blood –
> HERMIA O cross! – too high to be enthralled to low.
> LYSANDER Or else misgrafted in respect of years –
> HERMIA O spite! – too old to be engaged to young.
> LYSANDER Or merit stood upon the choice of friends –
> HERMIA O hell! – to choose love by another's eyes.
> …
> If then true lovers have been ever crossed,
> It stands as an edict in destiny. (1.1.132–51 *passim*)

In relation to the film's Macauley Connor himself (Stewart), Tracy is 'too high to be enthralled to low' since, as heiress to millions, she arouses the instinctive class resentment of the ostentatiously lower-class reporter, whose inexperience and youth are also emphasised as divisive issues. The other two suitors are encumbered by their own disadvantages: C. K. Dexter Haven (Grant) is Tracy's previous husband who had disqualified himself by his drinking and by striking and thus humiliating her, while George Kittredge (John Howard), the family's choice (chosen 'by another's eyes'), is a ponderous and moralistic politician. (It is tempting to suggest his name was created as a joking reference to two different 'George Kittredges' known by name in America, one a Democrat in Congress in the late nineteenth century, the other a prominent American Shakespearean scholar before the Second World War whose *Complete Works of Shakespeare* was widely in use, but a man seen outside Harvard as an archetype of the plodding pedant.) It is in her relationships with these men and with her father that Tracy's role might be seen as cutting up and re-pasting various Shakespearean parts. Her situation is in some ways comparable to Hermia's as a woman who is courted, if not by three, at least by two men, and is also in a fraught relationship with her father. Hermia is a character type to be repeated in Desdemona and Cordelia, and all three are reflected in the predicaments in the situation. Like Lear, Tracy's father reproves her for lacking a daughter's 'foolish, unquestioning, uncritical affection' and above all 'an understanding heart'. However, in relation to the true rivals in love, Dexter and Connor, she is placed as a Titania between Oberon and Bottom. Dexter is the jealous husband (or ex-husband in his case) who, after trying to get his own back by embarrassing her, is to be reconciled after her night of passionate dalliance in the garden and the pool with the plebeian Connor, who, despite his gaucheness, is also an imaginative writer and a poet. If she is not the Fairy Queen, Tracy is many times called a 'goddess' by Dexter and 'a radiant, glorious queen' by Connor, whose rapture is rather like Bottom's dream or 'rare vision':

> CONNOR There's a magnificence in you, Tracy … A magnificence that comes out of your eyes, in your voice, in the way you stand there, in the way you walk. You're lit from within, Tracy!

He is the one who, despite his early disdain, comes to see her not as a haughty woman without feelings, but as 'full of life and warmth and delight', not as 'iron' but 'flesh and blood', and he in turn acts as the catalyst for opening her eyes to the man she really loves, Dexter. Alcohol flows through the film, loosening tongues and minds to a new tolerance and changed visions at crucial moments, and at one point it is referred to in terms that recall love-in-idleness in the play: 'Just the juice of a few flowers, it removes the sting'. The final wedding reconciliation between Tracy and Dexter is similar to the reaffirmation of marriage between Oberon and Titania: 'Yes, George, I agree with you. In the light of day and the dark of night, for richer for poorer, for better for worse …', while Connor's memory of the night is as hazy and alluring as Bottom's, amounting in his case to 'two kisses and a late swim – all of which I thoroughly enjoyed and the memory of which I wouldn't part with'. The woman looking on, the press photographer Liz who, as is Helena's dilemma, loves but is not loved by Connor, also highlights the film's theme of acquiring tolerance for the irrational, in terms that could apply just as well to the night in the Wood of Athens: 'we all go haywire at times and if we don't maybe we ought to'. She finally gets her man, but there is still a strong suspicion, as there still hangs over Demetrius, that she is not his first or most glorious love. Reconciliation with the father comes at the end of the play, prompting Cavell to see echoes of *The Winter's Tale* but just as plausibly it evokes reference to the end of the *Dream*, although in that case the father, Egeus, seems to accept, silently rather than necessarily willingly, the order issued by Duke Theseus. Though Hermia is not given quite such an explicit or prolonged scene as either Tracy or, for that matter, Cordelia, in which father and daughter forgive and are forgiven, her father now sees Tracy as looking 'like a queen, like a goddess', while she feels at last 'like a human, like a human being', instead of being regarded as a remote goddess or woman with an iron heart. This family reconciliation parallels that between Titania and Oberon in the fairy kingdom.

One more important pattern links even more closely *The Philadelphia Story* and the *Dream*. The part of Tracy's young sister Dinah (from Diana) can be likened to Puck's marriage-making. Her final triumphant words are 'I did it. I did it all!', and it is she who most insistently reiterates at the end of the film the central image of an irrational but life-changing dream. She had been watching through the window the unfolding events, and later mockingly claims 'that was just the beginning, and it was no dream!', but she relates to Tracy, 'You know I did have the funniest dream about you last night', speaking of seeing Connor carrying something, and 'guess what it turned out to be, it was you'. Enigmatically she continues, 'of course he was gone. He was never there', and she confirms that 'Dexter says it's a dream too'. Just as Puck appreciates 'Lord what fools these mortals be' (3.2.115), Dinah the child could make the same wry statement about adults. Dream and the destabilising events in a green world are the emotionally transformative motifs that link *The Philadelphia Story* and *A Midsummer Night's Dream*. Screwball comedy has been treated elsewhere in this book as a genre influenced mainly by *The Taming of the Shrew*, but individual examples, such as this movie, exemplify my point that in a film different aspects, character changes, and motifs from the clutch of familiar plays by Shakespeare can emerge almost indiscriminately as semi-buried, possibly subliminal allusions to Shakespearean romantic comedy as a composite form.

If the metamorphic powers of an alien, 'green world' environment provides one structural pillar of the '*Dream* genre', another is created by the time scheme in which surprises are wrought over one night, which can be seen as akin to a dream or a nightmare depending on one's stance:

> HIPPOLYTA But all the story of the night told over,
> And all their minds transfigured so together,
> More witnesseth than fancy's images,
> And grows to something of great constancy;
> But, howsoever, strange and admirable. (5.1.23–7)

It provides the foundation for *Bringing Up Baby* (1938), although other than this the movie admittedly has fewer links with *A Midsummer Night's Dream*. Although a screwball movie, it is not a 'shrew-taming' type, since if anything the conventional roles are reversed, as in Shakespeare's *Venus and Adonis* or *All's Well That Ends Well* with the woman pursuing and the man coyly resistant. At one stage the conventions of gender reversal appear when the male appears in the female's negligee, which he explains by saying it is 'because I just went gay all of a sudden'. Also, the premise is that two women have designs on one man rather than Lysander and Demetrius both pursuing Hermia. The hapless and unworldly palaeontologist David Huxley (Cary Grant) is dedicated only to his job, which is assembling fossil bones (later he is given the pseudonym 'Mr Bone'), and is initially dominated by his humourless fiancée. As the fateful day and night in his life wear on, he becomes the object of pursuit by the rich but flighty, reckless, and accident-prone Susan Vance (Katherine Hepburn), who happens to have a tame pet leopard ('Baby' of the title). She makes no attempt to disguise her intentions: 'I'm going to marry him. He doesn't know it but I am.' Either mischievously or accidentally, she takes advantage of situations in which David is manipulated to appear to be stalking her (in fact she has stolen his golf ball and he attempts to retrieve it from her). She consults a psychiatrist in a restaurant about a man who 'follows me around and fights with me'. Dr Lehman concludes the man is 'fixated' on her, which is the exact opposite of the truth at that stage: in his words, 'our relationship has been a series of misadventures from beginning to end … I hope I never set eyes on you again!' Susan accepts and repeats the psychiatrist's explanation, 'the love impulse in man frequently reveals itself in terms of conflict'. This statement not only reflects again the popular Freudianism of the 1930s, but also, I would argue, reveals a level of literary allusion to the composite genre of Shakespearean comedy, since it applies to virtually all Shakespeare's comedies in a central way, and especially *The Taming of the Shrew*, *A Midsummer Night's Dream*, and *Much Ado About Nothing*. As the chaotic events of the ensuing night unfold, the dominant reference, as in *The Philadelphia Story*, is the *Dream*. The psychiatrist anticipates the strange events when he says that 'perfectly ordinary people act strangely without being crazy' (which applies as much to his own tic-afflicted twitchiness), and when Susan, David, and Baby go to dinner at her aunt's lavish home and estate – the green world of the film – all the characters are driven willy-nilly, like the characters in the *Dream*, into strange, hectic behaviour. They are trapped helplessly in situations to which they can only respond, ending up in prison, but the 'misadventures' stem from the presence of two leopards and a friendly dog (George) obsessed with bones. But more pervasively we become familiar with a kind of logic emanating from the way in which Susan leads her life irrespective of circumstances, as David points out in exasperation: 'You look at everything upside down. I've never known anyone like you.' Susan freely admits her whole life is chaotic, but that it is not aberrant but fun to lead life this way. Under her influence, the stiff academic David slowly relaxes into the topsy-turvy logic of events, and by the next morning he seems to have fully accepted it as his preferred way of life as well. Susan accidentally destroys David's brontosaurus, which has, over four years, been assembled as painstakingly as his former, orderly life, beginning the sequence with the words 'Everything's gonna be all right', to which David retorts 'Every time you say that, something happens'. She explains, 'All that happened, happened because I was trying to keep you near me. I just did anything that came into my head'. As the conversation proceeds, he thanks her and admits that he has just had 'the best day of [his] life':

SUSAN You don't mean it?
DAVID I've never had a better time.
SUSAN But I was there.
DAVID That's what made it so good.
SUSAN Did you really have a good time?
DAVID Yes, I did!
SUSAN That's wonderful. Do you realize what that means? That means that you must like me a little bit.
DAVID It's more than that … Yes. I love you, I think.
SUSAN That's wonderful because I love you, too.

Susan has also secured from her rich aunt the million dollars to fund David's museum, his initial reason for playing golf with the intermediary, Mr Peabody, which had led to his meeting with Susan. David's last, helpless words, as she falls into his arms over the ruins of the collapsed brontosaurus, are 'oh dear, oh no'. His final state, described by Cavell as 'in a trance of innocence',[28] is comparable to the dazed wonder of both Bottom and Demetrius at the end of the *Dream*, simply accepting the traces of the strange night they have experienced that has changed them both radically.

Although David claims it has been 'the best day' of his life, in fact it was during the night that the oddest and most transformative events have happened, and the time scheme is close to Shakespeare's 'midsummer night' in the *Dream*. In Shakespeare's play, despite the opening assertion in the play that 'four happy days' and four nights must pass before the wedding nuptials between Theseus and Hippolyta, only one night actually passes, in a spectacular use of the kind of 'double time scheme' used also in *Romeo and Juliet* and *Othello*. *Bringing Up Baby* begins with David and his fiancée discussing their coming nuptials, which are due to happen on the following day. In this sense the film follows a single rather than double time scheme and the action ends, exactly as does the *Dream*, about twenty-four hours later, with a rearrangement of the marriage partners after the confusions in the night in different settings. Cavell sums up in a way that could apply equally to the play and the film, although he is speaking only of the latter here: 'The exposition of the drama takes place, roughly, in the town, and is both complicated and settled in a shift to the countryside. It carefully alternates between day and night and climaxes around about midnight'.[29] The equivalent of the court in the *Dream* is the monumental museum in *Bringing Up Baby*, which is initially presided over by the repressively rational Alice Swallow and a statuesquely immobile David Huxley 'thinking', in the pose of Rodin's *The Thinker*, a setting that is finally invaded and virtually destroyed by the irrepressible life forces, Susan, Baby, and George. Later, the forest of Athens, with its unruly, 'upside-down' logic caused by fairy agencies, is mirrored in the film in various settings. First there are spaces of 'play' and recreation (the golf course, the restaurant), and second, as the night wears on, spaces of degenerating chaos at Susan's aunt's pastoral estate, and finally, the prison, presided over by Constable Slocum who is as incompetent and eccentric as Dogberry in *Much Ado*. The farcical nature of the events in the versions of emotional 'forest' provide examples of the kind of economical foreshortening through conflation of Shakespearean motifs that I have argued for in other films.

At the centre of the events is the tame leopard (and later its more dangerous alter ego that has escaped from the zoo) and George the dog. The way animals influence events has a weird range of references to the *Dream*, recalling both the effects of the turbulent fairy kingdom on the hapless mortal lovers in the play, and the transformation of Bottom, whose ass's head makes him a metonym for an asinine creature, an intersection of the human and animal worlds. Susan loves not only David but also, as she vehemently confesses, the leopard, which in a narrative truncation equates to Titania's amatory 'fixation' and erotic obsession with the transformed Bottom.[30] Titania's erotic and predatory behaviour towards Bottom tends to reverse gender roles, in the way we have observed in *Bringing Up Baby* in Susan's pursuit of David, whose position becomes uncomfortably entwined with the existence of Baby, George, and the wild leopard that he finally 'tames' with a chair before fainting with shock into Susan's arms. In a further set of distorted dramatic parallels, we find that the events over the night in both film and play are akin to comic nightmare rather than either 'dream' or reality, and they leave the various characters radically transformed – especially Demetrius, whose love for Hermia has now been completely displaced into love for Helena, just as David's for Alice has switched to Susan. One commentator, apparently without suspecting the possibility of Shakespeare's *Dream* as influence, describes what happens to David as 'a noirish induction by one con or another', which also applies exactly to Demetrius. The same critic concludes that *Bringing Up Baby* 'appears to be formulaic entertainment but ultimately proves troubling below the surface. It is in this complexity, as well as its fine comic sense, that *Bringing Up Baby* deserves the now-common claims to its artistry'.[31] The same kind of 'troubling' and even 'noirish' emotional complexity and 'fine comic sense' infuse, I suggest, Shakespeare's most anarchic play about love. Watching *Bringing Up Baby* while keeping in mind the generic elements of *A Midsummer Night's Dream* can be described as glimpsing the play through the distorting lens of the film. Once a connection, however oblique, has been noticed, the influence seems less unlikely, as is the case in *The Philadelphia Story*, which itself shares so much with *Bringing Up Baby*.

As suggested elsewhere in this book, the main lines of interpenetration linking Shakespeare and films are drawn during the first half-century or so of the history of movies, and later links are more often mediated between films themselves. A more recent film seems to exemplify this trend as not only can it be seen as directly harking back to Shakespeare's play, but it also presents itself as a self-conscious successor to both *Bringing Up Baby* and *The Philadelphia Story* in turn. In this way it makes explicit the parallels between these two films and also draws attention to the links of all three with Shakespeare's *Dream*. It is Woody Allen's *A Midsummer Night's Sex Comedy* (1982). In his customary, densely intertextual way, Allen incorporates references to Shakespeare's *Dream* into more than just his title, and he presents something of an homage to earlier cinema. Critics have noted pastoral echoes from Ingmar Bergman's *Smiles of a Summer Night* (1955) and general indebtedness to the gentle tones in Jean Renoir's films, but the two most overt links are with William Dieterle and Max Reinhardt's *A Midsummer Night's Dream* and (less often noted) *The Philadelphia*

Story. From Reinhardt, Allen takes a host of identifiable visual touches such as shots of an owl, a rabbit, the moon through clouds, and others. Overwhelmingly, the lasting memory is of Felix Mendelssohn's famous musical adaptation of Shakespeare's play, used in contexts and ways very similar to Reinhardt's. The lushness of the music complements the sheer beauty of the landscape in the wooded park, an environment sufficient to coax even such an inveterate urbanite as Woody Allen out of his customary urban haunt of New York. The strong mirroring of *The Philadelphia Story* comes in the central situation where one woman, in this case the Shakespearean-named Ariel (Mia Farrow), becomes the sexual prey for three men, namely her elderly fiancé, the professor of philosophy Leopold (José Ferrer), who bears comparison with Kittredge; the over-sexed doctor, Maxwell, who claims to fall in lust at first smell (literally); and Andrew (Woody Allen himself), who had an earlier, platonic relationship with Ariel. In both cases the main setting is a wooded park. A brook rather than a swimming pool is the centrepiece for erotic exchange, and a central image in both films is a man carrying a sodden woman, in one case because they have been swimming and in the other because they have crashed Andrew's absurd flying machine in the brook. In the *Sex Comedy*, the fiancé Leopold is not humiliatingly rejected by Ariel at the end, as is Kittredge by Tracy and Alice by David, but is conveniently disposed of by dying in a sexual climax with the other female guest, the doctor's secretary, Dulcy. Ironically, as the rationalist and antispiritualist, Leopold communicates back from the spirit world to say he is ecstatically happy. It is not easy to see a particularly happy ending for any of the others, since Andrew is still tied to his jealous and sexually frustrated wife Adrian, as Titania is perhaps unconvincingly reconciled with Oberon through his trick, and there is no sign that Maxwell, a man 'like one of those creatures in Greek mythology who's half-goat' and a devotee of lust but not love, will settle down peacefully with Ariel.

There are more reflections of the *Dream* to justify Woody Allen's parodic title, and to suggest that the film offers a critical interpretation of Shakespeare's original play. The woods are described as 'magical': 'on enchanted nights you can see things ... glowing things ... spirits'. Once again there is no attempt to offer simple one-to-one equivalents between characters, but it is interesting to see which roles are elided and merged. Leopold can readily be seen as Duke Theseus, Shakespeare's character who sceptically dismisses the 'imagination compact' of lunatics, lovers, and children and yet is, none the less, himself only an imagined, mythological figure. Although Leopold is the author of a book called *Conceptual Pragmatics* and one who proclaims 'there are no ghosts except in Shakespeare, and many of those are more real than many people

I know', it is he who makes constant references to imaginative literature, as in this quotation itself. He recites the medieval song 'Sumer is icumen in' and Shakespeare's 'The spring, the summer, / The childing autumn, angry winter change / Their wonted liveries' (*Dream*, 2.1.111–13), as well as giving passionate renditions of songs and 'The Lord's Prayer', which rises to a crescendo as a backdrop to abortive love-making on the kitchen table by a reluctant Andrew and rampantly mounting Adrian. At the end, more like Bottom than Theseus, Leopold is the plodding rationalist given insight into the true enchantment of the woods, which he now sees as 'filled with the spirits of the lucky men and women of passion who have passed away at the height of lovemaking'. In a more composite way, Andrew and Adrian as host and hostess to the gathering can be seen as versions of the unhappily married couple, Oberon and Titania, but Andrew also plays the role of an incompetent Puck. An amateur inventor, his flying contraption echoes Puck's willingness to put a girdle round the earth in forty minutes, and his 'spirit ball', which 'penetrates the unseen world' in ways that show 'there's more to life than meets the eye', provides a climax that shows either the past in an image of Andrew and Ariel embracing, or the future when Maxwell and Ariel embrace, before it finally explodes. There are also various points where, like Puck, Andrew either interferes with courtship or acts as clumsy matchmaker. Most significantly, the initial couples change their desires as quickly and mysteriously as Titania, Lysander, and Demetrius, and the women, like Hermia and Helena, become the bewildered foci of either sexual attention or indifference by first one man then the other. Andrew is with his wife Adrian, but now his old feelings for Ariel are rekindled; Maxwell comes with Dulcy but instantly lusts after Ariel; Leopold is affianced to Ariel but dies in flagrante delicto with Dulcy. All the time, as in *A Midsummer Night's Dream*, there is little illusion that we are watching love in any deep or sustained sense, but merely infatuation, fickleness, and lust; 'sex alleviates tension, love causes it', says Andrew laconically, and later, 'only a drunken, infantile idiot shoots himself over love'. All the characters are driven not by reason or emotions but by their libidos, even the pre-Raphaelite Ariel, who admits to having slept with 'everybody' (except Andrew) after she completed her convent schooling.

A third structural principle underlying the '*Dream* genre' is the initial situation in which two men pursue one woman, followed by complex plot devices to sort this imbalance out. The initial premise of *A Midsummer Night's Dream* is that Lysander and Demetrius both love Hermia, though she consistently loves only Lysander. Helena loves Demetrius but he does not return her love. The relationships are scrambled still further in the Wood of Athens, whose rules are set by the whimsical jealousies of fairies, and at one stage the two men love Helena. With the use of a juice that can alter people's desires, Puck eventually unscrambles the ever-changing equations until there is symmetry in couples: Lysander and Hermia can marry each other, and so can Demetrius and Helena. *An American in Paris* (1951) was one of the most successful, later musicals made by the 'Freed Unit' and directed by Vincente Minelli, who also directed *Gigi*, at Warner Brothers. Its advertising suggests that it was intended as a fusion of high and low culture, with its ostentatious visual references to French impressionist paintings, especially well-known works by Renoir, Utrillo, Dufy, Toulouse-Lautrec, Rouault, and Van Gogh, all used not only as scenic imagery to evoke a sophisticated Paris but also as tableaux vivants. The music is by Gershwin, and includes one of his most ambitious, 'classical' concertos. The balletic finale, ostentatiously expensive and comparable to – even surpassing – the expressionism of Helpman's choreography in Powell and Pressburger's *The Red Shoes* (1948), adds to the movie's air of cultural aspiration. One of the central characters is played by Nina Foch, who was at the time a member of the American Shakespeare Festival at Stratford, playing leading roles in *Twelfth Night*, *Measure for Measure*, and *The Taming of the Shrew*. The writer was Alan Jay Lerner, who, as a Harvard graduate, was among the most literary-minded Hollywood writers of musical drama, adapting to the screen such works as Colette's *Gigi*, the Arthurian legend in *Camelot*, de Saint-Exupery's *The Little Prince*, and most famously with Frederick Loewe, Shaw's *Pygmalion*. Furthermore, half-concealed within its plot, *An American in Paris* plays variations on the Shakespearean scrambled couples.

First, two women, Lise Bouvier (Leslie Caron) and Milo Roberts (Nina Foch), are in love with one man, Jerry Mulligan (Gene Kelly), a hard-up bohemian artist in Paris. He does not love Milo but is manipulated into accepting her patronage. Meanwhile a famous French singer, Henri Baurel, loves and expects to marry Lise, although she does not love him but feels obligated to him for helping her family during the war, as Jerry feels indebted to Milo for financially supporting his art. There is also a kind of 'left-over' individual, Adam Cook (Oscar Levant), who is a composer and does not fit into the final love pattern. The particular magic of cinema, aided by Paris and dance, does not need fairies or love-juice to resolve the problems. Through a combination of simple overhearing during a carnivalesque, semi-masked ball where identities become blurred and feelings unblocked, followed by a long sequence of dance that reveals true affinities of bodies circulating through the chaos of different scenery, which at one stage transforms into a wood and then into a flower market, Henri and Milo are led nobly and wordlessly to renounce their respective desires so that Lise and Jerry are free to marry. Essentially, like the *Dream*, the whole film turns on a series of private, individual dreams being either realised as wish-fulfilment or thwarted, and the style becomes more and more dream-like towards the end through the use of dance and the persuasive music of Gershwin, named 'An American in Paris', composed in 1928 and one inspiration for the movie. It would have been easy for the plot to manoeuvre the older, wealthy characters, Henri and Milo, into a final symmetry like Shakespeare's Demetrius and Helena, since their roles make them seem amply suited to each other; or, for that matter, Milo and Adam could have been paired, as the original ending envisaged. To some extent, one or other of the various couplings must be a part of the audience expectations, but these three characters are simply forgotten at the end, perhaps because such a result would distract attention from the affinity manifested through dance of Lise and Jerry (Caron and Kelly) as the central couple, and would unduly complicate a plot that clearly aims to be extremely simple to the point of thinness. In some ways this avoids an open-ended complication that is a potential puzzle in the *Dream*, the sincerity of Demetrius who ends the play still under the influence of love-juice. The 'Bottom-like' character is Adam, the frustrated, expatriate American composer, who egotistically fantasises that not only is he Gershwin as composer of 'Concerto in F', but also concert conductor, piano soloist and rapturous audience all rolled together. He may not get a fairy queen, but his own private obsession is played out in the lengthy dream or vision sequence, after which he must return to a more sober reality.

Down to the present day *A Midsummer Night's Dream* has been a favourite 'inset' drama in college environments, no doubt primarily because it is the play most firmly entrenched in educational syllabuses. *A Midsummer Night's Rave Party* is one fairly frivolous offshoot, while *Dead Poets' Society* (1989), set in the 1950s, uses the play more seriously. It presents a male student playing Puck, against his father's wishes, an adolescent rebellion parallel to Hermia's initial elopement. The equivalent to the Wood of Athens is a cave where the clandestine 'Dead Poets' Society' of boys meets nocturnally to read poetry, including their own. This empowers the shy student to overcome more of his inhibitions and confirm his metamorphic emergence into a new self-confidence. Here, however, the consequences are tragic rather than comic, though the experience of the play rehearsals and the teacher's attempts to liberate his students to 'seize the day' take a central significance from Shakespeare's play. The film develops as a more general critique of repressive authority, and when the boy's father refuses to accept his son's individuality discovered through acting and writing poetry, the boy commits suicide. Although there is no imposed happy ending, the play of sympathies dictates that moral authority lies against the various father figures, including the headmaster, and with the inspirational teacher (played by Robin Williams), who teaches the importance of imagination and the naturalness of change. In a sense it is akin to *Romeo and Juliet* in the way 'all are punished' by the injustice of the ending, and the fact that the primary reference is to *A Midsummer Night's Dream* reveals an unexpected level of deep similarity between these two Shakespearean plays, which not only were written at about the same time but comment on each other through the 'Pyramus and Thisbe' inset. In both plays the transition from youth to individuated adulthood, whether through love or creativity, is shown as a risky and dangerous psychic journey, which can lead alternatively to comic fulfilment or tragic consequences. The famous stage production of Shakespeare's play by Peter Brook in the 1970s may have been the catalyst for later versions of the *Dream* that explore the darker side of the forest's capacity for metamorphosis.

The influence of the *Dream* shows no sign of abating in modern movies. In *Get Over It* (2001), the college basketball hero, jilted by his girlfriend, tries to get access to her by auditioning for the cast of the school's musical, which happens to be based on Shakespeare's play. The entangled amatory consequences draw obviously on the love triangles in Shakespeare's *Dream*. *Were the World Mine* (2008) is also set in a school, which is rehearsing yet again a musical version of *The Dream* with complications that by now are familiar. Even the title of the movie is taken from Helena's lines to Hermia, 'Were the world mine, Demetrius being bated, / The rest I'd give to be to you translated' (1.1.190–1). These films take their place in a long line of generic 'repetitions with variations' in movies that draw on Shakespeare's *Dream*, and the pattern will no doubt continue to be replicated many more times over, partly capitalising on the well-known version of the play directed by Michael Hoffman (1999). *A Midsummer Night's Dream* joins *The Taming of the Shrew* and *Romeo and Juliet* in that each forms the basis of a genre specific to the individual play, as well as in most cases drawing on a composite genre incorporating aspects of different Shakespearean comedies. The fact that these three plays hold such a unique status is surely connected with the fact that they hold special places in early Hollywood cinema history through their respective, memorable realisations in the 1929 *Shrew*, Reinhardt's *Dream* (1935) and Cukor's *Romeo and Juliet* (1936). Hollywood has been 'translating' them ever since.

Art writing the script of love: playing roles in As You Like It

Though never gaining the celebrity of the two other Shakespearean movies produced in 1935–36 (*A Midsummer Night's Dream* and *Romeo and Juliet*), *As You Like It* was also made, this time in Britain, directed by the German-Jewish émigré, Paul Czinner, and starring his wife Elisabeth Bergner as Rosalind, alongside Laurence Olivier as Orlando. The leisurely and rather uneventful plot of the play relies on two of the more overt structural principles that feed into movies: the alternative environment of a 'green world', this time not threatening like the forest of Athens but a place where freedom and love have time to flourish, and the disguised heroine who is liberated to role-play a new perspective. However, its contemplative nature, unlike the non-stop action of the *Dream*, highlights another process, that of conscious fiction-making, where art is used not so much to describe or represent the experience of love directly, as to allegorise and even create it in self-consciously literary ways. It is not irrelevant that after Rosalind has escaped the conflict at court and retreated to the forest, she first encounters Petrarchan sonnets hanging on trees, as though the artifice of poetry dominates nature. Lovers begin 'writing their own script' by casting themselves and playing studied roles. Rosalind and Orlando in their pretences create their own fiction of a loving couple, each constructing the other as a compatible mate, negotiating differences by using hypotheses based on the recurrent word 'if', which is so important in the play. Shakespeare may have had in mind the classical myth of Pygmalion, with its analogy of an artist creating a sculpture so life-like that it is enlivened and provides the artist with his ideal, 'designer' lover.

Through her disguise and assumed identity of Ganimede, Rosalind creates herself in the persona of Orlando's lover, and Orlando is required under her instruction to 'play' as Rosalind's constructed lover. They have in fact already fallen fall in love at first sight, but then a long, leisurely time must pass in the forest before the fictional play-acting can merge with 'reality'. Orlando's impatience with 'thinking' rather than 'doing' acts as a prompt to betrothals and a return to court life, but in a fashion that retains the lessons that have been learned within the protected and artificial environment. The pastoral and literary Forest of Ardennes with its exotic French associations, in which the transformations of love are effected, is also Shakespeare's familiar Forest of Arden in Warwickshire, subject to 'the icy fang and churlish chiding of the winter's wind' but also creating the environment for merging the fictional and factual in a love relationship. This time it is a 'green world' without the *Dream*'s wildness (except for occasional touches such as a 'green and gilded snake'), and its prototype is the protective landscape derived from classical pastoral.[32] *As You Like It* may be less recognisable as an influence on filmed romantic comedy than the other play based on disguise, *Twelfth Night*, perhaps because the latter is more often a set text in colleges, but in its quiet and different way the former has also been influential through its own generic characteristic of socialising the initially literary process of playful self-fashioning through art.

Most clearly of all Shakespeare's comedies, *As You Like It* is built upon the structural device of juxtaposing contrasting environments. A status-conscious and competitive court, beset with power struggles within and between families and imaged in a wrestling match, is set against a pastoral 'play' area in which Rosalind and Orlando can explore love safely, largely through role playing and conversation.[33] In the spirit of Protestant companionate marriage,[34] they consciously develop friendship, rather than submitting to the rollercoaster emotions based on adolescent infatuation evident in the *Dream*, the largely unconscious play of mutual attractions in *Twelfth Night*, or resistance to family differences in *Romeo and Juliet*, and they create through play fictional parts (in the theatrical sense) that can in time become true roles to live by.

George Cukor's *Holiday* (1938) is in some ways a variation on the 'odd-couple' or screwball comedy stemming from *The Shrew*, but its very title suggests links with this aspect of *As You Like It*. The unconventional Johnny Case (Cary Grant) turns backward rolls in public and resists accommodation into the wealthy, patriarchal family's life with its emphasis on making money. He eventually turns away from his first love and fiancée, Julia (Doris Nolan). She takes after her acquisitive father, and is comparable to Bianca in *The Shrew* in her superficial commitment to conventional romance, which is revealed in this case to be heartless, calculating, and materialistically self-serving. Johnny gravitates instead towards Julia's rebellious and dynamic sister, Linda (once again Katharine Hepburn, who seems to revel in playing this kind of character). The abrupt ending shows Case and Linda escaping into the liberated, spirited, but apparently non-sexualised world of a 'holiday' on a liner, with his own equally non-materialistic and libertarian surrogate parents, Professor and Mrs Potter. Despite the fact that the character types played by Hepburn and Grant are clearly from the world of screwball comedy in cinematic terms, yet the process depicted lacks the coercion and conflict between its 'odd couple' that *The Shrew* manifests, and instead its structure is more comparable to *As You Like It*. There are two substantial critical analyses of the film and although neither mentions Shakespeare, the accounts are consistent with the one presented here.[35] The contrasting locales in Shakespeare's play, court and forest, find equivalents in the architecture of a single house, the Seton mansion. 'Downstairs' is presided over by the mercenary patriarch, Edward Seton Sr, and dominated by his values as a wealthy plantation owner (the link with slavery is ominous), who regards love as merely one means to the preferred end of a financially secure marriage. 'Upstairs' is the children's old playroom, presided over by the benign portrait of the girls' dead mother who had helplessly and unresistingly tolerated her husband's repressive family oligarchy. The playroom becomes Linda's chosen environment. She is just as much a rebellious outsider as Case himself, and she literally prefers to stay in this childhood haunt instead of joining the family party downstairs. The unambitious Johnny is enthusiastically greeted by Linda as 'like spring ... like a breath of fresh air', and he also instantly finds the room congenial and quite unlike the ballroom downstairs with its falsity and excess. He and Linda forge a strong pre-sexual friendship by sharing their compatible values, playing roles and exuberantly jumping on the couch and turning somersaults, to the disapproval of Julie, who is much more uncomfortable in this uninhibited environment, and her father who has never until now entered the room. The playroom provides the same kind of space for those characters willing to play roles and who are susceptible to its influence as the pastoral Forest of Arden:

> the resurgence of childhood energies ... spontaneity, improvisation and role-playing, transgressing the norms of accepted (and acceptable) patriarchal identities ... The film judges a relationship based on physical appearance (love at first sight) to be inadequate. It rejects patriarchal sexuality and romance, offering the companionate fun and friendship of the playroom in its place.[36]

One difference is that in *As You Like It* love at first sight is not denied but steadily confirmed through time and testing. However, more importantly, both the forest and the playroom centralise female consciousness and control (even when expressed through Johnny), just as the play allows Rosalind to preside. There are relativities in *As You Like It* itself, as the love between Celia and Oliver, instantaneous and expressed in a very physical way, contrasts with the Petrarchan platitudes of Phoebe, just as the film contrasts the conventions of traditional love with the playful physicality 'upstairs'. The film even has its Jaques in the brother Ned, a melancholy alcoholic, who also gravitates to the playroom, finding it unthreatening and satisfying to his contemplative bent, just as Jaques appreciates the forest's benign influence and relaxes in it. *Holiday* shows Cukor's characteristic Shakespearean literacy by quoting from *Romeo and Juliet*, Lady Macbeth, and *A Midsummer Night's Dream*, and in the terms of the argument I am pursuing here it has a strong generic connection with *As You Like It* and more generally to the composite drama of Shakespeare's group of romantic comedies.

Meet Me in St. Louis (1944) is the film credited as the first 'integrated musical', where the songs develop the plot rather than being independent cameos, and in some ways we also glimpse in this film vestiges of *As You Like It*. Although on stage Shakespeare's play reveals more functional and essential music than is noticed on reading, this is not the major point of intersection. On close inspection Shakespeare's play, at the heart of its generic make-up, shows a disintegration of families through the actions of a repressive father who happens also to be a usurping ruler, Duke Frederick. The action in the forest preludes a reintegration of family and government through the benign father and legitimate ruler, Duke Senior, and his daughter Rosalind. Restoration of legitimate authority in the state, signalled by Duke Senior's reinstatement and a series of marriages, including Rosalind's, is first enacted in the 'green world' of the forest, where characters may play fictional roles that gradually mesh with their own desired realities. In the series of resolutions, Duke Frederick and Orlando's initially hostile brother are also 'converted' in the forest, and these two characters simply become ciphers of the plot in its drive towards the happy ending, emphasising the transformative powers of the forest. If we see Dukes Frederick and Senior not as separate characters but as two sides of one father figure, then we have the essential situation played out in *Meet Me in St. Louis*, which can then be viewed as an economical foreshortening of *As You Like It*. Here the two fathers, repressive and benign respectively, are conflated into one figure, the generically named everyman, 'Mr Smith', whose first name is the same as the one Shakespeare chose in *The Tempest* for a similarly ambiguous father, 'Alonzo'. At first he is represented as blocking his eldest daughter's marriage hopes, by aborting the phone call in which her suitor was about to propose, and then without realising it he disintegrates the whole family by accepting a job offer to move to New York and away from their rather sleepy but beloved and upwardly mobile family existence in St Louis. In this guise, Mr Smith, however indulgently he is presented, is just as much an obstructive *senex* in terms of his daughters' desires as Egeus or Brabantio in *Othello*, and just as much a symbol of the kind of male authority that is resisted in Shakespeare's romantic comedies. The increasing family distress is registered most clearly in the rather weird and death-laden imagery of the youngest daughter, Tootie ('It'll take me at least a week to dig up all my dolls in the cemetery'), and the suppressed grief of the mother. It is finally voiced most articulately by the forceful Esther (Judy Garland). Significantly, the drama of the family is at its point of crisis just at the time when festivity is expected, Christmas. In a wintry and bleak household full of boxes packed ready for the move, Mr Smith has a change of heart as radical as Duke Frederick's, realises his folly, and announces they will stay in the family home. Immediately, the gift-giving festivities begin. There is, as film critics have pointed out, a socio-political point to be made about Hollywood's rejection of the bright lights of New York for the homely family values available in regional St Louis, comparable to the underlying assumption of *As You Like It* that love can be 'naturally' pursued and eventually fulfilled in a setting other than the conflict-ridden artificiality of the court. Duke Senior draws attention to the wholesome and unpretentious way of life that, in a more urban context, characterises St Louis, which is right in the middle of the USA in every way. There are also less obvious patterns linking *As You Like It* and *Meet Me in St. Louis*. The most obvious is the movement from family disintegration to reintegration, effected in *As You Like It* through the agency of the father figures, a reversal of values by one and benignity in the other, conflated in *St Louis* into one variable figure. This pattern is played out in a variation of setting that turns the green world of the Forest of Arden into the Smiths' regionally located and sylvan family home. In itself this is perhaps not so radical a resetting of the play's pastoral retreat as the shift to an urban ghetto in Christine Edzard's Canadian filmed version of *As You Like It* (1992), once we acknowledge that it is not the rustic leafiness that matters, but the potential for effecting emotional transformations in an emotionally protected environment beyond the 'painted pomp' (2.1.3) of court or city. In the movie, as in Shakespeare's forest, the notion of a single congenial 'home' can take on contrasting emotional associations and colourings, changing from a bright and love-filled upper-middle-class mansion to a dark and alienating place littered with removalists' boxes, observed in silent reproof by grotesque snowmen who are savagely destroyed by Tootie. Finally it becomes a warmly lit place of Christmas spirit and family togetherness. The movement of return is not a literal one back to a previous setting but metaphorically to the retransformed family home in St Louis. The emotional journeys undergone by the characters are charted most emphatically through the responses of Esther, whose role as matchmaker shows elements of Rosalind. There is even an exchange on 'little white lies' similar in spirit to Touchstone's discussion of the 'lie circumstantial' (5.4.79–80). In these and other aspects, the film becomes a subtle reflection on the genre and dramatic pattern underlying *As You Like It*, guided by a female consciousness in an emotionally defined setting, to a final ordering of relationships presented as socially harmonious and emotionally 'natural' – carnivalesque in the Shakespearean sense. Public ceremonies culminate both works – betrothals in *As You Like It*, the St Louis Day parade and fair in the film. Although the two works initially seem far from comparable, once the patterns of genre are noticed then similarities become plausible. Recognition of the underlying links does not so much draw attention to the skilful adaptiveness of writers (who were probably oblivious to the similarities) but to the fertile potential in this romantic comedy by Shakespeare.

Self-fashioning is also prominent in *Paris When It Sizzles* (1964), in which Audrey Hepburn plays a typist, Miss Gabrielle Simpson, helping an alcoholic scriptwriter (William Holden) to overcome his writer's block. It is a sophisticated, self-reflective film-within-a-film that becomes a kind of homage to movies like *The Lost Weekend* and *Casablanca*, and multiple genres like horror films, spy films, detective noir, the western, and 'good old romance', but which also employs and reflects on a gamut of generic characteristics of Shakespeare's romantic comedies. Although the central references used by the screenwriter (Richard/Rick) to explain the proximity of creativity and love are to *Frankenstein* and *My Fair Lady* – or more generally the myth of Pygmalion on which both are based – the process described also underlies Shakespeare's genre:

> Frankenstein – someone who creates or remakes another human being and either falls in love with it or it destroys him. It can go either way. That's what gives it such flexibility, Miss Simpson. Did you ever realise that Frankenstein and My Fair Lady are the same story? One ends happily and the other one doesn't. Think about that for a while.

Both Dr Frankenstein and Professor Higgins, like the sculptor of the Pygmalion statue, are artists who create a figure so life-like that they become real for the artist. In discussion, much play is made of film techniques like 'dissolves' and 'switches', giving more emphasis to the transformative qualities of cinema itself, shifting from life to art and back to life. Love is the alchemy that provokes and sustains the process, as writer and typist collaborate to write a film in which they take the parts of the central protagonists, dogged by a semi-fictional figure played by Tony Curtis who impotently rebels against the writer's lines:

> – I am not Maurice. I am Philippe.
> – My dear boy, you are a minor character and your name is of no importance … My god, you are a dull character.

And again, 'Can't you get this through your mind? You're only a bit part … Nobody cares anything about you. You're a mere literary convenience'. However, Maurice/Philippe ends up shooting the writer. Hepburn speaks of characters as though they are coming to life, wondering who they 'really' are, and by doing so she brings Richard back to the status of the writer as a 'liar and thief' stealing plots and characters. He is an ageing, alcoholic 'hack' who is chronically mercenary, while managing to 'fool the people'. When Gabrielle Simpson (Gaby) in the film-within-a-film says she loves the story, he retorts hopefully, 'You're not in love with the script. You're in love with me'. Writing the script together becomes an analogue for the mutual fiction-making of Rosalind and Orlando in *As You Like It*, where art is used not to express love but to create it, by role playing lovers who are 'writing the script' together and in the process creating themselves as a loving couple. It is significant that Rosalind and Orlando fall in love immediately, at first sight, and their sojourn in the forest is a leisurely exercise in making their initial, fictive image of each other into a lasting truth, in effect creating each other as beloved other. The process is essentially literary, beginning with Orlando writing sonnets about Rosalind and hanging them on trees. Shakespeare's characters, like Rick and Gaby, are seen constructing each other, negotiating difficulties to create harmony through a set of mutually sustained fictions. Like the artist sculpting a Pygmalion with which he then falls in love, the respective sets of characters in both play and film continue to make fictions they seek to live by, until one, like Orlando, is pressed to prompt a return to some kind of reality by protesting 'I can live no longer by thinking' (5.2.48). In this kind of pastoral, utopian romantic comedy, the hypothetical or 'make-believe' world must now give way to a more uncomfortable and 'real' world of official responsibility and marriage. However, the genre posits, such a transference is based on a new stability, after the characters' passage through a process of self-realisation towards self-fulfilment, having 'found themselves' in an unfamiliar and testing environment.

There are other films depicting romantic love that reveal some facets of *As You Like It* and develop this play's generic 'repetition and variation'. *Roman Holiday* (1953) casts Audrey Hepburn as a crown princess who tires of her regal duties and, when in Rome, absconds into the city life, where she experiences love with Joe, a 'commoner' reporter (Gregory Peck). Although Rosalind is forced to abscond from court into the forest, the sequence involving juxtaposed settings between the world of officialdom and politics, with its utopian commitment to feelings and self-realisation, is the same in both play and film. The backdrop of everyday Rome, presented with a touch of travelogue in its own right, is the equivalent of the green world of the Forest of Arden. In her gesture of 'slumming', Princess Ann needs at least to adopt some new role in order to remain incognito, and although Rosalind's full disguise as a man may not have been considered so plausible in a 1950s film, Ann does at least have her hair cut short like a man's, and she contemplates the attraction of living a normal life free from state responsibilities. Like Rosalind, she finally returns to her allotted position at court, but unlike Shakespeare's heroine, for reasons of royal protocol she cannot take with her the man she loves. In itself, *Roman Holiday* was perhaps the stimulus for other, similarly plotted movies such as *The Princess Diaries* (2001) and its sequel (2004), in which the heroine undergoes a series of educative processes to fit her as a future queen while not losing touch with the non-royal world she has grown up in.

More recently, the educative potential of disguise and role playing in *As You Like It* has been more explicitly referenced and made functional in the teenage movie, *Never Been Kissed* (1999), no doubt made to cash in on the popularity of other Shakespeare movies among college students in the late 1990s, *Romeo + Juliet* and *A Midsummer Night's Dream*. Josie (Drew Barrymore) is a twenty-five-year-old copy-editor of the *Chicago Sun Times* who is given the chance to be a reporter, dispatched to return to her old high school to write a story about it. The new role of the job constitutes her 'disguise'.[37] Her return triggers bad memories of her own schooldays as 'Josie Grossie', a plain girl who had been bullied and ignored. She has been ordered to report adversely on the current English teacher, but in the event she falls in love with him. It is the teacher who triggers Josie's own self-therapy, and he does so with the aid of *As You Like It* in the classroom. Josie impresses him with her knowledge of conventions of pastoral literature, and he proceeds to bring the play to bear on her own life, allowing her to self-fashion herself with a more positive self-image. The teacher presents Shakespeare's play as one about the possibilities of self-transformation and self-realisation, by learning from its emphasis on disguise and role playing:

> SAM Welcome to Shakespeare's *As You Like It*. 'All the world's a stage, and all the men and women merely players'. Anyone have any idea what Shakespeare meant by that? It's about disguise, playing a part. It's the theme of *As You Like It*. Can anyone tell me where we see that?

It is an astute insight, since Jaques' speech is so often treated as a set-piece in anthologies rather than a comment on the action and themes of the play. Josie's essay on the play shows how much she can apply it, not only in relation to the play but also to her own life. Other touches seem to be parallels with *As You Like It*, for example, the sex education class and surrounding discussions are a contemporary equivalent of the frank discussions between Rosalind and Orlando. The adjustment of gender expectations and compromise between a man and a woman gives a modern equivalent of the 'pre-nuptial' discussions in the play.

Another facet of *As You Like It* shows a different kind of repetition-with-variation in Shakespearean comedy that reappears in some film comedies, this time involving contrasting character types rather than plot structure. The relationship between Touchstone the courtier and Audrey the country girl builds upon that in *Love's Labour's Lost* between Don Adriano and Jaquenetta, both ill-suited couples linking a fastidious or pedantic man with an earthy woman, as though the intellect is attracted to the body. This pattern is found in films such as *Bringing Up Baby* and *Ball of Fire* (1941), which was co-written by Billy Wilder, in which an unworldly professor researching slang becomes enmeshed with a nightclub performer, 'Sugarpuss O'Shea' – which in turn may also look back to Shaw's *Pygmalion* and forward to *My Fair Lady*. The cinema of love is an intertextual and interrelated field, drawing in both broad and nuanced ways on Shakespearean precedents collectively and singly.

Notes

1. Altman, *Film/Genre*, 17.
2. Quoted James Harvey, *Romantic Comedy in Hollywood: From Lubitsch to Sturges* (New York: Da Capo Press, 1998), 316.
3. Hunter, *John Lyly*, 314.
4. Maltby, 'Comedy and the Restoration of Order', 224.
5. See Leo Salingar, *Shakespeare and the Traditions of Comedy* (Cambridge: Cambridge University Press, 1974), chs 3 and 5.
6. See especially Northrop Frye, *A Natural Perspective: The Development of Shakespearean Comedy and Romance* (New York: Columbia University Press, 1965), which drew on other essays by Frye, and C. L. Barber, *Shakespeare's Festive Comedy* (Princeton, NJ: Princeton University Press, 1959).
7. See Salingar, *Shakespeare and the Traditions of Comedy*, 218–40.
8. Grant, *Film Genre*, 40.
9. See Frye and also Leslie A. Fiedler, *The Stranger in Shakespeare: Studies in the Archetypal Underworld of the Plays* (New York: Stein and Day, 1972); Janette Dillon, *Shakespeare and the Solitary Man* (London: Macmillan, 1981).
10. Shakespeare's plays-within-plays are mentioned incidentally as the first sources for American musicals by Rick Altman, *The American Film Musical* (Bloomington: Indiana University Press, 1987), 105, but he does not amplify.
11. See Enid Welsford, *The Fool: His Social and Literary History* (London: Faber & Faber, 1935); R. H. Goldsmith, *Wise Fools in Shakespeare* (East Lansing: Michigan State University Press, 1955); Robert H. Bell, *Shakespeare's Great Stage of Fools* (London: Palgrave Macmillan, 2011).
12. Rowe, 'Comedy, Melodrama and Gender', 47.
13. Samuel Crowl, 'Shakespeare and Film Genre in the Branagh Generation', in Anthony R. Guneratne (ed.), *Shakespeare and Genre: From Early Modern*

Inheritances to Postmodern Legacies (London: Palgrave Macmillan, 2012), 191–203, 192.
14 Grant, *Film Genre*, 39.
15 Rowe, 'Comedy, Melodrama and Gender', 43–4. Rowe contrasts romantic comedy to screen melodrama, suggesting that the latter has at its heart not female resistance but passivity, suffering, and victimisation.
16 Linda Jenkins, 'Locating the Language of Gender Experience', *Women and Performance: A Journal of Feminist Theory*, 2 (1984), 5–20, 11, cited in Rowe, 'Comedy, Melodrama and Gender', 42.
17 Dan Sallitt, 'Ernst Lubitsch: The Actor vs the Character', repr. in Gregg Rickman (ed.), *The Film Comedy Reader* (New York: Limelight Editions, 2001), 154–8, 154.
18 At least one critic has argued for the centrality of the genre of romantic comedy in this film: see Celestino Deleyto, *The Secret Life of Romantic Comedy* (Manchester: Manchester University Press, 2009), ch. 2, 'Comic Negotiations: Laughter, Love and World War II – *To Be or Not to Be*'.
19 Richard Armstrong, *Senses of Cinema: Billy Wilder*. Online: http://archive.sensesofcinema.com/contents/directors/02/wilder.html (accessed 12 September 2009).
20 Gehring, *Romantic vs. Screwball Comedy*, 67.
21 Gehring, *Romantic vs. Screwball Comedy*, 120.
22 Quoted in Gehring, *Romantic vs. Screwball Comedy*, 68.
23 Gehring, *Romantic vs. Screwball Comedy*, 79.
24 Gehring, *Romantic vs. Screwball Comedy*, 80, 95.
25 Neale, *Genre and Hollywood*, 211–12.
26 John Dover Wilson, *Shakespeare's Happy Comedies* (London: Faber, 1962); H. B. Charlton, *Shakespearian Comedy* (London: Methuen, 1938); Harley Granville-Barker, *Prefaces to Shakespeare: First Series* (London: Sidgwick & Jackson, 1927); Muriel Bradbrook, *The Growth and Structure of Elizabethan Comedy* (London: Chatto & Windus, 1955).
27 Cavell, *Pursuits of Happiness*, 154.
28 Cavell, *Pursuits of Happiness*, 128.
29 Cavell, *Pursuits of Happiness*, 129.
30 Cavell, noting that in making the film only one leopard was used, suggests that 'while in this narrative fiction there are two leopards, in cinematic fact there is only one; one Baby with two natures; call them tame and wild; or call them latent and aroused'. *Pursuits of Happiness*, 128.
31 S. I. Salamansky, 'Bringing Up Baby (1938): Screwball and the Con of Modern Culture', in Jeffrey Geiger and R. L. Rutsky (eds), *Film Analysis: A Norton Reader* (New York: W. W. Norton & Co., 2005), 282–99, 298.
32 See the classic account by Renato Poggioli, *The Oaten Flute: Essays on Pastoral Poetry and the Pastoral Ideal* (Cambridge, MA: Harvard University Press, 1975).
33 See, respectively, Thomas F. van Laan, *Role-Playing in Shakespeare* (Toronto: University of Toronto Press, 1978); D. P. Young, *The Heart's*

Forest: A Study of Shakespeare's Pastoral Plays (New Haven, CT: Yale University Press, 1972); Harold Jenkins, 'As You Like It', *Shakespeare Survey*, 8 (2002), 40–51.

34 Notions of companionate marriage being advantageous to women have been sometimes contested, for example, see Paula McQuade, 'Love and Lies: Marital Truth-Telling, Catholic Casuistry, and *Othello*', in Dennis Taylor and David N. Beauregard (eds), *Shakespeare and the Culture of Christianity in Early Modern England* (New York: Fordham University Press, 2003), 415–38.

35 Kathrina Glitre, *Hollywood Romantic Comedy: States of the Union 1934–65* (Manchester: Manchester University Press, 2006), 54–8; Andrew Britton, *Katharine Hepburn: Star as Feminist* (London: Studio Visa, 1995), 119.

36 Glitre, *Hollywood Romantic Comedy*, 56, 57.

37 See Richard Burt, 'Afterword: Te(e)n Things I Hate about Girlene Shakesploitation Flicks in the Late 1990's, or Not-So-Fast Times at Shakespeare High', in Courtney Lehman and Lisa Starks (eds), *Spectacular Shakespeare: Critical Theory and Popular Cinema* (Teaneck, NJ: Fairleigh Dickinson University Press, 2002), 205–32, 219. In this essay, Richard Burt provides lengthy analysis of this film as one based on an ideology of 'conservative feminism'.

3

'The guy's only doing it for some doll': musical comedy

'If music be the food of love, play on.'
Twelfth Night

Ever since the seventeenth century, Shakespeare's plays have been adapted into musical forms, whether lyric, symphonic, balletic, or operatic,[1] and movie scores and popular music of the last fifty years bear his marks.[2] Many books have been written covering different aspects of the subject, among which Julie Sanders's *Shakespeare and Music: Afterlives and Borrowings* has a pithy chapter on filmed musical comedies.[3] A part of the reason is that the plays themselves, especially the comedies, are dotted with songs and music with different dramatic and thematic significance in each case: 'one could argue that no other genre (comedy or otherwise) is so continually tied to music as [Shakespeare's] romantic comedy'.[4] *Twelfth Night* especially is laced with different kinds of music from the 'moody' kind indulged in by Orsino, through Feste's plaintive ballad lyrics, to the late-night, drunken 'caterwauling' led by Sir Toby. A play that begins and ends with a song,[5] it contains many snatches and almost certainly lengthy renditions of overtly or unobtrusively referenced music whose sources are now no longer current. Recognising this dimension, the wonderful but neglected Russian filmed version of *Twelfth Night* (1955), directed by A. Abramov and Yan Frid, is almost entirely backed with music. Among the other romantic comedies and later romances, most in theory and perhaps all in practice would have ended in song and dance. Harley Granville-Barker observed that *Love's Labour's Lost* is 'never far from the actual formalities of song and dance',[6] a fact that was enough to inspire Kenneth Branagh in making his film. There is an argument that Elizabethan and Jacobean plays came to include more music and dancing when they were written specifically for indoor theatres such as Blackfriars,[7] but there is more than enough referencing within plays written for the Globe, especially among Shakespeare's comedies, to establish a genre that had claims to originating musical comedy on the popular stage.

In addition to all the songs where the play supplies their words, there are many 'cues' for a popular song or ballad of the time, which no doubt prompted full renditions: for example, Moth's 'the hobby-horse is forgot' in *Love's Labour's Lost*, quoted also in *Hamlet* where the phrase is followed by the stage direction 'hautboys play', and the stage direction in *I Henry IV*, 'Here the lady sings a Welsh song'. Another example comes in *Much Ado About Nothing*, where a person simply reading the text might miss the song and dance:

> MARGARET   Clap's into 'Light o' love'. That goes without a burden. Do you sing it, and I'll dance it.
> BEATRICE   Ye light o' love, with your heels. Then if your husband have stables enough, you'll see he shall lack no barns.
> MARGARET   O illegitimate construction! I scorn that with my heels. (*Much Ado*, 3.4.40–6)

'Light o' Love' seems to have been one of Shakespeare's favourite songs, since it is referred to also in *The Two Gentlemen of Verona* and *The Two Noble Kinsmen*.[8] Among the many ways in which Shakespeare's practice anticipated musical comedies, he even forecast distinctions made by film theorists such as the implicitly metatheatrical device of the 'backstage plot' (in *A Midsummer Night's Dream* and *Love's Labour's Lost*), musical interludes (*As You Like It* and elsewhere), and even 'integrated' musicals where the song lyrics are inextricably linked into the plot (Feste's songs in *Twelfth Night* might be an example, recurrently reflecting on the action itself). Furthermore, musicals often build upon the conventions of pastoral,[9] and although this genre derived from classical writers such as Theocritus and Virgil and from the Italian Renaissance writer Tasso, its more immediately familiar examples for the modern world are Shakespeare's *As You Like It* and *The Winter's Tale*. This chapter will examine some of the broadly defined ways in which his romantic comedies in particular are among the cultural influences that fed into the 'Hollywood musical' genre, despite concerted attempts in the 1930s to claim it as an indigenous American form.

Musical comedies, although usually regarded as a unique creation of Broadway and Hollywood cinema with occasional glances back at nineteenth-century music hall, in fact rely often on conventions close to those operating in Shakespeare's romantic comedies. At times lip service to Shakespearean comedy is paid by historians of modern romantic comedy, for example Kathrina Glitre in her recent *Hollywood Romantic Comedy: States of the Union 1934–65*. However, Glitre, like others, in her concern not to overstate 'generalised assumptions of romantic comedy as an unchanging, transhistorical tradition' by relying on 'the perceived similarities between the dramatic tradition and the Hollywood genre, at the expense of recognising developments',[10] in fact tends towards the opposite danger of not perceiving such similarities at all except in the broadest terms. A more detailed and forthright approach is offered by Irene G. Dash in her entertaining and informative book, *Shakespeare and the American Musical*, where what she says about stage musicals has equal relevance for films:

> Sometimes Shakespeare scared people, especially those writing about the American musical. They didn't know what to do with him. Despite Shakespeare's texts being in the forefront of the development of the organic musical and being popular, these adaptations were basically overlooked. But they shouldn't have been. Right from the start, from the time that Richard Rodgers and Lorenz Hart decided to turn to a Shakespeare play [*The Comedy of Errors*] rather than write their own story, his works were central.[11]

The success story of Shakespearean adaptation into musicals continues, and as Sanders demonstrates, 'the Shakespeare musical has come of age right up to date and is enjoying a new lease of life, indeed a new relevance, in the present age'.[12] My own argument turns on perceiving links through genre rather than momentary effects, quotations, allusions, scenic similarities, and details. I suggest that Shakespeare's own plays are generically both imitative and experimental, and that films that show their influence are similarly bifold (or multifold). His narratives hold within them the potential for recontextualisations and adaptations to different historical and cultural circumstances, and the structure of musical comedies in film provides examples of generic adaptation and transplanting into the modern period. Details of plot do not matter so much as the underlying (or overarching) narrative patterns that provide repetition and variation, depending in this case on the centrality of music in the play as a whole.

The overall point concerning the ubiquitousness of music in all Shakespeare's plays, and not only the comedies, can be made by reference to the voluminous research findings presented by scholars such as Edward W. Naylor in *Shakespeare and Music*, Frederick W. Sternfeld's work on music in the tragedies, and Peter Seng in *The Vocal Songs in the Plays of Shakespeare*.[13] More pointedly in the context of modern musicals, Ross W. Duffin in his remarkable collection, *Shakespeare's Songbook*, argues persuasively that the many allusions to song titles and ballads that occur in Shakespeare's plays of all genres would have been cues to renditions of each song at more length, thus providing far more musical material than appears at first sight from the texts, and more than is ever used in modern performances.[14] Duffin's argument is that Shakespeare would not see a need to supply extended lyrics since (without strict copyright regulations) they would have been well known as popular songs, and also would have been associated with their own well-worn musical scores. He makes the point graphically in speaking of modern times:

> A modern play that included, in passing, such disparate and even fragmentary lines as 'Stormy weather,' 'Hey Jude,' or 'You can get any thing that you want' would easily be recognized as containing allusions to popular songs. People would immediately think of the tunes and, to some extent the rest of the lyrics of those songs and would realize that those members of the audience who didn't recognize the song references and the associations they conjured up were missing part of the message.[15]

In the light of the reference to 'Hey Jude', a kind of corollary emerges from the evidence that the Beatles made musical references to Shakespeare, more so as their own cultural impact grew, in a spirit of '*both* a parody and a bond'.[16] Paul McCartney was even invited by Kenneth Tynan to write music for songs in the National Theatre production of *As You Like It* (he declined). An approach was also made to Donovan, who also declined, though he did incorporate allusions to Shakespeare's song 'Under the Greenwood Tree' into his own 1967 album in which he specifically acknowledges Shakespeare's work.[17] Moreover, the evidence suggests that the action of a play would have stopped to give way to the song as a whole whose content and message, for example in the context of *Twelfth Night*, would have sprung from and reflected themes unfolding in the play as a whole:[18] in ways roughly comparable, I argue, to the musical film. The more obvious point still is that music is a powerful part of the affective experience of a play or film, establishing tone, atmosphere, and emotional colouring in ways that words alone could not. To make the equivalence even closer, judging from Duffin's compilation, there seems to have been a noticeable similarity in the number of musical scores in each play – about ten per comedy – again like the pattern in modern musicals where we regularly find more songs (about twenty, usually) but interpolated in a similar fashion and for similar reasons.

In the discussion that follows I should clarify that although, in most cases, musicals appeared first 'live' on Broadway and, if successful, were later filmed, here I shall be considering only the filmed versions. Always there are significant differences between the stage and screen versions and often the different dating is significant for historical context, but since this discussion concerns genre and especially film genres, rather than particularities, this seems to be a justifiable procedure.

A widely admired, scholarly book on a single Hollywood genre is Rick Altman's *The American Film Musical* (1987). Altman has modified some of his conclusions in more recent works, but the general themes are still significant and provide a starting point. He points out that all a genre definition can give is a description of resemblances between works that share a 'consecration of a particular grouping of semantic elements as acceptable, desirable, even normal', which over a period of time can lead to 'the establishment of any specific manner of interconnecting those elements'.[19] He points out that the musical in particular always mutated according to changing cultural priorities under the influence of history. It changed, for example, from a 'Jolson' type (from *The Jazz Singer* (1929), accepted as the first musical), built on melodrama of the odd-man-out, to 1930s stories of 'star-crossed young lovers' (Altman's phrase, significantly quoting from *Romeo and Juliet*) who usually reach a hard-won happy ending in marriage. Musicals contributed patriotically in the Second World War and afterwards, in recapturing national American history in the 1950s. In the 1960s they reached out to a new, younger, and financially endowed demography, and beyond to families. Incorporating the historical changes into his 'semantic' analysis, Altman groups musicals under three main sub-genres. 'The fairy tale musical' (including themes such as 'sex as battle' and 'sex as adventure'), 'the show musical' (including 'the backstage musical'), and 'the folk musical' (looking back with some nostalgia to American history). Rather than offering 'the Shakespeare musical' as another, I shall suggest that all three of Altman's categories, to some degree, are influenced by Shakespeare, whose comedies underlie some of the generic attributes defining cinematic musical comedies. In a tantalising phrase that he does not follow into its Shakespearean frame of reference, Altman himself offers a clue in invoking Frye's reference to 'New Comedy':

> The comic plot most familiar to the Western world, called 'New Comedy' by Northrop Frye and identified with major writers from Menander to Molière, reveals a pair of young lovers frustrated in their desires by an older figure, often the girl's father, whose allegiance to cultural values (birth, class, money, etc.) is ridiculed and eventually overcome by the young lovers' seemingly natural and just cause (often energetically defended by a tricky servant). The New Comedy system thus aligns youth, servants, and spectators in defense of love (and 'nature') against the older blocking character and the conservative world which he represents ('culture').[20]

Altman goes on to argue that 'the debt of the fairy tale musical – and of the musical in general – to romantic comedy radically dislocates the meaning of the term "comedy" in the familiar but misleading label "musical *comedy*"', suggesting that the New Comedy structure 'involves the opposition of the young (love, energy, justice, nature) to the old (money, conservation, power, culture)', both competing for the same desirable object, like a woman who is both marriageable and a daughter.[21] While not disagreeing with Altman's terms and analysis, I would suggest three interrelated modifications. First, Frye's description of New Comedy, though ostensibly an argument based on historical sources in classical comedy, is in fact an attempt to illuminate, and is in turn derived from, Shakespeare's romantic comedies in particular,[22] which is the model most familiar to modern film-makers and audiences. It is quite a circular argument. Frye was exploring the sources of Shakespeare's plays, but these sources in turn, I would argue, have been replaced by the Shakespearean mode as a source behind modern media. Second, Shakespearean romantic comedy itself mutated in different plays in ways that become relevant to musicals, changing the central conflicts significantly. For example, his later plays with happy endings overlook the power struggle between young and old, concentrating instead on initial fragmentation and eventual reunification of whole families and in particular fathers and daughters. Third, the Shakespearean influence on the musical lies not only in the reception of his romantic comedies and his romances respectively, but also the tragedy of love, *Romeo and Juliet*, which, mainly through the example of *West Side Story*, creates yet another sub-genre, 'musical tragedy', which will be analysed in Chapter 6. In subtle, elusive, and sometimes structurally dispersed ways, Shakespeare's influence on the modern film musical is important at the level of genre but has never gained full critical recognition. However, a caveat: given the sheer magnitude of the corpus of films, which runs into the thousands, I cannot analyse more than a handful of examples where the influence seems reasonably justifiable, hoping that readers' attention will be awakened to see similar patterns in other musicals.

There is nothing sacred or even precise about the terms 'musical' and 'musical comedy', since they are often used with a wide application. The usual pedigree is traced from origins in the minstrel show, vaudeville, and other forms of variety entertainment such as turn-of-the-century farce.[23] Altman has researched the early descriptions of such movies and concludes that 'the variety of generic terms used to categorize films now regularly described as musicals is remarkable', citing many titles in the years 1929 and 1930 that were advertised as almost anything from 'epic' and 'drama' at one end of the spectrum to 'musical farce' at the other. But it is significant that 'comedy' recurs often, as do phrases like 'comedy drama', 'romantic comedy', 'subtle comedy', and romance'.[24] 'Musical' as a stand-alone term was never used before the end of 1930, by which time the period, which is now hailed as the genre's most productive age as measured in output if not quality, was over. The 'single, well delineated genre' is a critical construct, and like film noir, the musical, or musical drama, as a coherent, descriptive grouping it is a phenomenon noticed in retrospect. Steve Neale, engaging in particular with Altman's *The American Film Musical*, says 'the musical has always been a mongrel genre' with its roots in different forms, and he expands by quoting from J. Collins that it is 'multifaceted, hybrid, and complex'.[25] Given such critical latitude, there seems nothing wrong in theory, then, with inspecting examples without too many filmic preconceptions, and from a point of view that keeps in mind the possible influence from a range of sources and influences that can include Shakespeare's canonical romantic comedies. Altman himself, though not mentioning Shakespeare, places comic drama, comedy, romantic comedy, and romance as important to the evolution of the so-called musical,[26] as though the music itself need not be the central, defining element when a comic presentation of love in drama is represented in a certain way. And wherever the term romantic comedy occurs, Shakespeare's name should come in tandem, since he can be given credit for perfecting the staged version, mixing influences from the plays of John Lyly and prose romances to create his own unique form of romantic comedy, and later dramatised romance.[27] Perhaps a more descriptive name might be comedies of courtship.

The term 'musical' has other limitations in this context. It is too broad and porous, first because virtually all films use music in ways that are fundamental to emotionally manipulating audiences, and second because opera, for example, is normally excluded from its ranks, though operetta, such as the films in which Jeanette McDonald and Nelson Eddie appear, is included. Besides, the term suggests a technical resource that does not automatically suggest a particular content, set of conventions, or themes as, for example, the term romantic comedy does. Equally it is also too narrow because arguably the episodes we most remember about many of the 'great' examples, those made by Busby Berkeley and the ones in which respectively Fred Astaire, Ginger Rogers, and Gene Kelly appear, present not only the music but, just as importantly, dancing. In this context, once again we can, if we look, find a surprising amount of dance in Shakespeare's romantic comedies, at least from *Love's Labour's Lost* onwards, again missed when reading the plays since references to dance are even more cryptic than those to songs whose lyrics are supplied by Shakespeare. The primacy of dance is signalled in dialogue, visually revealed in performance, but not always highlighted by stage directions.[28] Dancing operates sometimes as a visual metaphor for sexual compatibility between a couple – Romeo and Juliet are the obvious examples – while ensemble dancing may express 'communal solidarity' as it invariably does in musicals.[29] There are precedents, for example, at the end of *The Merry Wives of Windsor* at the cost of the excluded, scapegoated figure, Falstaff, in *As You Like It* where a stage direction announces 'A dance' before the Epilogue, and *Much Ado About Nothing* where Benedick calls 'Strike up, pipers', after which there is a 'Dance'.

Shakespeare in musicals

The name Shakespeare on the credits may distract film historians in assigning a movie to a genre. Although Mankiewicz's *Julius Caesar* (1953) fits closely the criteria for Greco-Roman epics, it rarely features in studies on that subject, and is instead sidelined into the faintly antiquarian slot of 'Shakespeare film'. A similar fate befell Warner Brothers' 1935 *A Midsummer Night's Dream* in relation to the Hollywood musical. If it were billed as written by any other screenwriter it would be recognised as predominantly a musical, but because of his name it is discussed exclusively as a Shakespearean adaptation. Once again, as in the case of *Julius Caesar* and epic, when seen in generic terms the film clarifies the pervasive, Shakespearean influence behind the genre of musical as a whole, and in Chapter 2 we consider its contribution to cinematic romantic comedy as a closely related genre. Even *A Midsummer Night's Dream* itself as a play could be classified as an early musical, so pervasive is the medium in a play popularly regarded as having been written to celebrate a wedding in a great house where obviously dancing and singing were appropriate, as Hartnoll notes:

> The music of fairyland sings Titania asleep, 'You spotted snakes with double tongue' – a prayer for her safe repose (II.2). It plays again perhaps between Acts III and IV, when the Lovers *sleepe all the Act* (i.e. on the stage throughout the act-interval). It returns at the end of the play when an air of supernatural blessing is shed around by the entry of the *King and Queene of Fairies, with their traine* and their final song, which embraces the *actual* noble household within the beneficent sleep-world of the play. Titania's amorous aberration in loving Bottom in his ass's head is beautifully pointed by her being wakened by Bottom's clownish singing of 'The Woosell cocke, so blacke of hew' (III.1), a splendid contrast to the fairies' lullaby; and by Bottom's reply to her offer of music – Wilt thou hear some musicke, my sweet love? – CLOWN. 'I have a reasonable good ear in musicke. Let us have the tongs and the bones.' – *Musicke Tongs, rurall Musicke* (IV.1) ... the true norm is sounded by Theseus with his horns and hounds (*Winde Hornes ... Hornes and they wake*).[30]

Purcell (*The Fairy Queen*, 1692, where Purcell's music is incidental rather than settings of the text) and Mendelssohn (1842) are only the best known of many composers who have drawn on and developed the play's repeated use of music and foregrounded the innate musicality of its structure, manoeuvring lovers through harmonious patterns of relationships like voices in a madrigal.

The 1935 *Dream* exhibits stylistic eclecticism covering, among other influences, the elements brought from Europe by émigré directors Max Reinhardt and William Dieterle of German expressionism and gothic imagery reminiscent of *Nosferatu* (1922). Vaudeville farce characterises the rude mechanicals, and ballet dominates through Mendelssohn's music and the choreography by Bronislawa Nijinsky (sister of Vaslav). The choice of star actors from among Warners' employees indicates the generic range of references – Dick Powell (young, matinee romantic lead), Oberon played by Victor Jory (often cast in sinister roles and here with a touch of Dracula), Puck played by Mickey Rooney (known as a mischievous, frenetic, and somewhat demonic child star), Joe E. Brown (physical and facial comedy). Bottom is played by James Cagney (gangster movies), Titania by Olivia de Havilland, who was discovered for this film by Reinhardt in her school's production of the *Dream*, and later to become one of Hollywood's most famous female stars. However, the overall film genre is unmistakably the Hollywood musical. In particular, the camerawork in filming the fairies is influenced by the unique overhead, kaleidoscopic shots made famous by Busby Berkeley, used as a trademark in many Warner Brothers musicals in one of the form's early heyday periods, 1933 to 1937.

While trying sometimes to disguise or suppress their reliance on an Elizabethan playwright, at other times Hollywood musicals are unusually explicit in raising Shakespeare as an 'issue' and a reference point, interlacing reverence with affectionate parody. On the release of the *Dream* in 1935, Warner Brothers issued a lot of spin-off publicity befitting the movie's ambitious length (140 minutes when played in full) and its considerable financial investment (£1,500,000), as happens routinely today with most films but was then more rare. The studio recorded a series of publicity statements by some of the film's personnel, each appearing through the velvet curtains across a proscenium arch, visually emphasising not only Shakespeare's theatrical pedigree but also cinema's roots in traditional theatre. They present glowing tributes not only to the movie but to its Shakespearean material, and each speaks of the 'courageousness' of making such a film, 'as new to the talking screen as sound was to the silent' (Frank McHugh, Quince, the Carpenter). A five-minute short called *Warner Brothers Studio Café* showed Joe E. Brown having lunch with Pat O'Brien (then rehearsing the Warner Brothers musical drama, *Stars Over Broadway* (also 1935)) after the release of the *Dream*, and the dialogue, which purports to be unscripted, runs this way:

O'BRIEN I caught *The Midsummer Night's Dream* last night. Boy, that is a pip.
BROWN Like it?
O'BRIEN Never realised Shakespeare could write such terrific comedy.
BROWN Say, the things that Shakespeare wrote 300 years ago, comedians are still using … Listen *A Midsummer Night's Dream* is so different from anything else that's ever been produced I'm mighty proud to have appeared in it …
O'BRIEN The picture will be popular for 300 more years. Never seen you playing a female impersonator before.
BROWN That wasn't my idea. That was Bill Shakespeare's.

A musical short of some twenty minutes' duration, *Shake Mr Shakespeare* came in the wake of the *Dream* but stands alone as a somewhat surrealistic homage to Shakespeare on screen. For a long time lost, it is now available among the 'extras' on the DVD of the *Dream*. A Hollywood director falls asleep over his volumes of Shakespeare's plays, whereupon characters come to life in a dream sequence, heralded by Mickey Rooney as Puck with 'lord, what fools these mortals be', to step out of their respective plays. Signature lines are recited: 'To be or not to be …', 'What's in a name …', 'Life's but a walking shadow …', 'Then must you speak of him as one who loved not wisely but too well …'. They sing to the sleeping director 'We're going to Hollywood', and others like Richard III and Julius Caesar appear. Exchanges from *Romeo and Juliet* are turned into comic colloquialisms ('Romeo, where the heck are you? … Oh tell me why the heck art thou giving the run-around to me?'), and the lovers quarrel over whether they will sign with Warner Brothers or MGM. The balcony scene becomes an occasion for a marriage contract that is as much a movie contract, concluded by Juliet's 'Why don't you come up and see me sometime?', misquoting Mae West's famous line in *She Done Him Wrong* (1933). Hamlet appears in the graveyard playing catch with Yorick's skull and using it as a bowling ball. When the ghost appears Hamlet greets him with 'Hiya pop'. On the cue 'Hollywood calls for many Hamlets', twelve of them appear all dressed identically in black and do a tap dance on gravestones. At the Roman forum Mark Antony is expected but Henry VIII appears 'in the wrong play', and after chants of 'We want Anthony' he appears and delivers 'Friends, Romans, countrymen …' in song and dance. Cleopatra promises that 'the man who kisses me will need a lot of money', to which Antony responds, 'I need a lot of money'. She then turns into a contortionist 'getting tossed around again' by two muscular acrobats. Finally, Shakespeare himself appears from between his books, intoning, 'Is it for this I spilled such magic ink?', to be answered, 'Oh listen all, things have changed, this is different ... Today the screenplay is the thing'. When Shakespeare objects, the song breaks out, 'You gotta shake Mr Shakespeare', a fight erupts, the director wakes and finds the characters gone, and he is somnambulistically in the arms of the cleaning lady. Of all the things one could say about this little oddity of a short movie, one notices primarily the assumption that the audience will be familiar with the characters and lines, the playful irreverence with which Shakespeare is treated as if his plays are taken to be popular entertainment, and the sense of inevitability that he will be taken up by Hollywood in a new idiom – 'You gotta shake Mr Shakespeare'. It is a clarion call announcing his assimilation into the medium of film.

Samuel Crowl has shown how well integrated into *Love's Labour's Lost* (2000) are songs from American musicals of the 1930s and 1940s, 'many first sung by Fred Astaire in the musicals he made with Ginger Rogers and written by such masters of the genre as Cole Porter, Irving Berlin, George and Ira Gershwin, and Jerome Kern'.[31] He shows that in each example the song follows a linking part of the narrative – an image from the poetry or an incident triggers an association that leads into a song – so that the music is not meretricious but thematic. Equally, the dances occur more or less as they may have done in the play itself: 'Branagh's film finds in the American movie musical a patterned grace, elegance, and wit that serve as a twentieth-century equivalent to Elizabethan romantic comedy.'[32] This reinforces various statements made by Branagh himself, that the inter-war years were an especially appropriate period in which to set the play and that the cinematic genre burgeoning in the later years of that period was the musical, which offered an alternative, fictional world. He was also keen to make his film into an appreciative homage to the form, with a nod also to *Casablanca*.[33] All this information confirms the manifest influence of the Hollywood musical on Branagh's film, but to reverse the emphasis, it also demonstrates that Branagh's *Love's Labour's Lost* inverts the chronology and highlights the prior influence of Shakespearean comedy on Hollywood musicals themselves. The play is, after all, among the earliest in which Shakespeare, albeit 'cautiously, even flirtatiously', turns to dancing, singing, and music to carry the play's 'theme of the unfinished, the broken and the incomplete', deferring marriage beyond the closure.[34] For another reason, which Branagh may have realised, *Love's Labour's Lost* as a play became poignantly apt for an immediately post-war generation, since Peter Brook's famous stage production, which put the play on the map for the first time since the Elizabethan age, came in 1946, and elements of it become relevant in the film version of *On The Town* in 1949.

So far as I know, *On the Town* (1949) has never been compared with *Love's Labour's Lost*, but the structural and thematic similarities are surprising. This movie is one of those where the Shakespearean influence is almost certainly carried unconsciously and indirectly through genre. Shakespeare's play has a plot that is simple but unprecedented among the comedies, since its surprising ending, which defers marriage beyond the time of the play, violates the generic expectations of resolution in a romantic comedy. Four men, either voluntarily (the Duke of Navarre) or involuntarily (Berowne), choose to live in an all-male 'academe', studying and abjuring the company of women. Immediately, four women appear on an incidental political mission. Trying to keep to the spirit if not the letter of their vow, the men 'entertain' the women al fresco with witty badinage, invitations to dance, and game-playing disguise. The playful spirit is received by the women 'as bombast and as lining to the time', but emotional engagement is provocatively left dangling by constant disruption. Consistent with conventions of romantic comedy, the men programmatically fall in love with the women, and vice versa, but the ending of the play is left as lacking in conventional closure as the frustrated dances. At the moment when marriage becomes an issue, news of the Princess's father's death is announced by a mysterious and cryptic messenger, Mercade, and the women are prompted to depart hastily. They promise to marry at the end of a year, if the men can succeed in keeping new vows to spend the year in various quite distressing tasks that entail privation and are by no means easy. That is all (apart from a song and a dance), despite Branagh's 'feel-good' epilogue in the film, which shows the men coming back from war a year later and marrying the women. In Shakespeare's broken closure, however, a year is 'too long for a play':

> Our wooing doth not end like an old play:
> Jack hath not Jill. These ladies' courtesy
> Might well have made our sport a comedy. (5.2.860–2)

On the Town shows three sailors coming off their warship with its all-male crew in order to spend one day's rest and recreation in New York. Far from trying to avoid women, they are driven by long-repressed libidos to create at least short-lived liaisons with three responsive women. All activities are largely group-driven rather than individual, enacted outdoors or in public places like a museum and the top of the Empire State Building, despite one woman's forthright invitation to 'come back to my place'. While openly displaying desire to the point of lust, the men avoid intimacy and continue to work as a male group. This is marked by their common sailors' uniforms, which becomes a problem when they need to disguise themselves as women to escape police attention (the men in *Love's Labour's Lost* disguise themselves as Muscovites). The day of shore leave is spent in hedonistic sight-seeing and frenetic wooing through song and dance. Despite a certain amount of misunderstandings and separations, they all end the day on the brink of permanent relationships. However, at the end of the day the men go back reluctantly to their vessel and to their all-male life, which by implication opens them up to danger and possible death in war. The last scene is visually dominated by the bleak wharf and warship, and a song that turns on duty and 'work' ('I Feel I'm Not out of Bed Yet') that returns us to the morning. The women, now individuated only by wearing different coloured dresses, wave goodbye from the wharf to the sailors, equally anonymous in their uniforms and among hundreds of others identically dressed, as the ship pulls out. The camera pans up past the ship's metallic weaponry to the New York skyline, leaving the film as a paean to the navy and the city rather than emotional self-realisation of individuals or fulfilment in love. Marriage is mentioned as a wistful hope lying in the future, and *On the Town* ends, like *Love's Labour's Lost*, as undoubtedly a romantic comedy but with inconclusive courtship and more than a touch of regret.

One film historian, although making no reference to Shakespeare, gestures towards the generic similarities of the respective endings, suggesting a post-war insecurity as the root social cause:

> Though the film ends with the promise of reunion, this 'utopian' resolution is fraught with uncertainty. The film's narrative concludes with the men returning to their ship, thus invoking yet another separation similar to those so common to wartime films. *On The Town*'s narrative depends on the tenuousness and pressure of time – one day – in which the sailors seek to gratify their different desires for pleasure. Time poses constraints on the characters.[35]

The description applies, coincidentally, with some exactitude to *Love's Labour's Lost*. On a sardonic note, as the sailors return to the ship we see three more disembarking, with the implication that many more such affairs will be initiated, never to be concluded. Another musical, *Anchors Aweigh* (1945), shows two sailors (Gene Kelly and Frank Sinatra) facing similar urgency in their amatory pursuits, having only two days of shore leave. The ending is less personal and more triumphalised, orchestrated into a celebration of the US Navy as a whole. The final shot of the pairs of lovers embracing, to the navy choir singing 'Until we meet once more / Here's wishing you a happy voyage home', allows this film to avoid the unanswered questions and soften any uncertainty and pain that might lie behind the deferral of fulfilment.

Although *On the Town* was made in 1949, it is set in 1944, the year when its two 'live' sources – Jerome Robbins's ballet *Fancy Free* set to Leonard Bernstein's music, and the Broadway version of *On the Town* itself – were both made and set. The implication is that since the war was still in progress, marriage was barely an immediately viable option, as Branagh himself must have noticed in choosing the pre-war context. Although in the play it is the women rather than the men who leave at the end, the backdrop has included negotiations in a wartime situation, a reported death causing a hasty retreat, games of role playing, deferral of the 'world without end bargain' of marriage until peacetime, and the necessary truncation of the day-long courtships as evening draws on. Yet another rudely disrupted entertainment, 'The Nine Worthies', is also part of the inconclusive ending. The emphases in the play and the musical may be different, and I do not want to claim *Love's Labour's Lost* as a straightforward source for *On the Town*, but the respective works have strong and structurally significant resemblances of a generic kind. As a footnote, in *This Is the Army* (1943), a young soldier who wants to follow his father's First World War initiative in producing an all-soldier concert decides conscientiously not to marry his fiancée until the end of the war. The film-maker almost certainly did not have *Love's Labour's Lost* in mind, but at least the example suggests an experience common at the time.

Allusions to Shakespeare

Paradoxically, the high road between musicals and Shakespeare is not through comedy but a tragedy. As Duffin shows, there are nine references to ballads in *Romeo and Juliet* itself,[36] and it is mentioned frequently enough in films, especially in the 1940s, to qualify it as a reference point in movie history long before *West Side Story*. The balcony scene alone become a minor convention or even cliché. *Stage Door Canteen* (1943) is a revue for and about the US armed forces during the Second World War, and a vehicle for celebrity singers, dancers, comics, and actors. The famous stage actress Katharine Cornell plays herself giving the balcony speech by Juliet while serving soup to a soldier. She is followed by the darling of the troops, Gracie Fields, singing an anti-German song. The juxtaposition enlists Shakespeare as an Allied wartime morale-booster, just as he was in the British documentary films of Humphrey Jennings, such as *Words for Battle* (1941) and *Listen to Britain* (1942), and Olivier's *Henry V* (1944) made in celebration of the RAF. America also appropriated him as part of the war effort, not through the more obviously propagandist history play but through *Romeo and Juliet*. Fleeting romances often doomed by wartime separation provide a theme of *Stage*

Door Canteen. Meanwhile, in *Playmates* (1941), John Barrymore plays an out-of-work actor who gives a lesson in Shakespeare to the leading lady, using the example of *Romeo and Juliet*. This self-parodying performance is said to be marked by the 'sad and sorry spectacle of Barrymore at the end of his professional tether'.[37] In the musical *State Fair* (1945), an overt reference to Shakespeare comes by way of the by now almost obligatory ditty in American musicals referencing *Romeo and Juliet*:

> HER I'm not a girl for sentimental tripe
> I never go for the Romeo type.
> HIM Over a dewy eyed Juliet
> No-one has seen me drool yet.

However, *Romeo and Juliet* was not the only Shakespearean reference in the history of musical films. *The Show of Shows* (Warner Bros, 1929) contains a scene from *Henry VI Part Three* played by John Barrymore, while *The Underpup* contains 'Lo! Hear the Gentle Lark', Sir Henry Bishop's musical setting of stanza 143 of *Venus and Adonis*, which the movie complements with the anonymous song, 'I'm Like a Bird'. *Casanova in Burlesque* (1944), a vehicle for the comedy of Joe E. Brown, uses the plot of *The Taming of the Shrew* (nine years before *Kiss Me Kate*) and refers to other Shakespearean plays, having songs such as *Willie the Shake*.[38] In the plot, according to publicity, 'A stripper discovers a professor who spends summer teaching Shakespeare and winter as a burlesque comic'. Later, *Catch My Soul* (1974) is reputedly a successful and 'unintentionally hilarious' musical version of *Othello*.[39] *Thank God It's Friday* (1978) contains a song utilising *Romeo and Juliet*. *West Side Story* (1961), although obviously not a comedy, is the most famous example of film musical adaptation of *Romeo and Juliet*. The tradition goes on, since Baz Luhrmann's *Romeo + Juliet* (1996) is a musical tragedy while much later *10 Things I Hate About You* (1999), despite being classified as a 'teen-pic', is also a musical comedy version of *The Taming of the Shrew*. Other examples of Shakespeare lying behind musicals are noted by Thomas Hischak in breezy fashion:

> *A Midsummer Night's Dream* got a jazz facelift in *Swingin' the Dream* (1939) and the pastoral comedy appeared Off Broadway as *Babes in the Woods* (1964). Even the melancholy Dane discovered rock in *Rockabye Hamlet* (1976) but Broadway only welcomed him for two weeks. *The Two Gentlemen of Verona* lost the title's 'the' and became the musical *Two Gentlemen of Verona* (1971) in Central Park and then on Broadway. *Twelfth Night* is Shakespeare's most musical play with more songs than any other so it is understandable that it has been musicalized four times: the delightful *Your Own Thing* (1968) spoofed the Bard and rock musicals and

had a long run Off Broadway; the musically interesting *Music Is* (1976), which lasted only a week on Broadway; *Love and Let Love* (1968), which did not do much better Off Broadway; and the stylish African American musical *Play On!* (1997) which used music by Duke Ellington.[40]

Sadly for us, none of these was turned into a movie, though detailed and appreciative eye-witness accounts of *Your Own Thing* and *The Two Gentlemen of Verona* are provided by Irene G. Dash in *Shakespeare and the American Musical*. *Babes in the Woods* should not be confused with the risqué, 'camp' film of the same name made in 1962, which is in many ways an American 'Carry On' film, while *Hamlet in Rock* (2008) might substitute for *Rockabye Hamlet*.

References to Shakespeare often acquire multiple significances in a particular context, the most complex example being *Singin' in the Rain* (1951), which is, like *On the Town*, a classic musical from the Arthur Freed unit at MGM. (In fact, a character based on Freed appears in the former.) *Singin' in the Rain* is set in 1927, the year in which 'talkies' were inaugurated in *The Jazz Singer*, which is alluded to by name. When a fictional star of the silent screen, Don Lockwood (Gene Kelly), literally falls into the car of aspiring student stage actress Kathy Selden (Debbie Reynolds), the latter mocks Lockwood's 'pantomime' acting in movies: 'If you've seen one you've seen them all', she says, in a derisive and unsympathetic dismissal of the genre, which the film itself does its best to challenge. She goes on to say, 'Acting means great parts, wonderful lines, words. Shakespeare. Ibsen' – again a dismissal of the silent movies in which he stars. He mocks her back with 'You're going to New York, and someday we'll all hear of you – Kathy Selden as Juliet, as Lady Macbeth, as King Lear! You'll have to wear a beard!' Now angry, she retorts, 'At least the stage is a dignified profession. Why are you so conceited? You're nothing but a shadow on film. You're not flesh and blood'. They part with his sarcastic words, 'Farewell Ethel Barrymore'. Given the manifest innocence of Kathy in contrast to the worldly, famous film star, 'Shakespeare' is here aligned with dignity, sincerity, eloquent language, and 'flesh and blood', set against the trivial and insubstantial world of silent films. However, this can easily be turned into an accusation of cultural snobbery against popular culture like musicals themselves: 'You can study Shakespeare and be quite elite', as one of the songs proclaims. More subtly, this running debate comments on the perennial ambiguity with which Shakespeare, like classical, live theatre itself, was regarded in the unashamedly populist genre of musicals in an equally mass medium of film.

The reference later takes on different resonances. When Lockwood discovers that the only work Kathy can get is not playing Shakespeare but being one of the 'Coconut Grove girls' in a floor show stepping out from a giant cake, he finds a reason for more sarcasm: 'Well if it isn't Ethel Barrymore. I do hope you'll favour us with something special. Say, Hamlet's soliloquy, or a scene from *Romeo and Juliet*. Don't be shy, you make about the prettiest Juliet I've ever seen. Really.' His thinly veiled pique at being told he is not a serious actor returns with his faintly derisive description of Kathy later: 'She's an actress on the legitimate stage.' When love begins to blossom he follows her onto a movie set, again referring to Shakespeare as he switches on lights, one by one: 'A lady is standing on her balcony in a rose-trellised garden ... You sure look lovely in the moonlight, Kathy', leading into the song 'You Were Meant for Me'. They sing and dance as a duet for the first time, and as is standard in film musicals, this gesture aurally and visually suggests sexual compatibility and mutual romance: 'The idealised representation of sexual desire as heterosexual romance and union is one of the mythic and ideological functions of much popular culture, including the musical. Dance, in which the partners move in harmonious physical rhythms, has served as a ready sexual metaphor at least since the hot dance jazz of the 1920s.'[41] Even before Lockwood and Kathy realise they are in love, their bodies moving in unison betray the fact. The critical point in the film is achieved with a little help from Shakespeare, not structurally from *Romeo and Juliet* despite the references, but from romantic comedy.

In *Singin' in the Rain* a further reference adds another hint of influence. The character Cosmo Brown (Donald O'Connor) is presented as having the functions of a Shakespearean clown, and he is the next to make explicit reference to Shakespeare, this time in a comic context:

> Big people have little humor. Little people have no humor at all. In the words of that immortal bard Samuel J. Snodgrass as he was being led to the guillotine:
>
>> Now you could study Shakespeare
>> And be quite elite
>> And you can charm the critics
>> And have nothing to eat
>> Just slip on a banana peel
>> The world's at your feet
>> Make 'em laugh
>> Make 'em laugh
>> Make 'em laugh
>> ...
>> Don't you know everyone wants to laugh.

Despite the diversionary phrase 'Samuel J. Snodgrass as he was being led to the guillotine', the 'immortal bard' is named as Shakespeare and equated with a critical 'elite' opposed to Cosmo's kind of slapstick, but the subtext, suggested by the prior sequences in which 'legitimacy', sincerity, and feelings are attached to the plays of Shakespeare, is that he himself knew how to 'Make 'em laugh'. However throwaway the references to Shakespeare seem to be in *Singin' in the Rain*, they are integrated into the guiding themes at a level that suggests genre. Tensions between 'legitimate theatre' and film musicals go both ways, suggesting that the former is being inexorably superseded by the latter, yet movies can be given respectability by the former even as it is gently mocked. Shakespeare was a key and contested figure in these debates that had persisted since movies began, and nowhere more so than in the specific genre of musicals that periodically sought to assert more uplifting and 'legitimate' cultural capital than its surface light-heartedness would suggest.

Brief allusions in another 'backstage' musical, *The Perils of Pauline* (1947), invoke acting values of a slightly different kind. Set just before and during the First World War, this movie again takes us behind the scenes in the period of silent movie-making when the film is retrospectively set. To some extent it is based on the life of a real actress who played in serials that were very popular in the silent era. 'Pearl White' (Betty Hutton) is a spirited and rebellious young woman who stands up for herself and for all exploited workers, from downtrodden women in a sewing factory to actors: she knocks out a casting agent who makes a pass at her. Pearl ends up risking life and limb in cliff-hanging movie serials. She is first 'discovered' as a performer by a group of self-styled 'thespians' in a stage company performing *Romeo and Juliet*, and her vigorous comic style and singing ability are adjudged to make her 'an ideal curtain-raiser for Shakespeare', providing a vaudeville act before the serious drama. In this case, reference to Shakespeare is used to spark debates about performing styles. The traditional stage is represented as old-fashioned and ponderous but honest, pitted against the new medium of movies, utilising sensationalism, opportunism, and a different kind of 'ham' acting with unsubtle gestural movements. It is seen as a medium that 'costs you nothing but your self respect' and depends on 'illusions'. However, the critique and ridicule of theatrical values operates reciprocally. While fault is found with Shakespearean stage practice, which is seen as outdated, the world of silent movies, however much a beacon of industrial and technological progress, is artistically exploitative and illusionary. The outbreak of war disrupts both. In terms of the plot, Shakespeare has little continuing function, except that the ending has an emotive element from *Romeo and Juliet*, but the early allusion does act as a central reference point in an important debate about the medium of film, as it does in *Singin' in the Rain*. Once again, it is Shakespeare himself who raises some of the terms of the disputes, since he regularly challenges his own illusions from within (as in Fabian's 'If this were played upon the stage I would condemn it as an improbable fiction' in *Twelfth Night*) and undermines actors even in his own plays as mere 'shadows':

> If we shadows have offended,
> Think but this, and all is mended;
> That you have but slumbered here,
> While these visions did appear;
> And this weak and idle theme,
> No more yielding but a dream.
> (*A Midsummer Night's Dream*, Epilogue 1–6)

Puck's words apply equally to Shakespearean comedy and movie musicals, a mutual challenge that significantly binds the two through their illusionism, actors who are 'shadows', dreams, and shared generic qualities around romantic love.

Contrasted settings and backstage musicals

Several of Shakespeare's romantic comedies alternate between two locales or settings, and the contrasts and transitions are important to the plays' structures and meanings. *A Midsummer Night's Dream* moves from Theseus's palace to the Athenian woods, and back again; *As You Like It* from the court to the Forest of Arden (Ardennes) and back to court; *The Merchant of Venice* from the romance atmosphere of Belmont to the financial world of Venice and back to Belmont. Recognising the fertility of the pattern, Shakespeare adopted it also in some tragedies such as *King Lear* (the court and the heath), *Othello* (Venice and Cyprus), *Timon of Athens* (the city and the forest that meets the beach), and even in *Macbeth*, in which Banquo is murdered while riding in the very Wood of Dunsinane that at the end of the play 'moves' to the palace. While it would be foolish to claim that such structuring would not have evolved without Shakespeare's example, yet these plays established the dramatic effectiveness of such a flexible locational dynamic in a universally accepted theatrical repertory. Like so many other tried and trusted devices in dramaturgy, this one entered cinematic practice. In particular, the potential offered by the 'green world' presented the opportunity for creating the 'backstage musical' sub-genre. Here I will examine some examples from romantic musicals that seem to show an influence from

Shakespeare's romantic comedies, in playing against each other a professional setting and a recreational.

Something to Sing About (1937) was made just two years after Reinhardt's *A Midsummer Night's Dream* and both films coincidentally star James Cagney in roles unusual for him but that hold similarities. In the *Dream* he is Bottom, who becomes the love object for an infatuated Fairy Queen, while in *Something to Sing About* he is a talented but rather hapless tap dancer or 'hoofer' from New York, a 'hempen homespun' who happily marries his long-standing sweetheart but becomes the victim of publicity linking him romantically with a Hollywood love goddess, the fairy queen of her own brittle, fabricated world. The contemporary publicity for the movie boasted 'A Cagney you have never seen!', though in fact the audience had recently seen a similar Cagney as Bottom, not so foolish but just as homespun, and romantically linked with the Fairy Queen herself. Through the portability of Cagney's 'star appeal' in related roles, these similarities serve at least subliminally to link Shakespeare with the rather modest but interesting 'backstage musical', *Something to Sing About*. The dramatist himself does make one obtrusive, visual appearance, when a bust of Shakespeare appears right in the middle of the frame, separating on the left the Hollywood speech trainer with his European accent (perhaps like Reinhardt's?) from Cagney on the right with his Brooklyn accent and down-to earth values. As the trainer tries unavailingly to teach Cagney how to produce vowels that are 'round like a pear', Shakespearean theatrical diction is associated with high acting, but the bard's presence is enigmatic and ambivalent. The division between left and right is highly significant in the film's design. Cagney begins in New York in his familiar jazz band, but is 'discovered' and whisked westwards to Hollywood to make his career in films. When he flies from east to west, the film shows a small aeroplane, perhaps a toy, flying from right to left, and when he returns it flies from left to right, in the same alternating pattern, when his girlfriend/wife visits him in Hollywood and returns to New York. As in Shakespeare's comedies, the two locations take on contrasting moral and thematic significances. New York is represented as a place of camaraderie, loyalty, sincere feelings, ordinary decencies, and genuine love. Hollywood, like the court in *As You Like It*, is marked by conflict and competitiveness, where people deceive each other for the sake of publicity, and where fights break out. New York embraces people as they are, while Hollywood tries to change them in ways that falsify their true identities and compromise their integrity through pretentiousness. When Terry Rooney (Cagney) finally has enough of the illusionary fabrications and is appalled at how he is misreported as being about to marry his leading lady, he flies back (left to right) to his band, which is now deserted by its audience without his presence, and to his wife, who once again can sing while he dances. The cabaret theatre quickly fills again with their reassuring presence, and we assume they will live happily ever after, without any more contact with the destructive charisma of Hollywood. The contrast in this case makes some internal comment on the musical as a naturalised American form, since there was genuine friction between east and west, between New York's Broadway, often seen as 'legitimate' musical theatre and emotionally 'natural', and the magical but escapist illusions of 'Tinseltown', a debate that is played out in different ways in other musicals such as, for example, *Singin' in the Rain*. But the point to be made here is that, whether by conscious design or unconscious reception of a generic legacy, the Shakespearean model of twin locations lies at the heart of the film's meaning, just as the bust of his head and shoulders separates the screen into two differentiated spaces in the early scene.

In some ways the sub-genre of 'backstage musical' inevitably has two locations by virtue of its very nature. There is offstage life where actors are represented as 'real people' with their own emotional lives and dilemmas. They are sometimes shown in their homes, or more usually in temporarily rented apartments or borrowed rooms (*Anchors Aweigh*), befitting their insecure lives. On the other hand, there is the space of the staged performance that they are rehearsing, usually the setting for the finale, which is choreographed and seamlessly performed by the actors not as ordinary people but in roles as perfected, fictional stage personae. Invariably there is a thematic connection between the two worlds, as there is between Shakespeare's 'plays within plays' – Peter Quince's 'Pyramus and Thisbe' and Holofernes' 'The Nine Worthies' – and the plays that incorporate them. The clue to the connection is through metatheatre, a device by which actors in the play draw attention to the play's artifice, thus paradoxically establishing a level of 'reality'. Shakespeare was the dramatist who most regularly exploited this dimension in his comedies, and it lends itself perfectly to the idea behind backstage musicals, where stage illusion and emotionally complicated reality are routinely switched.

Musicals of family romance

Another among Rick Altman's musical sub-genres is 'the folk musical', and the most relevant examples are the later ones by Rodgers and Hammerstein in the post-war years. It is self-evident that the later musicals, which are the product of the various collaborations between Rodgers, Hart, and Hammerstein, are very different in ethos from those examined earlier in this chapter from the 1930s and 1940s. These differences can almost certainly be explained by the need for family reunification after the wartime separations, and this in itself brought to the fore a different set of Shakespearean models, the late romances, which are based on family separation and reunion. The settings of these movies reflect neither the witty smartness of New York on the east coast nor the youthful glamour of Hollywood on the west, but rather the working middle classes and a range of ages, and are often located in the Midwestern, farming centre of the United States – such as Oklahoma, Iowa (*State Fair* (1945 and 1962)), or at least a wholesome, working port in local New England (*Carousel* (1956)). An alternative pattern in these movies uses exotic foreign parts coming under American cultural influence in the Second World War and the Cold War (Polynesia in *South Pacific* (1958) and Siam in *The King and I* (1956)), inviting multiple comparisons with *The Tempest*.

Shakespeare had chosen settings for his late romances that were similarly exotic for his times. Pericles travelled the high seas, losing his wife and daughter in the process. Bohemia is the setting for *The Winter's Tale*, and an almost deserted island for *The Tempest*. Like the family musicals, they also have social settings that are close, even closed, communities – the incestuous court of Antiochus in *Pericles*, the claustrophobic court of Leontes and the pastoral community in *The Winter's Tale*, and the small company brought together on the island in *The Tempest*. Furthermore, they do not present in a sustained form the kind of romantic courtship that would indicate kinship through genre with Shakespeare's romantic comedies, since the coupling of young lovers is presented more summarily than in the earlier plays. Instead, we are given a broader range of emotional experiences, spanning whole families over a longer time scheme. However, this does not mean that Shakespeare's influence is not present in the later musicals, simply that their writers find analogies in a different set of plays. *Oklahoma!*'s thematic concentration on jealousy, its sombre, narrative inclusion of domestic violence and even death, bears comparison with the dark tones of the first half of *The Winter's Tale*, while other threads suggest a generic relationship the musicals share with Shakespeare's last plays or romances. Centrally these include separation and reunion of families (somewhat incongruously anticipated in the very early *The Comedy of Errors* as a contrived device for a denouement, when even the otherwise absent mother is returned). It is this changed set of Shakespearean analogies and distant sources that give to these later musicals a very different atmosphere and thematic concentration. Richard Rodgers, Lorenz Hart, and Oscar Hammerstein had all attended Columbia University, and the buried references to plays that are less well known than *A Midsummer Night's Dream* and *Romeo and Juliet* may well have been stirred by their earlier studies and interest in Shakespeare.

Carousel, initially a Broadway musical performed in 1945 by Rodgers and Hammerstein and based on a play from Budapest written in 1909, was made into a movie in 1956. It has been described as one of the first musicals to have a tragic plot, although without a tragic ending. In this sense it is more like tragi-comedy, Shakespeare's late plays in general, and *The Winter's Tale* in particular, ending in family reunification. Billy is dogged by memory of his violence towards his wife, out of frustration because he has been sacked by a jealous employer from his job as carousel barker and is unable to get another job, just as Leontes must spend sixteen years in a state of perpetual shame and anguish, recalling his treatment of Hermione that led to her apparent death. The moment when Billy strikes his wife is only reported, not shown, but it is crucial to the plot, as the film starts when he is dead and remorseful for the 'one bad thing' he did in his life. His situation is precisely the same as Leontes' violent and jealous accusations of Hermione in the first half of *The Winter's Tale*. Even though Billy is an accomplice to a robbery, the thing that makes him more remorseful is striking his wife. He dies (by an act of guilt-stricken suicide in the stage play, an accident in the film) before he can see his unborn child. Similarly, Leontes is informed of the birth of his daughter without seeing her. Fifteen years later (not quite the sixteen in *The Winter's Tale*), again like Leontes, Billy is given a posthumous 'second chance' while in literal purgatory ('the back door to heaven'), condemned to arranging stars. His state is akin to Leontes' living purgatory in the middle of the play, his conscience constantly goaded by Paulina. Billy is allowed to return to earth for one day to see his daughter Louise, who is now a delinquent, and he notes that she is replaying his own indiscretions. He is allowed to go to her graduation and pass on his knowledge to her in a moving father/daughter reconciliation, yet again echoing the tone of muted relief on Leontes' rediscovery of Perdita. Billy strikes even her, but it feels to her like a 'kiss' not a blow. Louise is also reconciled to his memory and implicitly forgives him, making the ending mirror that of *The Winter's Tale*. The final section is the graduation speech about not being ashamed of what your parents have done, followed by the song 'You'll Never Walk Alone', full of imagery likening life to surviving storms – a recurrent theme in at least two of Shakespeare's late romances, *Pericles* and *The Tempest*, and an image used by Florizel to describe Perdita in *The Winter's Tale*. If received with Shakespeare's play in mind, the ambitious, balletic waltz becomes a kind of parallel to the sheep-shearing scene in which Perdita is sixteen and now the central figure of the play. Other similarities can be noted: in the film a young man proposes to Louise but insinuates she is below him in social status, repeating that her father was a carousel barker who hit his wife. In *The Winter's Tale* this class prejudice is expressed by Polixenes rather than his son Florizel, but his dismissive and angry tone is as vituperative as Leontes' earlier verbal violence directed at Hermione.

Finding such links between *Carousel* and *The Winter's Tale* might stand as a fairly typical example of the influences I am suggesting throughout this book, no doubt invisible to the 'naked eye' yet possibly persuasive to somebody acquainted with Shakespeare's romance. It does seem arguable from the evidence of their other films that Rodgers and Hammerstein at least appreciated and learned from Shakespeare's plays, even if knowledge of individual texts may have been latent in their imaginations. There is a hint in the film that even if generic similarities were conscious and deliberate, they may not be willing to say so: there is an incidental reference to *Julius Caesar* that seems to mock high culture, or perhaps the plebeian taste of the censorious and religious characters in this group who are not sympathetically portrayed:

> WIFE I was telling Julie about that musical extravaganza we saw in New York. [*Singing*] 'I'm a tomboy, Just a tomboy, I'm a madcap maiden from Broadway'.
> HUSBAND We also saw *Julius Caesar*. Ain't that a better show to tell her about?
> WIFE Not for me. I took one look at them men in nightgowns and went right to sleep.

It is a sly, metadramatic moment, since the audience is aware that it is watching a 'musical extravaganza' that had been on Broadway in New York in 1945 – and at this moment the thing most worrying them is the 'tomboy' teenager Louise, Billy's daughter. Mankiewicz's film of *Julius Caesar* played in 1953 and may be what they had seen, though it was not a Broadway 'show'. Shakespeare hovers tantalisingly close, yet just beyond reach, which is also oddly appropriate in a family musical depicting what amounts to the return to earth of a ghost.

Much ado about Nathan

Mankiewicz went on to direct in 1955 one of the most famous of all musicals, *Guys and Dolls*, based on a Broadway musical (1950) that was in turn adapted from New York stories by Damon Runyon, who had been called 'Shakespeare of the Speakeasy'. Many of Runyon's stories can once again be heard exactly as they were read on radio in the late 1940s,[42] and among them we find such works as 'The Melancholy Dane', while Richard III makes an appearance in 'A Story Goes with It'. The musical was unusual in having its source announced as a work by a 'literary writer', and the main story used as the basis for the Broadway musical and later film, *Guys and Dolls*, was 'The Idyll of Miss Sarah Brown'. With the help of a little speculative pattern recognition we might hypothesise that at least a subliminal source for the musical's generic structuring may have been *Much Ado About Nothing*.

Both the play and the musical present two sets of lovers and turn on the reluctance of men to enter marriage, complemented by one pair of females who are willing and even eager for a match (Hero and Adelaide respectively), and another pair less so (Beatrice and Sarah Brown). Beatrice's reluctance seems to stem from having been jilted in the past, while Sarah Brown has not closed the door on the idea of a love relationship, though she puts it below the demands of her Salvation Army mission and also possibly harbours over-high expectations if we judge from her song, 'I'll Know …'. The double structure of love pairings, one mutually willing and the other resistant, is the basis for both narratives. In *Much Ado* Claudio falls in love with Hero, but before marrying they are estranged by an external plot to discredit the woman. Beatrice and Benedick have both volubly sworn against marriage, especially with each other, but, again as the result of an external plot, they end the play betrothed. Both strands depend to a large extent on pretence and external manipulation, both constructive and destructive. In *Guys and Dolls* a reluctant Nathan Detroit has been affianced to Adelaide for fourteen years, apparently in love with each other, but the delay is much to her distress since she has already pretended to her mother that she has been married for many years and has five children – in tacit agreement with Benedick's final belief in the function of marriage, 'the world must be peopled'. They are persuaded to elope, but Nathan is still unwilling to marry and also is implicated in an illegal crap game that prevents him. With a lie he jilts Adelaide yet again, an estrangement finally resolved by a serendipitous meeting that establishes that Nathan missed the tryst because he was, much out of character, attending a prayer meeting at the behest of Sky Masterson. While different from the Claudio–Hero plot, it has significant thematic similarities in that lies, fictions, and pretence characterise both liaisons, and also ironically allow the relationships to recover and end in marriage. The betrothal in both works is essentially built on a trick, and the words sung in the movie could just as well be applied to both sets of lovers in *Much Ado*: 'Love is the thing that has nipped them, / And it looks like Nathan's just another victim'.

Meanwhile, the relationship between the hardened semi-criminal Sky Masterson and the saintly Salvation Army bandleader Sarah Brown bears even closer resemblance to that between Benedick and Beatrice. In both, the partners are initially settled against marriage to anybody and particularly not each other, and considerable antipathy and disapproval mark their early encounters. Shakespeare's characters are brought together essentially by a social conspiracy to make each believe the other is in love. While Sky and Sarah are not manipulated in quite this way, the event happens through adoption of an equally unlikely fiction, as the chronic gambler Sky is persuaded to bet against the proposition that he cannot take the steely Sarah, resistant to seduction, to Havana. He manages the feat by promising Sarah he will fill the mission with 'one dozen genuine sinners' for her Thursday revival meeting if she will accompany him to Havana. She agrees, and with her inhibitions loosened by 'Dulce de Leche', which she thinks is non-alcoholic though its basis is Bacardi rum, the two find mutual feelings of attraction in an inebriated haze. The similarities to *Much Ado* are at the level of the 'double-relationship' genre of romantic comedy set up by Shakespeare in his play, and the second pairs of lovers in particular are comparably strong both in antagonism and in love, especially with the casting of Marlon Brando in the film. He brings the star quality of dangerous outsider and rebel rather than lover, just as casting Frank Sinatra as Nathan imports the persona of the man-about-town congenitally evading commitment. The star quality brought by Jean Simmons at this stage of her career had an ambiguous air, carrying memories of roles in classical adaptations such as a haughty Cleopatra in Shaw's *Caesar and Cleopatra* (1945), the coldhearted young Estella in David Lean's *Great Expectations* (1946), and Ophelia in Olivier's *Hamlet*; yet also Kanchi, a highly sensual Himalayan native in Powell and Pressburger's *Black Narcissus* (1947), and a sexually maturing teenager shipwrecked on a lush island in the first version of *The Blue Lagoon*. (The last mentioned film opens with a male choir of hardened sailors singing a hymn at a sea-funeral, juxtaposed with the young girl in Victorian dress with her governess.) Her image is often described as 'demure', but presumably it was the paradox of a stern exterior with hidden depths of repressed sexual vitality that suited her to Sarah Brown's role. Beatrice can be played in a similar way, the combination beautifully captured in Shakespeare's image of her sitting in the orchard hidden in 'the pleachèd bower / Where honeysuckles, ripened by the sun, / Forbid the sun to enter' (3.1.7–9).

Another generic similarity with *Much Ado* is the inclusion in the pattern of each a group of comic law enforcers. In Shakespeare's play, Dogberry and his bumbling colleagues are initially ineffectual, but, as it turns out, they are the ones who somewhat accidentally apprehend the malefactors in the plot to discredit Hero. They do not oppose love since they are not directly connected with the two love plots, just as the police in *Guys and Dolls* are just trying to prevent the crap game, and they equally ironically and accidentally also help to solve the love problems. The comic role of incompetent law enforcers is the same in *Much Ado* and *Guys and Dolls*, and is repeated in many other films, from Chaplin's films to *Keystone Cops* movies to *West Side Story*, making it arguably another small sub-genre of movie history leading back to Shakespeare.

Surely one of the oddest analogies between *Guys and Dolls* and *Much Ado About Nothing* is raised by the most memorable of Adelaide's songs, in which she laments getting a cold 'with psychosomatic symptoms', suggesting that the single female is susceptible to neurosis that in turn causes inflammation of the eye, ear, nose, and throat:

> In other words, just from worrying if the wedding is on or off
> A person can develop a cough.
> ...
> [*Adelaide sneezes*][43]

The stimulus for her complaint is a popular psychology book on psychosomatic illness that she is reading and from which she quotes, and she speculates that the endlessly deferred wedding is causing her apparently endless cold. It may seem a strange and adventitious connection, but one that is irresistible, to suggest that Beatrice is afflicted in the same way, speaking 'in the sick tune'. Hero and Margaret tease her, whereupon they break into singing 'Light o' Love' as already quoted, but it is not enough to shake her illness that Margaret and Hero interpret as love-sickness:

> BEATRICE [*To Hero*] 'Tis almost five o'clock, cousin. 'Tis time you were ready. By my troth, I am exceeding ill. Heigh-ho!
> MARGARET For a hawk, a horse, or a husband?
> BEATRICE For the letter that begins them all – h.
> ...
> HERO These gloves the Count sent me, they are an excellent perfume.
> BEATRICE I am stuffed, cousin. I cannot smell.
> MARGARET A maid, and stuffed! There's goodly catching of cold.
> ...
> BEATRICE ... By my troth, I am sick.
> MARGARET Get you some of this distilled *carduus benedictus*, and lay it to your heart. It is the only thing for a qualm.
> HERO There thou prickest her with a thistle.
> BEATRICE Benedictus – why Benedictus? You have some moral in this Benedictus.

MARGARET Moral? No, by my troth, I have no moral meaning. I meant plain holy-thistle. You may think perchance that I think you are in love. Nay, by'r Lady, I am not such a fool to think what I list, nor I list not to think what I can, nor indeed I cannot think, if I would think my heart out of thinking, that you are in love, or that you will be in love or that you can be in love. (3.4.38–86 *passim*)

The exchange is full of puns and double entendres, and among other things it exemplifies the point that Shakespearean comedy is full of references to musical refrains and dances that are not entirely clear from the written text alone. More pertinently, however, it establishes that Beatrice has a cold (she is 'stuffed'). Margaret jokingly recommends the remedy of *Carduus Benedictus* or Holy Thistle, a common remedy used by Elizabethans for a range of illnesses. It was something of a favourite with John Hall, Shakespeare's son-in-law, who prescribed it for one patient suffering from pulmonary illness with difficulty in breathing, to another for healing pustules caused by a fever, another for fever, while for another it was prescribed in the form of drops to cure deafness for a woman suffering from 'melancholy' – in fact, all these patients were women, though this may be coincidence.[44] Margaret's reference to the herb is, of course, designed to set off a sly, punning connection with Benedick and being in love – more or less the logic employed by Adelaide in her self-diagnosis. Benedick's equivalent ailment is toothache, and Don Pedro, Claudio, and Leonato draw the same conclusion that his resultant 'sadness' emanates from love (3.2). It is a curiously precise analogy, possibly accidental or subliminally connected, but at the very least it shows that Shakespeare had trodden the same associative path, and that he had the knack of anticipating what will still 'make 'em laugh' in the popular medium.

The most conspicuous differences between Shakespeare's romantic comedies, and, for example, Ben Jonson's satirical plays, lie in the depiction of lovers who, broadly speaking, are treated sympathetically rather than ridiculed. They contain frequent interpolations of music and a fictive 'green' setting outside that is presented as an alternative to urban realism, where play and disguise are possible. All these elements are gathered into the endings of the comedies, as they usually are in the ensemble endings of musicals. Both genres, romantic comedy and musical comedy, share an enacted festivity and triumph of love, usually manifested in song that celebrates social inclusiveness, anticipating the all-cast chorus line at the end of musicals. At their source they are both capable of exhibiting the triumph of lawless love over repressive laws, of the libido over willed moralism, and the social celebration of Saturnalia over institutional repression. At each stage of the liberating process leading up to such closures, the irresistible compulsiveness of love drives the plot. In the words of a song in *Guys and Dolls*, 'The guy's only doing it for some doll', or in those of Shakespeare, 'Such is the simplicity of man to hearken after the flesh' (*Love's Labour's Lost*, 1.1.214–15).

Notes

1 There is a large body of material on this subject, most comprehensively Bryan N. S. Gooch and David Thatcher (eds), *A Shakespeare Music Catalogue*, 5 vols (Oxford: Oxford University Press, 1991); and see in particular Peter J. Seng, *The Vocal Songs in the Plays of Shakespeare: A Critical History* (Cambridge, MA: Harvard University Press, 1967); F. W. Sternfeld, *Music in Shakespearean Tragedy* (Abingdon: Routledge, 2005 [1963]); David Lindley, *Shakespeare and Music* (London: Thomson Learning, Arden Critical Companions, 2006); Julie Sanders, *Shakespeare and Music: Afterlives and Borrowings* (Cambridge: Polity Press, 2007); Ross W. Duffin, *Shakespeare's Songbook* (New York and London: W. W. Norton & Co., 2004).
2 Adam Hansen, *Shakespeare and Popular Music* (London: Continuum, 2010); Stephen M. Buhler, 'Musical Shakespeares: Attending to Ophelia, Juliet, and Desdemona', in Robert Shaughnessy (ed.), *The Cambridge Companion to Shakespeare and Popular Culture* (Cambridge: Cambridge University Press, 2007); Wes Folkerth, 'Popular Music', in Richard Burt (ed.), *Shakespeares after Shakespeare: An Encyclopedia of the Bard in Mass Media and Popular Culture* (Westport, CT and London: Greenwood Press, 2007), vol. I, ch. 5.
3 Sanders, *Shakespeare and Music*.
4 Gehring, *Romantic vs. Screwball Comedy*, 74.
5 James Schiffer, 'Introduction: Taking the Long View – *Twelfth Night* Criticism and Performance', in James Schiffer (ed.), *Twelfth Night: New Critical Essays* (London and New York: Routledge, 2011), 1–44, 20; see also in the same volume David Schalkwyk, 'Music, Food, and Love in the Affective Landscapes of *Twelfth Night*', 81–98. Most recently, see the indispensable book by Christopher Wilson and Michela Calore (eds), *Music and Shakespeare: A Dictionary* (London: Bloomsbury, 2005).
6 Harley Granville-Barker, *Prefaces to Shakespeare* (Princeton, NJ: Princeton University Press, 1947), vol. II, 442, quoted in Crowl, *Shakespeare and Film*, 156.
7 See Andrew Gurr and Farah Karim-Cooper (eds), *Moving Shakespeare Indoors: Performance and Repertoire in the Jacobean Playhouse* (Cambridge: Cambridge University Press, 2014), 208–11.
8 For the words, see Duffin, *Shakespeare's Songbook*, 253–5.
9 See, for example, Tim Carter, *Oklahoma!: The Making of an American Musical* (New Haven, CT: Yale University Press, 2007), 187–90.

10 Glitre, *Hollywood Romantic Comedy*, 13.
11 Dash, *Shakespeare and the American Musical*, 1.
12 Sanders, *Shakespeare and Music*, 92.
13 Edward W. Naylor, *Shakespeare and Music* (London: J. M. Dent & Sons, 1896); Sternfeld, *Music in Shakespearean Tragedy*; Seng, *The Vocal Songs in the Plays of Shakespeare*.
14 Duffin, *Shakespeare's Songbook*.
15 Duffin, *Shakespeare's Songbook*, 40.
16 Hansen, *Shakespeare and Popular Music*, 92.
17 Hansen, *Shakespeare and Popular Music*, 95.
18 See R. S. White, 'Functions of Poems and Songs in Elizabethan Romance and Romantic Comedy', *English Studies: A Journal of English Language and Literature*, 68.5 (1987), 392–405.
19 Altman, *The American Film Musical*, 116.
20 Altman, *The American Film Musical*, 143–4.
21 Altman, *The American Film Musical*, 144.
22 Frye, *A Natural Perspective*.
23 Neale, *Genre and Hollywood*, 107, referring to several historians of the musical.
24 Altman, *Film/Genre*, 31–3.
25 Neale, *Genre and Hollywood*, 105.
26 Altman, *Film/Genre*, 66–7.
27 See R. S. White, *Let Wonder Seem Familiar: Endings in Shakespeare's Romance Vision* (London: Athlone Press, 1985), ch. 3.
28 See Alan Brissenden, *Shakespeare and the Dance* (Atlantic Highlands, NJ: Humanities Press, 2001 [1981]), chs 3 and 4.
29 Grant, *Film Genre*, 40.
30 Phyllis Hartnoll (ed.), *Shakespeare in Music: A Collection of Essays* (London: Macmillan, 1966), 22.
31 Crowl, *Shakespeare and Film*, 118.
32 Crowl, *Shakespeare and Film*, 156.
33 See, for example, Branagh's comments in an interview recorded by Ramona Wray and Mark Thornton Burnett, 'From the Horse's Mouth: Branagh on the Bard', in Mark Thornton Burnett and Ramona Wray (eds), *Shakespeare, Film, Fin de Siècle* (London: Palgrave, 2000), 165–78, esp. 174–6 and *passim*.
34 Brissenden, *Shakespeare and the Dance*, 35.
35 Dixon, *American Cinema of the 1940s*, 228.
36 Duffin, *Shakespeare's Songbook*, 523.
37 Clive Hirschhorn, *The Hollywood Musical* (London: Octopus Books, 1981), 199.
38 Hirschhorn, *The Hollywood Musical*, 236.
39 Hirschhorn, *The Hollywood Musical*, 402.

40 'Shakespeare Musicals', in Thomas Hischak, *The Oxford Companion to the American Musical: Theatre, Film, and Television* (Oxford: Oxford University Press, 2008), 669–70.
41 Grant, *Film Genre*, 40.
42 www.otr.net/?p=drun (accessed 4 July 2015).
43 Song lyrics can be found at: www.lyricsondemand.com/soundtracks/g/guysanddollslyrics/index.html (accessed 1 January 2015).
44 Joan Lane (ed.), with medical commentary by Melvin Earles, *John Hall and His Patients: The Medical Practice of Shakespeare's Son-in-Law* (Stratford-upon-Avon: The Shakespeare Birthplace Trust, 1996), 35, 141, 145, 337.

4

Of errors and Eros: a brief digression on twins

In *The Boys from Syracuse* (1940), based on the original Broadway production in 1938, Richard Rodgers composed the music and Lorenz Hart the lyrics, and they signal very clearly the musical's origins in *The Comedy of Errors*. There is certainly nothing hidden, disguised, or unintentional about the reference in this case. The immediate source is credited as the Broadway stage play written and produced by George Abbott, but lest anybody be under any illusion the final credits announce that 'This picture is after "A Comedy of Errors" by William Shakespeare (– Long, long after.)'. No doubt the main composer of choice for the project was Hart, whose Shakespearean interest is entertainingly described by Irene Dash, who devotes a whole chapter to an exegesis of the stage version of *The Boys from Syracuse*:

> These two young New Yorkers were well qualified to transpose Shakespeare into the new musical idiom. Lorenz Hart knew not only this play, but most of Shakespeare's work. His love for the bard dated back to his childhood. The story goes that when he went to camp, his trunk was so heavy his counsellor couldn't lift it. No wonder: Shakespeare's *Complete Works* had replaced his clothes. That summer, Hart earned the nickname 'Shakespeare.' He carried his love of the plays into adulthood.[1]

There was a more general, quasi-industrial issue at stake in the choice of Shakespeare's play as a source. As Tim Carter explains in his book-length study of *Oklahoma!*, during the late 1930s and early 1940s the Theatre Guild in America made a conscious effort to add cultural capital to the musical as a form, in an attempt to gain a new status as a serious genre, 'folk opera'.[2] Ironically, given the attempt also to claim it as the first indigenous American cultural form, the elevated status was to be reinforced by references to 'the classics' and especially Shakespeare's plays. For example, in 1940 an idea was floated, involving among others Kurt Weill, to turn *Much Ado About Nothing* into a musical, and later *Twelfth Night*.[3] *The Boys from Syracuse* was a part of this ambitious plan to take the musical form 'upmarket', despite its generally farcical tone that owes so much to popular culture.

Although the movie is a very loose adaptation of Shakespeare's play, without any attempt to replicate the language, in fact the differences are quite superficial compared with the central structure and narrative, which are surprisingly close to the play's. It could have been set in any two places as it has been in countless local stage productions – New York and Boston, London and Edinburgh, and many others depending on the location of the performance – but at the cost of mystifying some in the audience it retains the ancient Greek settings of Plautus's *Menaechmi* (which the film does not acknowledge), the cities of Ephesus and Syracuse. The opening intertext satirically promises that 'there were men in those days – and women – and politicians – and graft – and double-crossing – and all the modern improvements we enjoy today'. Much of the more obvious visual comedy anticipates *The Flintstones* in self-conscious anachronisms from the classical world imposed upon 1940s America. Newspapers are stone tablets with headlines spruiked with the same kind of 'extra, extra, read all about it' that is the conventional call of street vendors in older movies. Heroes give autographs, chariots flout rules of the road like taxis and indulge in car chases, complete with hand signals. There is a 'Grecian Gladiators Guild' advertised while the 'Wooden Horse Inn' stands in the background, and money is exchanged via a cash register. Such anachronisms abound and are made the source of farce.

The movie was made in the first full year of the Second World War, and this is significant to its comedy. In 1940 America had not joined the European Allied forces, and there was some leeway for the unfolding events in Europe to be portrayed as a restricted squabble that could be seen light-heartedly, or at least presented in 'insular' fashion, as an 'escapist musical'.[4] There was a feeling that the war would not last long, and there are filmic references that make light of it: the first scene shows a soldier in a toga saluting like Mussolini while smoking a cigar like Churchill, announcing that the war between Ephesus and Syracuse is over. It is not over, however, for the Syracusan father Egeon, and the story follows closely Shakespeare's tale of illegal immigrants being mistaken for locals because Egeon's long-lost sons are identical twins (the Antipholuses, both played by the tenor Allan Jones, married in 'real life' to Irene Hervey who is Adriana), as are their servants (the Dromios, both played by the moronic comic actor Joe Penner). However, while the plot and the generally farcical tone follow Shakespeare's imitation of Plautus, other significant aspects of the movie point to some ways in which Shakespeare himself subtly modified his classical source and signalled his own future development in comedy. In order to see that he already had in mind the sentiments of romance that raise questions of 'what does such an experience *feel* like?', one has only to contrast the heartless buffoonery and comedy of situation in Plautus's version. Adriana reproaches the unmarried Antipholus for his apparent indifference with genuine, emotional distress:

> How comes it now, my husband, O how comes it
> That thou art then estrangèd from thyself? –
> Thy 'self' I call it, being strange to me
> That, undividable, incorporate,
> Am better than thy dear self's better part.
> Ah, do not tear away thyself from me;
> For know, my love, as easy mayst thou fall
> A drop of water in the breaking gulf,
> And take unmingled thence that drop again
> Without addition or diminishing,
> As take from me thyself, and not me too.
> (*The Comedy of Errors*, 2.2.123–32)

An unmistakable addition from the world of fictional romance is the overarching family history of the Egeon family, separated by shipwrecks and finally reunited as siblings with their father and mother (left out in the film for simplicity). This part of the plot is essentially taken from the prose romances that were Shakespeare's own favoured reading, works such as Sidney's *Arcadia* and Greene's *Pandosto*, stretching back to their generic sources in Heliodorus's Greek *Aethiopian History*. He was to combine elements from these works again and again, in *Twelfth Night* and more particularly his last plays, *Pericles*, *The Winter's Tale*, and *The Tempest*. This emphasis on family separation and reconciliation was the strand that was also developed in the musicals written by Rodgers in his later collaborations with Oscar Hammerstein. The film shows Shakespeare's subsequent direction in comedy, away from situational farce and towards romance in the other sense of comedy of courtship between lovers. Ironically, it is in the love story enacted between Antipholus of Ephesus and Adriana of Syracuse that the romantic comedy that we associate with Shakespeare truly emerges. The songs in *The Boys from Syracuse* tell their own story in this vein: 'This can't be love because I feel so well', 'Falling in love with love is falling for make-believe … is playing the fool … is such a juvenile fancy … I was unwise with eyes unable to see'. The love song whose title comments significantly on the theme of the play is sung by the two Antipholuses in a lyrical, mirror-image duet: 'Who are you?/Who am I?':

> If that's what – you – can – do,
> I wonder who – are – you?

Questions of identity are so obviously central to Shakespeare's plot that they are raised to thematic level, and though comic in its outcomes, his play provides a metaphysical dimension:

> ANTIPHOLUS OF SYRACUSE
> He that commends me to mine own content
> Commends me to the thing I cannot get.
> I to the world am like a drop of water
> That in the ocean seeks another drop,
> Who, falling there to find his fellow forth,
> Unseen, inquisitive, confounds himself.
> So I, to find a mother and a brother,
> In quest of them, unhappy, lose myself. (1.2.33–40)

The Boys from Syracuse uses the unlikely plot and farcical tone of *The Comedy of Errors* to fuel a musical by elevating the relatively subsidiary, although premonitory, element of love in the play to a central role in the movie. This brings it into the mainstream genre of romantic, musical comedy and also accurately suggests what Shakespeare himself was to make of the story when he returned to twins in the romantic comedy *Twelfth Night*, which begins with a similar predicament. Even more clearly than *Errors*, it is a generically hybrid play with elements of farce, most obviously the gulling of Malvolio, but it is also unmistakably a romantic comedy ending with marriages. In a similar way, the film turns a comedy of *Errors* into a comedy of *Eros*, aligning it with a genre familiar to film-goers as musical comedy.

Before leaving *The Comedy of Errors* we might note with curiosity that it has spawned a different and expanding sub-genre in that most eclectic and hybrid cinematic tradition of all, Indian movies. Whether the film comes from the large Hindi 'Bollywood' studios or from other film-making communities and languages, these have the hybrid nature of building into one plot several genres, such as comedy, romance, tragedy, and thriller. They can also turn any plot into a de facto musical at least in certain sections, and this is probably the most recognisable trait of Indian cinema. India is a country where twins hold special local significance and are widely considered as, in some mildly superstitious way, special and lucky. To add to the mystery surrounding twins there, apparently authenticated but intriguing facts emerge, such as a village in Kerala that over the last sixty years has seen almost six times the number of twins born than the global average.[5] As we shall see, several Indian films have re-sourced *The Comedy of Errors*. Others use twinship as the central cause of 'errors' while not having actual twins, such as the classic Bollywood comedy *Gol Maal* (1979) where the central character maintains a complex double life by merely pretending he has an identical twin who is socially and temperamentally different from him. The influence behind it is more likely to be Shakespeare's *Errors* than Oscar Wilde's *The Importance of Being Earnest*, because of the curious celebrity of the former in India, in different language-speaking communities. Richard Allen argues that there is a special affinity between *The Comedy of Errors* and Indian cinema more broadly, since mistaken identities and misrecognition are such common themes in the national cinematic traditions.[6] The play 'is both a template for and version of Bollywood misrecognition comedies more broadly'.[7]

Bhrantibilas, which translates as 'play of errors', is a Bengali prose work published in 1869 and apparently a direct adaptation of Shakespeare's play, showing a merchant from Calcutta (Kolkata) with his servant, who are mistaken for locals when they travel to another city. It was dramatised in Calcutta in 1888 and has been regularly performed since then.[8] In 1963 it was filmed, again in Bengali and under the same name, *Bhrantibilas*, and then in 1968 remade as a Hindi (Bollywood) musical under the name *Do Dooni Char* ('two twos are four'). The complications are professional, with a banker and assistant mistaken for merchant and servant.

Yet another version, *Angoor* (1982), has become the best known of the versions. It is mainly in the Hindi language, but uses Urdu sometimes to signal the theme of the alien national necessary to the plot. It begins with an image of an antique black-and-white portrait, which looks suspiciously unlike Shakespeare, accompanied by the words: 'This is William Shakespeare ... This story is based on the play *The Comedy of Errors*. Several writers have penned stories revolving around twins but Shakespeare is the only one to write a story based on four twins.' The first scene shows the father of Ashok and Ashok being reproved by the mother for confusingly calling their twins by the same name, and they are rapidly persuaded to adopt two foundling boys, both of whom they equally perversely call Bahadur, who become servants to the Ashoks. The family is separated in a shipwreck (depicted in realistic footage presumably taken from a newsreel) and the time scheme jumps to when the sets of twins are grown up, proceeding with the same comic strategies used by Shakespeare. If anything, the film milks the situation for more 'errors' than the play, providing multiple permutations based on mistaken identity. Although the general tone is comic and there are some songs to give the Bollywood atmosphere, the movie edges into the disturbing issues briefly raised but not fully developed in Shakespeare's play. The 'alien'

Ashok, frightened that he faces a plot to steal his money, becomes genuinely afflicted with incipient paranoia, while the 'local' Ashok becomes subject to shame and accusations of madness. There is domestic violence, public violence, and crime requiring police attention, and more than one character contemplates suicide by hanging, even going to the length of buying a rope for the purpose. In another gratuitous twist, the women involved are drugged, and they act contrary to their expected personalities. The whole experience over twenty-four hours is described by several as a 'nightmare', but by morning not only are the 'errors' corrected by revelations of the twinships, but they are all reunited with even their elderly, widowed mother, though one of the Ashoks mistakes the cook for her. The whole treatment is not at all subtle, and it even becomes a little wearying in the repetitiveness and obviousness of the jokes, but the makers of *Angoor*, by choosing to adapt *The Comedy of Errors* into India's distinctively inclusive genre, do draw out from Shakespeare's play some of its unmined and disturbing issues of deracinated identity, social and individual turbulence, and the nature of roles.

The Comedy of Errors was adapted in India again, this time without acknowledgement to Shakespeare, into the Hindi *Bade Miyan Chote Miyan* (1998) ('large Miyan, small Miyan'). This time the setting is Mumbai's underworld society of criminals and police, giving the opportunity to open up potentially serious problems of the local police twins being accused of crimes perpetrated in fact by the alien thieving twins, since with the help of modern technology the perpetrators are caught on videotaped evidence. Once again completely farcical in the vein of Shakespeare's comedy, the adaptation finds hidden depths implicit in its unlikely plot.[9] In 1997 *Ulta Palta* ('reverse reflex'?) was made in the Kannada language with music, and here the first set of twins come to work in a new town and are confused with a much richer, local industrialist. Next, in 1998 came a television programme in Hindi called *Dam Dama Dam* ('Dam Dam Dam'), with two actors playing all four roles. This is, of course, not uncommon, since it is easy to do in movies where quick changes are not required and actors can be made up and clothed at leisure. It is the case in the latest, and in some ways the most polished of all, *Double di Trouble* (2014), this time made in Punjabi and again with a musical component. The twin sets are here father and son rather than brothers or master and servant, but in other ways the confusions from Shakespeare are kept, such as the mistakes over the ring, which causes both marital friction and a nearly botched financial deal. In this version the dual settings are functional in social and economic ways – instead of having the outsider twins come from the country to a rather vaguely defined and confusing city, they come from a clearly disadvantaged town, rife with corruption and gang vandalism, to pursue a law case in the wealthier, middle-class Chandigarh – from the lawless to the measured grids of Le Corbusier's elegant, planned city. Although the dominant tone is farcical and there is no doubt it will end satisfactorily for all, there is some awareness of the emotional frustrations endured by the characters. What are comic 'errors' to the audience at times become serious crises of identity. Both father figures are driven to contemplate suicide, feelings of either being insane or living in an insane world are recurrent, and the 'local' father is driven to exclaim with heartfelt distress, 'This city is driving me crazy'. Reactions of the police, who become involved with the apparent theft, satirically monitor the mounting impression of uncontrollable madness in the normally staid society of Chandigarh. However, the complications are finally explained in the phrase 'A mirror? Same to same', the visiting father and son get the verdict they wish for from the court, and all ends convivially in a dance. This movie seems destined to become a minor classic among '*Errors*' movies, with a comically versatile performance from the actor playing both fathers, the brilliant Dhamendra, and powerful music in the Bollywood style (despite the Punjabi origin) from the heart-throb Gippy Grewal and others. But it looks unlikely to stem the small flood of Indian examples of the adaptable 'comedy-of-errors genre'.

Believing we have a lost twin wandering somewhere in the world, and even more disturbingly a doppelgänger (double-goer) who is an exact, real or apparitional, likeness, were recognised by Freud as examples of 'the return of the repressed', forgotten experiences that had haunted the child's unconscious. It is significant that he took this example of the uncanny or *unheimlich* (unfamiliar) from fiction, a short story by E. T. A. Hoffman called 'The Sandman' (1817), just as he constructed other theories on the basis of Shakespeare's plays. Given Freud's saturation in Shakespeare, this may even be a return of the repressed occurring in his own mind, a forgotten reading of *The Comedy of Errors* almost coming back to consciousness. Despite the play's classical origin and farcical tone, as so often happens in Shakespeare's comedies the human implications are potentially troubling, especially when the situation involves an encounter with a woman who is convinced that she is your wife, or an irate businessman to whom money is owed. The Antipholuses and Dromios, and their movie descendants, do not find such experiences as funny as their audiences, and there are moments where their anxiety at either living in a mad world or being mad themselves shows through. Beneath the simple theatrical premises of identical twins lies a more general, and often even more disturbing, set of conventions surrounding mistaken identity and disguise, to which we now turn.

Notes

1 Dash, *Shakespeare and the American Musical*, 15–16.
2 Carter, *Oklahoma!*, 3–18 *passim*.
3 Carter, *Oklahoma!*, 8.
4 Dixon, *American Cinema of the 1940s*, 3.
5 'Indian Village with 250 Sets of Twins', *Telegraph* (UK), 11 May 2009.
6 Richard Allen, 'Comedies of Errors: Shakespeare, Indian Cinema, and the Poetics of Mistaken Identity', in Craig Dionne and Parmita Kapadia (eds), *Bollywood Shakespeares* (New York: Palgrave Macmillan, 2014), 165–92.
7 Craig Dionne and Parmita Kapadia, 'Introduction: Shakespeare and Bollywood – The Difference a World Makes', in Craig Dionne and Parmita Kapadia (eds), *Bollywood Shakespeares* (New York: Palgrave Macmillan, 2014), 14.
8 See Rajiva Verma, 'Shakespeare in Hindi Cinema', in Poonam Trivedi and Dennis Bartholomeusz (eds), *India's Shakespeare: Translation, Interpretation and Performance* (New Delhi: Dorling Kindersley, 2006), 276–9, which mentions still more versions.
9 Perhaps it deserves mention that there was another musical in 1981 based squarely on *The Comedy of Errors*, which was mercifully not filmed. *Oh Brother* was set in an Iran flowing with oil during its revolution.

5
Comedy of disguise and mistaken identity

Gendered disguise

If Shakespeare's comedies in general provide cinematic romantic comedy with a composite generic blueprint, and if *A Midsummer Night's Dream* offers a specific model for love's confusions, another linking, generic element that emerges is romantic comedy based on disguised identity. This chapter raises the acute problems concerning the nature of influence that have been mentioned earlier. On the one hand, there is very little direct evidence that Shakespearean comedy had anything much to do with disguise in cinematic romantic comedy. For example, the most important book on the subject, *Hollywood Androgyny* by Rebecca Bell-Metereau, includes not a single reference to Shakespeare.[1] Yet on the other hand, the conventions of disguise can easily be seen as building upon an unbroken theatrical tradition leading back at least to Shakespeare's *Twelfth Night*, *As You Like It*, and *The Merchant of Venice*, needing no overt acknowledgement to establish the influence. The ways in which disguise is handled in at least some films suggests the device is unlikely to have come out of the blue into the new medium, and they are so reminiscent of Shakespeare's practice in his repeated narrative incidents surrounding disguised heroines that an indirect influence seems arguable. If anything, without that illustrious antecedent one might conclude that the sheer fictiveness and implausibility of the device would set it at odds with the often photographic realism and unsparing close-ups typical of most movies. It seems like a convention that might work on the stage but simply would not work in movies. However, the example offers one of the most obvious of all the ways in which Shakespearean precedents helped to shape modern film genres. A reminder is timely here that this study concerns not 'sources' but 'influence' in a more pervasive sense of the dominance of Shakespeare in the assimilation into movies of theatrical genres and their attendant conventions. Moreover, it is not just the mere fact that disguise complicates the plot that is part of his abiding legacy, but more significantly the psychological and social significances assigned to disguise as adapted into modern contexts are anticipated in his comedies, in particular the often profound issues of identity as it is defined through appearance, gender, and class.

An essay that came relatively early in the development of cinematic theory, Annette Kuhn's 'Sexual Disguise and Cinema' in *The Power of the Image: Essays on Representation and Sexuality*,[2] has become a classic reference for discussion of disguised gender in movies. Kuhn's account does not claim to consider antecedents, sources, or influences. Her analysis is located firmly within the context of 'classic narrative cinema' and her main point of reference is the feminist work by Laura Mulvey on scopophilia (the pleasure of looking, 'the gaze') in movie aesthetics.[3] But even without mentioning Shakespeare's name, each of the points made by Kuhn about movies using sexual disguise applies directly to Shakespeare's comedies based on the same trope, mainly the most well known, *Twelfth Night*, *As You Like It*, and *The Merchant of Venice*. For example, there is the closeness of disguise and play-acting, and performance as 'an activity that involves pretence, dissimulation';[4] 'a vision of fluidity of gender options; to provide a glimpse of "a world outside the order normally seen or thought about" – a utopian prospect of release from the ties of sexual difference that bind us into meaning, discourse, culture'[5] – a 'green world' in short. Disguise represents a challenge to notions that sex differences are natural, absolute, and fixed, and imply instead that identity can be created by superficial means such as clothing. Part of the convention is the need to provide some sort of explanation for adopting a disguise, such as employment (compare Viola as Cesario, servant to the Duke); carrying out a job that literally could not be done without disguise (Portia in the courtroom); safety and survival in a dangerous environment (Rosalind as Ganymede in the forest); comedy derived from the audience knowing of the disguise while other characters do not ('discrepant awareness', in the term coined by Shakespeare scholar Bertrand Evans[6]); a play on the discrepancy between 'illusion and reality'; a certain kind of closure that is at least anticipated if not effected, turning on revelation of the 'real' gender of the cross-dressed figure: 'A natural perspective, that is and is not' (*Twelfth Night*, 5.1.214). All these issues are familiar discussion points in Shakespearean criticism, and they are some of the aspects of the subject that we may find reflected in some movies.

Ever since its origins using masks in ancient Greece, drama has involved a central emphasis on suppression of the actor's identity through devices such as dissimulation and disguise, with resultant confusions over identity. Some, like Plato and Elizabethan Christian

Puritans, have condemned theatre for exactly this tendency, arguing that as a mode of communication it depends on lying and deceptiveness rather than truth-telling. Others, like the dramatists themselves and their audiences, have obviously revelled in the possibilities opened up, not only for exploiting comic situations in social groups, but also for exploring profound issues about identity itself, and especially about what happens to people when they fall in love. It allows dramatists and actors to be 'truth-telling' in a quite unique, imaginative sense. A whole set of fictional and dramatic conventions grew up in early modern literature and drama around events such as a character disguising or being mistaken for somebody else, mirroring deeper changes in personality under the influence of love. These first appeared in Italy in a genre known as *commedia erudite*, among them an early source for *Twelfth Night*, Pollastra's *Parthenio Commedia* (1516).[7] The most influential Elizabethan romance, Sidney's prose work *Arcadia* (or 'works', since an 'Old' *Arcadia* was rewritten, now the unfinished 'New' *Arcadia*), shows two princes disguising themselves, one as a shepherd and the other as a woman, in order to gain access to the women they love. The women have in turn been hidden away from society in a pastoral retreat because of their father's misguided attempt to avoid the destiny predicted for them by an oracle, 'an uncouth love, which nature hateth most'. The 'man–woman' (Pyrocles/Cleophila) in particular inspires a complex set of love emotions from the woman he loves (Philoclea, who thinks 'he' is a 'she'), her father (Basilius), and also her mother (Gynecia), who is the one who sees through the disguise and recognises Pyrocles as a man. The result is not only comic but provides a complex anatomy of sexual desire in its various manifestations and psychological consequences. Edmund Spenser's poetic romance, *The Faerie Queene*, uses disguise often in a moral context that suggests duplicity and evil, except in one important instance. Britomart, who is almost certainly a prototype for Shakespeare's disguised heroines,[8] not only is Amazonian by temperament but she is also a female knight, dedicated to learning about and teaching Friendship and Chastity, clad in armour and behaving in a warlike manner, encountering and overcoming enemies of love and friendship. Like Portia, she rescues her future lover Artegall. Meanwhile, John Lyly in his play *Gallathea* (1588) represents two young women disguising themselves as men in order to deceive the gods and avoid their fates. They subsequently fall in love with each other, in a way that can be fulfilled (given Elizabethan attitudes) only by one of them finally metamorphosing into a biological male. Their compatibility is figured in a dance to the harmony of music, and the resolution is provided by the goddess of love:

VENUS Then shall it be seen, that I can turn one of them to be a man, and that I will!
DIANA Is it possible?
VENUS What is to Love or the Mistress of Love unpossible? Was it not Venus that did the like to Iphis and Ianthes; how say ye? Are ye agreed? One to be a boy presently?
PHILLIDA I am content, so I may embrace Gallathea.
GALLATHEA I wish it, so I may enjoy Phillida. (*Gallathea*, 5.3.142–6)

While lesbian desire is covertly countenanced but not endorsed in Lyly's play, heterosexual coupling is hailed as the triumph of love, even if it is effected partly under circumstances involving disguise.

These works by Sidney, Spenser, and Lyly were well known to Shakespeare, alongside Thomas Lodge's prose romance *Rosalynde*, which is the close source for *As You Like It*, and together they provided him with a stock formula of gender disguise that he adopted as 'repetition with variations' in some of his romantic comedies. He immediately leapt upon Lyly's dramatic example by showing a disguised woman following her fickle lover in *The Two Gentlemen of Verona*. Later, and more famously, the plots of *As You Like It*, *The Merchant of Venice*, and *Twelfth Night* turn on women disguising themselves as men. Lyly, who wrote his plays for performance by boy actors as part of a line of academic drama written for young males, may have been the first to use disguise in an English romantic comedy, and in his *Gallathea* disguise is a datum for a complex, comic situation. However, Shakespeare goes even further in following Sidney's *Arcadia* and Lodge's *Rosalynde*, dramatising this situation as a vehicle to explore complex feelings and emotional states as part of love's journey.[9] In doing so, my argument runs, he initiated at least a sub-genre of romantic comedy that became highly significant in cinematic versions of love comedy, including musicals. Shakespeare so effectively assimilated, transformed, and surpassed his immediate models and sources that they in turn have been largely forgotten, while his own efforts have created a classic performative canon. His plays' enduring popularity rests mainly on the fact that he was never one to accept highly artificial events at the level of mere conventions that we must take for granted, suspending disbelief, if the fiction is to work in the theatre. Instead, he perceived and drew out a human significance in the conventions themselves, capable of giving analogies for feelings and actions in the world outside the theatre. The convention that made the disguises plausible on the Elizabethan stage, namely the already androgynous figure of the boy actor, no longer holds currency, but Shakespeare's treatment digs beneath this surface artifice, allowing the possibility of disguise raising issues other than simply gender appearance. For example, it can be used to circumvent social restrictions on love, by adopting an assumed class difference or some variation on mistaken identity, each of which, I shall suggest, becomes important for the cinematic genre of romantic comedy. Disguise in Shakespeare's comedies is an aspect of that great standby for student essays on Shakespeare, his ongoing concentration on aspects of 'appearance and reality' as it operates especially in sexual matters. This recognition becomes important to the ways in which movies draw on the generic convention. The assumed identity may place the heroine in a position of humiliating subjection (*The Two Gentlemen* and *Twelfth Night*) or allow outspoken independence (*As You Like It* and *The Merchant of Venice*), but underlying both routines is a similar process. The dizzy illusions of blind love at first sight and impelled by desire can be tested in a less risky, hypothetical proximity, so that with luck and over time love may be consolidated into more reliably companionate attachment. The sequence provides a mechanism for lovers to get to know the 'real' identity of a person they think they love but initially hardly know.[10]

Coming after Shakespeare's works in both chronology and influence were the Jacobean dramatic romances of Beaumont and Fletcher, which extensively use the convention of disguised gender in ways that highlight by contrast the novelty of Shakespeare's treatments. These collaborating playwrights, whose plays were very popular in their time, use disguise in more ideologically conservative ways. They underwrite essentialism in stressing the 'naturalness' of sexual difference rather than questioning, challenging, or expanding its boundaries. *Love's Cure* presents not only a woman dressed as a man but also her male sibling disguised as a woman, only to show that the man is effeminised by his assumed role and needs to be 'corrected' by the literal discovery of his all too active 'male member', which is restored to potency by love. His Amazonian sister is seen as equally aberrant and she needs to fall in love in order to embrace her femininity. 'Nature (though long kept back) will have her own' becomes the theme of the play. By contrast, the action of *Twelfth Night* subverts Sebastian's statement 'nature to her bias drew' (5.1.258) by implying that sexual roles are not necessarily immutable or explained by 'nature' alone but have an element of 'nurture' or counterfeiting and social construction.[11] Meanwhile, Beaumont and Fletcher's *The Loyal Subject*, again representing a male-to-female cross-dressing, draws on *Twelfth Night* but reverses Shakespeare's ambiguities by once again using the device 'to affirm subjects' obedience to sovereigns and women's subordination to men',[12] as does *The Maid's Tragedy* where a woman disguises herself as her brother. Such examples are no doubt partially explained as ways to please the monarch of the time, James

I, who was notoriously anxious about, and opposed to, disguise and cross-dressing in his realm, just as Shakespeare's comedies must have reflected something of the authorised gendered ambiguity of Elizabeth I in the 1590s, a queen who described herself in these famous words: 'I know I have the body of a weak and feeble woman, but I have the heart and stomach of a king, and of a king of England too.' After Beaumont and Fletcher, cross-dressing became a more or less unbroken tradition in the theatre in revivals of Renaissance plays, enhanced by a new sexual frisson in 'breeches roles' when women were allowed to act when the theatres reopened in the Restoration. Behind the tradition, and acting as origins in England and America, lay Shakespeare's comedies. Behind his plays lay, in particular, Lyly's plays, and the prose romances *Arcadia* and *Rosalynde*.

Generally speaking, in his romantic comedies Shakespeare uses the apparently common Elizabethan convention of disguise to explore complexities and anxieties concerning sex and gender in ways that anticipate modern preoccupations, and in this sense they directly and indirectly inform the development of film in the twentieth century. Probably the most familiar way of discussing this in modern criticism is in terms of gender transgression, fluidity of sexual categories, and ambivalence about gender itself. Feminist critics in particular have dealt with the issue in these and other ways, some focusing on the possibilities for gender redefinition and integration implicit in cross-dressing,[13] others denying altogether that there are any women in Shakespeare's plays, only a male dramatist using boy actors to represent them from his generation's attitude to women in general.[14] Others raise even more radical possibilities of androgyny, bisexuality, and transsexualism that challenge conventional understandings of sexual desire. However, most of my discussion of movies below will be devoted to suggesting that the reasons behind Shakespeare's use of disguise can act as metaphors for identity shifts or self-discovery not confined to gender. The Elizabethans themselves were aware of the possibility that clothes are only an outward sign of a consistent identity, partly through theatre itself, and in particular the use of boy actors to play women, and also because contemporary sumptuary laws insisted that the clothes one wears should signify not only one's gender but, just as importantly to them, one's class. This becomes important in movies. Theatre was tenuously exempted from these laws except in the eyes of hard-line Puritans:

> The stage was a privileged site of transgression, in which *two* kinds of transvestism were permitted to players: changes of costume that violated edicts against wearing the clothing of the wrong rank as well as the wrong

gender. As fools and players were licensed, given official sanction to do that which, unsanctioned, was liable to prosecution, so also licenses to wear clothing forbidden by the various statutes were issued by Queen Elizabeth, as by her predecessors.[15]

Actors, then, were already involved in different kinds of impersonation adopted in order to present fictional identities, all socially suspect since not only could a male transgressively 'play' a female who could then 'play' a male, but also an impoverished actor could play an aristocrat, and a ragged commoner could even play a king. The whole business of acting, at its heart, obviously depends on the suppression or layering of one identity or person under another guise. Disguise in the broadest sense, then, was central to Shakespeare's drama as it is to theatre in general, in many more ways than one, and I shall be suggesting that this fertility has been tacitly imitated, adapted, and repeated in many films in the genre of romantic comedy.

Gendered disguise in Shakespearean comedy is justified in the plots as a device used either to give a woman self-protection (Rosalind and Viola), and also access to the man she desires (Julia in *The Two Gentlemen* and Viola), or to undertake a task she could not carry out as a woman (Portia), and the effect often includes pathos alongside comedy. The two examples of men disguising as women are more unequivocally comic – the punitive ridiculing of Falstaff by dressing him up as the fat woman of Brentford in *The Merry Wives of Windsor*, and the impersonation by Flute of Thisbe in the play presented by the rude mechanicals in *A Midsummer Night's Dream*, which parodies theatrical conventions on the Elizabethan stage:

> QUINCE Francis Flute, the bellows-mender?
> FLUTE Here, Peter Quince.
> QUINCE Flute, you must take Thisbe on you.
> FLUTE What is Thisbe? A wand'ring knight?
> QUINCE It is the lady that Pyramus must love.
> FLUTE Nay, faith, let not me play a woman. I have a beard coming.
> QUINCE That's all one. You shall play it in a mask, and you may speak as small as you will.
> BOTTOM An I may hide my face, let me play Thisbe too. I'll speak in a monstrous little voice: 'Thisne, Thisne!' – 'Ah, Pyramus, my lover dear, thy Thisbe dear, and lady dear.'
> QUINCE No, no, you must play Pyramus; and, Flute, you Thisbe.
> BOTTOM Well, proceed. (1.2.38–53)

Apart from these examples, it is invariably the heroine who dons the disguise under some kind of compulsion or choice. For example, 'she' is made less physically and socially vulnerable than she would be if dressed in her 'maiden weeds' as Rosalind intends, or undertake an occupation otherwise debarred to women, as Portia enters the courtroom, and Viola becomes servant to Duke Orsino:

> Conceal me what I am, and be my aid
> For such disguise as haply shall become
> The form of my intent. I'll serve this duke.
> Thou shall present me as an eunuch to him. (*Twelfth Night*, 1.2.49–52)

The expedient of being a 'eunuch' is not mentioned again and Viola seems to drop this plan, but she does adopt a disguise of a male servant and messenger.

However, as I have emphasised, Shakespeare invariably makes conventions functional in emotional as well as narrative terms, uncovering some human, metaphorical dimension to the disguise rather than just a pragmatic motivation, but the deeper significance is different in each case. *The Two Gentlemen of Verona* is where he first used the device, and here it is relatively uncomplicated, allowing Julia to survive dangers while also emblematising her humiliation in having to observe helplessly from close range her lover's betrayal when Proteus shamelessly woos Silvia. In *Twelfth Night*, Viola's disguise as the male Cesario in close proximity to the man she loves points to greater emotional complexities and ambivalences over gender itself, which are both enabled and compounded by the Elizabethan audience's awareness that female characters are played by boys. This work, like Sidney's *Arcadia*, depends on the possibility that one character can be either male or female, or even both in different contexts, or effectively androgynous. Although she is liberated in one sense to be close to Orsino, and she is given anonymity and the class mobility of a nonentity, instead of being known through her nationally alien and also aristocratic status, yet in another sense she becomes trapped by her male disguise. Not only does she yearn to express her love but she also becomes the unwilling object of Olivia's amatory desires, bewailing her entrapping need to remain silent: 'What I am and what I would are as secret as maidenhead' (1.5.206–7). The final pairings of Viola and Orsino, and Olivia and Sebastian, would have been made even more ironic for Elizabethan audiences who knew full well they were watching four males and no females. In *The Merchant of Venice*, however, Portia's disguise as the lawyer's clerk does not really draw attention to gender identity as such, but to the desire and responsibility of one lover to rescue the other from danger, like Britomart in *The Faerie Queene*. It enables Portia to save Bassanio from death at the hands of Shylock by advocating a literal legalism or quibble in the courtroom setting. In this example, the relevance of Portia's sexuality is effaced by the professional legal robes, and the only element of specifically gender difference lies in the fact that she could not be a lawyer as a woman. Meanwhile, Rosalind's disguise in *As You Like It* gives her freedom, not only to conceal her aristocratic status but also to move from one gendered position to the other through vivacious role playing. This is so effective that she sexually attracts Phoebe. The interplay between Rosalind and Orlando, as well as her advice to Phoebe, seem to suit the emphasis on companionate marriage that was emerging in Elizabeth's Protestant England, where sexual partners were expected to respect each other's point of view. The contrast is the coercive 'taming' metaphor of marriage at work in *The Shrew*, although even in that play disguise operates in the 'romantic' sub-plot of Bianca's courtship. Such disguises are not confined to the early comedies since Shakespeare returns to them in *Cymbeline*, when Imogen disguises herself as a boy. In another late example of mistaken identity, although one not involving gender, Perdita in *The Winter's Tale* is not consciously disguised but under the impression she is a shepherd's low-born daughter instead of a princess and heir to the throne. Here the division between inner and outer identities relates to her noble status as a triumph of nature over nurture, and the later unravelling will allow her to marry into royalty herself – a trope not only looking back to ancient romance but forwards to eighteenth-century novels like *Tom Jones* and some Hollywood comedies.

The main dynamic in all these examples of Shakespeare's disguised heroines is one of concealment and eventual revelation for more than simple narrative reasons. One of the messages that can be conveyed is that the emotional logic of love, recognition, and compatibility may continue to operate irrespective of superficial appearances. Conversely, it sometimes implies that a lover can change personality and identity under the transforming effect of attraction to another person.[16] At its simplest, disguise may cause comic and erotic predicaments, as in the very first story of inverted gender roles concerning Omphale in ancient Greek mythology. In summary, the device in Shakespeare's hands becomes a flexible, versatile way of presenting and challenging multiple notions of the self, spanning the influence of love, of psychological identity and public persona, of recognition, self-concealment and self-revelation, mostly representing 'the ordeals of awareness and reorientations of ideals and desire before [the central characters] can truly merit one another's love'.[17] The issues raised adhere sometimes to sexual desire and sometimes to class difference, as they do in the movies we shall now consider.

Cross-dressing in films

Although 'breeches roles' in which women impersonate men occur in operas like *Fidelio* and *The Marriage of Figaro* and sometimes in film comedies – even occasionally in male-dominated genres like westerns and war films – yet the device has not produced films as celebrated as the few that show men disguising themselves as women. More familiar are the films such as those in the screwball genre that show women *acting* in stereotyped male roles rather than 'dressing up'. In the early German silent film directed by Ernst Lubitsch, *Ich möchte kein Mann sein* (*I Don't Want to Be a Man* (1918)), a vivacious 'tomboy' rebels against her oppressive parents, preferring the lifestyle of men. She has her hair cut like a man's and wears an evening suit and top hat, deceiving even a man who implausibly finds himself her new guardian, and flirting with her, convinced that she is male. This may be an early and sympathetic portrayal of the 'new woman' in post-First World War Western society, including suffragettes and future 'flappers'. *The Oyster Princess* (1919), also directed by Lubitsch, bears comparison, dealing with a similar situation in which a girl impersonates a boy in order to escape the social expectations placed upon women. The device has lasted throughout movie history: in *Lady Oscar* (1979) a woman dresses as a man but never moves away from her self-perception as a woman, and in Disney's *Mulan* (1998), which has some plot resemblances to *Twelfth Night*, a young woman poses as a male warrior in order to fight in an all-male army. *First a Girl* (1935) has already been described in the Introduction, and right down to the present day (witness *Butch Jamie* (2007)) changes are rung on the figure of the woman disguised as a man. As Bell-Metereau points out, in most cases such films 'end with the happy woman relinquishing her masculine role and settling down in happy subordination to a man', as in the plays of Lyly and Beaumont and Fletcher, although some 'allow her to have a man and maintain her autonomy'.[18] Shakespeare in plays such as *The Two Gentlemen of Verona* and *Twelfth Night* shows us the 'happy subordination' in a heterosexual role, while an argument can be made that Rosalind in *As You Like It* and Portia in *The Merchant of Venice* have asserted new rights that at least qualify them for some autonomy. Marjorie Garber, whose book on cross-dressing is among the most substantial in the field, is also a Shakespearean scholar, and she frequently glances back at the theatrical roots in the Elizabethan theatre. In the world of modern media, *Shakespeare in Love* (1998) and *She's the Man* (2006) have overt links, but thereafter we find a wide spectrum of source material. Garber also acknowledges the limitations of this connection as a source study for film, demonstrating other socio-sexual practices and the innate theatricality of role playing involved in transvestism and transgenderism that have led to a proliferation of movies, especially in the 1990s when sexual mores had become more relaxed than in previous ages. Earlier films, like *Sylvia Scarlett* (1935), *Victor Victoria* (1982), and *Orlando* (1992), have more 'literary' sources and nuances but are still rooted in a set of contemporary social and sexual contexts rather than invoking Shakespeare. The musical *Yentl* (1983) (based on *Yidl Mitl Fidle* (1936) and also on a more recent short story by Isaac Bashevis Singer (1960)) may be right in the middle of the spectrum, since its Jewish heroine (Barbra Streisand) does not disguise herself as a boy for some amatory reason but because girls were not allowed to study the Jewish Talmud. However, the intersection of learning the law in a very Jewish context invites comparison with *The Merchant of Venice*, and it does have outcomes in love and a form of 'marriage'. Although the cultural politics are very different in the play, feminist critics in particular have pointed out that Shylock shares with women an 'outsider' status indicated in the need for Portia to disguise herself in order to practise law, and that there is even a tradition of female actors playing the role of the Jew.[19]

In *She's the Man* (2006), the original device of gendered disguise is used in a movie made for a teenage college audience and signalled as Shakespearean adaptation. Issues in *Twelfth Night* are arguably oversimplified and reduced to matters of anatomy and convention, making disguise more a matter for mirth, titillation, or teenage anxiety than Shakespeare's exploration of emotional blockage and the difficulties of oblique communication in adult relationships. These works also probably traded on the 'footballing heroine' in British films like *Gregory's Girl* (1981) and the Anglo-Indian *Bend It Like Beckham* (2002), where the female is not disguised but excels in a male sporting team and the tomboyish environment of a girls' football team, respectively. Gender expectations and conventions underlie these movies, and this in itself is analogous to the female disguises in Shakespeare, allowing the heroine to behave in ways not available to her *in propriam personam*. A recent Indian (Punjabi) remake of *She's the Man*, *Dil Bole Hadippa!* (roughly translated as 'the heart says hurray!') (2009), sets *Twelfth Night* in a men's cricket team, and the heroine is Veera disguised as Veer, pretending to have a twin sister. At the same time, even when they are not made obvious, such devices can be adapted to replicate the socially and emotionally normative nature of Shakespearean comedy, in which marriage secures connections between people along affective lines according to who 'really' loves whom in a heterosexual context, rather than who *ought* to marry whom. In *Twelfth Night* Duke (or perhaps Count)

Orsino does not marry his equal in rank, Countess Olivia, and nor does Olivia, who ends up with Sebastian as a male simulacrum of Viola. The corollary in romantic tragedy is that Juliet marries the man she loves, Romeo (whom she significantly meets in disguise at a masked ball), and not the man her family considers appropriate, Paris.

Male impersonation of a female, curiously enough, has led to more celebrated movies than the reverse, perhaps because it is seen in the modern world as a more inherently comic situation (as in the cameo in *Bringing Up Baby* already mentioned, where Cary Grant appears wearing a woman's nightdress) than a woman disguising herself as a man. In early movies, Charlie Chaplin (*A Woman* (1915)) and Stan Laurel (*Babes in Toyland* (1934) and *The Dancing Master* (1943)) dressed as women, as did other leading male actors, for comic effects. In the tradition of stand-up comedy, female impersonation has led to the phenomenon of Barry Humphries' unpredictable alter ego 'Edna Everage', while in films it has generated high camp works like *La Cage aux Folles* (1978), *The Adventures of Priscilla, Queen of the Desert* (1994), and *The Birdcage* (1996), and more ambiguous depictions in *Cabaret* (1972), *The Rocky Horror Show* (1975), and Ed Wood's strange 'documentary', *Glen or Glenda* (1953). *I Was a Male War Bride* (1949) portrays Cary Grant disguising himself as a woman in order to enter the United States under the 'War Bride Act'. In these examples any connection with *Twelfth Night*, *As You Like It*, *The Merchant of Venice*, and the other plays is so remote and culturally indirect that it is of little critical significance, except to confirm them as precedents of a transgender narrative pattern behind movie genres. However, the most well known of these films show that issues of identity are raised that bear some comparison to Shakespeare's treatment of gendered disguise.

The greatest film comedy whose plot runs a gamut of disguise, impersonation, cross-dressing, and assumed identity is Billy Wilder's *Some Like It Hot* (1959). In many ways it is the most sophisticated, comprehensive, and unsettling outcome of the range of genre characteristics from which *Twelfth Night* is constructed, as well as owing something to Flute the bellows-mender playing Thisbe. Unlike the plethora of modern imitations that avoid cross-dressing in favour of some other more socially plausible kind of mistaken identity, this movie grasps rather than shirks the comic and even romantic potential of transvestism. The two male musicians disguise themselves as women, Jerry (Jack Lemmon) as 'Daphne' and Joe (Tony Curtis) as 'Josephine'. They assume female identities in order to secure the only employment available to them, in an all-women band, and also to escape the attention of the mafia after they witness a mob murder. Even the reasons behind the disguises are similar to those in Shakespeare, employment and self-protection in a dangerous world, as Bell-Metereau, using a fleeting comparison to Shakespeare's comedies, indicates:

> As in Shakespearian comedies and a number of silent film treatments of the motif, qualities of gentleness, pacifism, and distaste for violence are favorably presented as reasonable feminine alternatives to the masculine values of aggression and combativeness. *Hot* sets up two realms – the frightening, masculine underworld of the city, and the comforting, feminine refuge of the all-girl band – and it is clear that any sane person would choose the latter.[20]

It is a part of the comedy in *Some Like It Hot* that instead of having women disguise themselves as men to protect themselves in a male world, here men disguise themselves as women to escape their implication in the male world. Again, the point is made by Bell-Metereau that this disguise presents cross-dressing 'as a necessary survival mechanism, and escape from physical danger and not a perversion'.[21] The pretences by Jerry and Joe lead to obvious and farcical predicaments dependent on the fact that the audience is never invited to accept the cross-dressing as truly convincing, as in the case of Flute as Thisbe, but also they extend into more complex terrain in the radical destabilisation of gender definitions and roles reminiscent of *Twelfth Night*. The exercise may bend the mind a little, but *Some Like It Hot* can be seen as a direct gender reversal of Shakespeare's play while retaining the play's basic emotional structuring. Here it is the males who disguise themselves as women while it was Viola who disguised herself as a man, but the problematical consequences are oddly comparable, even down to the fact that the disguises are visually presented in such a way that Daphne and Josephine are akin to the twins, Viola and Sebastian. As men, they are unmistakably different from the women in the band, especially Marilyn Monroe, but in wearing similar, distinctive wigs, make-up, and clothes, and assuming higher-pitched voices, they take on the aspect of 'a natural perspective, that is and is not'. To the other women in the band they feel the need to explain the ways in which they differ by stressing their privileged education. In *Twelfth Night* (as in Sidney's *Arcadia*), the disguised woman becomes a love object for both a man and a woman, and the resolution is made possible by the 'unveiling' of the masculine twin who can be paired with Olivia, as well as the female who is paired with Orsino. The situation creates profound frustration in Viola. She is sexually drawn to Orsino and can on stage be placed in situations of erotic intimacy not only to enhance the comedy but also to emphasise her discomfort. In Tim Supple's stage and film version, for example, she speaks to Orsino

Comedy of disguise and mistaken identity 161

while he is naked in the bath. Concealed genital difference is played upon, as to both Orsino and Olivia she can enigmatically say, 'What I am and what I would are as secret as maidenhead' (1.5.206–7), and she can muse to herself, 'A little thing would make me tell them how much I lack of a man' (3.4.293–4). The language of Orsino in describing her reveals his semi-conscious perception of her female identity:

> Dear lad, believe it;
> For they shall yet belie thy happy years
> That say thou art a man. Diana's lip
> Is not more smooth and rubious; thy small pipe
> Is as the maiden's organ, shrill and sound,
> And all is semblative a woman's part. (1.4.29–35)

In *Some Like It Hot* the female disguise of male Joe as Josephine places him on the train in excruciatingly frustrating physical proximity to Sugar, played by Monroe at her most fleshly and in lingerie, just as Viola's proximity to Orsino discomforts her, but the disguise forces Joe to suppress masculine responses as strenuously as Viola must hide her womanly feelings. The result is comic in the film, poignant in the play. As a way out of his dilemma, he creates a different disguise as a male millionaire with an accent that sounds ridiculous ('nobody talks like that', mocks Jerry). This disguise as the pompous and vain Shell Oil magnate, just as bizarre in its own way as 'Josephine' is to Joe, bears resemblances to the ridiculousness of Malvolio dressing in yellow and wearing cross-gartered stockings. Viola's equivalent verbal option of disguise-upon-disguise is to speak of her 'father's daughter' in the third person, creating a female persona for herself. It could even be said that in the film Sugar at some level intuits the true sex of Josephine, as Orsino does Cesario's, since she is, as the film makes clear she has always been, at least subliminally, attracted to saxophone players. In *Twelfth Night*, nobody except possibly Feste sees through Viola's disguise, while in *Some Like It Hot* it is part of the plot's joke that Spats Colombo's mafia group easily penetrate the disguises by noticing the musical instruments' cases, one riddled with their bullets, and they recognise the transvestites as the male witnesses to the 'rubbing out' of 'Toothpick Charlie' and his group. Meanwhile, Viola is equally frustrated by the unwanted attentions paid to her by Olivia, who thinks Viola is indeed the male Cesario, mirroring exactly the situation in which Jerry as 'Daphne' is placed with Osgood. Shakespeare unties the 'knot' by providing a twin brother for Viola, but in the film script the absence of a genuinely female Josephine is turned into the ultimate joke and the film's comic climax. Given the latitude of reversing genders and having two separate male characters,

Wilder's resolution 'unveils' Josephine as Joe, who is now free to marry Sugar, while Daphne, even as Jerry, seems stuck with a male paramour, Osgood (Joe E. Brown), in a transsexual relationship, culminating in Osgood's laconic acceptance: 'Nobody's perfect.' Not only does Osgood prevent Jerry from shedding his disguise, but Jerry's own words, 'I'm a girl', reflect his recognition that his disguise has become himself. The ending is as teasing as the myth of Gallathea (and its dramatic form in Lyly's play) where an actual sex change is effected in order to provide a betrothal. The situation is well on the way to a reconceived and equally plausible ending of *Twelfth Night*, leaving Viola remaining as Cesario and being paired with Olivia, in a relationship based on a false identity that is both homosexual and heterosexual at the same time, while her alter ego brother Sebastian is paired with Orsino as homosexuals. There is, after all, an ambivalent open-endedness about *Twelfth Night* in the provisionality of Orsino's proposal:

> Cesario, come –
> For so you shall be while you are a man;
> But when in other habits you are seen,
> Orsino's mistress, and his fancy's queen. (5.1.381–4)

The tone may be different in the two works but the result is curiously comparable, with disguise rendering gender difference and sexual preference almost arbitrary and free-floating. The reversals are not neatly exact but the nature of the complications is similar, and if we add an awareness that Shakespeare's boy actor plays the role of Viola who then 'plays' the masculine Cesario, we get another set of ironic similitudes with Jerry playing Daphne 'playing' the fictional heir of the Shell Oil company who woos Sugar. The complexities open up more teasing questions about the 'true' identity (if there is one, beyond the effaced actor) of Joe and Viola respectively. Shakespeare could not, or would not, wish to press the situation to a more openly homosexual closure in his play, and even *Some Like It Hot*, as Ed Sikov points out in *Laughing Hysterically: American Screen Comedy of the 1950s*, was openly challenging laws against homosexuality in ways that were subversive in 1959.[22] *Some Like It Hot* is, at least in part, a scrambled but strangely similar twentieth-century adaptation of *Twelfth Night*, although it seems unlikely the makers were intending this. It is not a case of direct or even indirect borrowing, but a matter of genre, harking back to Shakespeare's distinctive comedy of disguise.

To treat the central issues of cross-dressing in this way presupposes that Shakespeare, at least in *Twelfth Night*, was not presenting transvestism as a naive convention of the theatre but as a vehicle for seriously

Comedy of disguise and mistaken identity   163

interrogating ideas of gender and identity, in ways that reverberate up to the 1950s at least, and calling into question 'our complacent, drab view of sexual possibilities'.[23] With variations, this happens also in *Tootsie* (1982), although compared with the often surrealistic anarchism of *Some Like It Hot*, this film now seems quite tame and dated. There are many reasons for this, one of which is that the earlier film, for historical reasons, completely avoided a conscious feminist discourse, but the later one depends to a large extent on the fact that the time of its release was the high-water mark of 'second-wave' feminism in America. After a period of militant political activity in the 1960s and 1970s, including the publication in 1970 of Germaine Greer's *The Female Eunuch* and Kate Millett's *Sexual Politics*, the main goals of the movement seemed close to achievement, since in 1982 itself an Equal Rights Amendment to the United States Constitution only narrowly failed to pass through Congress with the unexpected support of the conservative President Ronald Reagan. Such was the degree of public support for equal rights by this time that many laws were passed and court decisions established rights of equality without the need for an Amendment to the Constitution. Although these advances were arguably something of a false dawn since the full demands of 'second-wave' feminism have still not been implemented, by 1982 the principles and issues had largely been placed in the public arena in a form that could neither be denied nor treated with such hostility as they had been earlier.

Playing to the 'middle ground' and without risk to its middle-class target audiences, *Tootsie* could be addressed relatively benignly to the 'rights' movement at its moderate end, while distancing itself from the 'militant' wing:

> JULIE'S FATHER I thought you'd be more like one of them 'liberators'.
> DOROTHY You know, I'm not really like the woman in the show. I mean, that's just a part of me. I'm not that militant.
> JULIE'S FATHER Don't get me wrong. I'm all for equality. Women ought to be entitled to everything and all et cetera, except sometimes I think what they really want is to be entitled to be a man.

Once again, the issues raised by Shakespeare indirectly, mediated through screwball comedy, are raising their heads. The statement by 'Dorothy' (the disguised, out-of-work actor Michael Dorsey, played by Dustin Hoffman) has multiple ironies, since 'she' is 'not really like the woman in the show' in several senses. Not only is Dorothy an actor rather than the hospital administrator she is playing (or at least improvising upon), but 'she' is also a 'he' anyway. However, the sense that follows ('I'm not that militant') refers to the fictional character's readiness to attack men in the television soap opera they are watching, for patronising and sexually degrading the women on the programme and on the set. Julie's father responds with a statement that probably would have been endorsed by a majority of at least the college-educated population in 1982, that equality is a good thing in itself but that 'militants' take it too far in claiming the right to 'be a man'. It was virtually a cliché of the time and it seems that this is the underlying political position of the film itself, apparently oblivious to the fact that it portrays a man claiming the right to be a woman. This was a major point of criticism expressed by feminists, who no doubt were dismissed as 'militant' extremists. They pointed out quite reasonably that the impersonation denies a female actor the right to employment, and that the patronising premise is that a man in disguise can voice women's demands more assertively and with more success than a woman:

> FEMALE TELEVISION EXECUTIVE You are the first woman character who is her own person, who can assert her own personality without robbing someone of theirs. You're a breakthrough lady for us.

It is not difficult to see why this might create hostility in female audiences. Moreover, the disguised man proves himself even 'more like a woman than a woman' in not only gaining the character part ahead of his actress friend, but also becoming the focus of two men's sexual attentions. 'She' is entering the terrain occupied by Shakespeare's Helena in the *Dream* and entering Viola's predicament, since as a man in his own figure he cannot maintain even one heterosexual relationship. Dorsey's eventual acceptance that he likes Dorothy better than himself is a concession to the topical debate that males should show and develop a female side, a view that some critics have attributed to Shakespeare not only in his androgynous heroines but in characters like Hamlet. However, even this can be turned around, as some unconvinced reviewers pointed out, to suggest that it is doubly objectionable that female identity is merely a projection of the male's, and also that 'new age' men could exploit women's position by claiming or even pretending with false consciousness to share female knowledge and goals. Marjorie Garber summarises this feminist line of argument:

> Some feminist critics have seen Hoffman's star turn as an example of the preempting of women's roles by men in a Hollywood where there are few enough good parts for actresses. This is very similar to Showalter's argument about male literary critics who wanted to get in on the action and 'read like a woman,' now that feminism had become respectable and indeed theoretically exciting. In fact, Rebecca Bell-Metereau, like Showalter, notes that in the film Michael Dorsey directly suggests an allegorical reading of the actor as woman: putting on make-up, trying to make himself attractive, sitting by the phone waiting for that all-important call.[24]

As well as infantilising such stereotypically 'female' images, one could also note that the actual women in the film are, without exception, presented as helpless victims, not least the woman to whom Dorsey becomes attracted, Julie Nichols (Jessica Lange), who is the plaything of the promiscuous director and in need of either surrogate male support or of behaving 'more like a man' to escape victimhood. To the credit of Julie, however, she herself three times rebuffs Dorsey's sexual overtures, once after he, as a man, takes advantage of his knowledge of what Julie wants from a man (not 'role-playing' but an honest statement of sexual desire), then as a woman when Julie takes it she is being seduced into a lesbian affair, and again at the end of the film when she finds he has throughout been acting as a deceptive traitor, allowing her intimately to confide in him as with a woman. He virtually quotes Viola in his plaintive words, 'I'm not the person you think I am', and finds himself a target of hostility just as 'Cesario' is attacked as deceitful by both Orsino and Olivia. Another aspect of the film that could have riled feminists is that Dorsey as a male is depicted from the opening scenes and throughout the whole film as socially dysfunctional (especially with women) and professionally uncooperative. His behaviour does not radically change when he is masquerading as a woman, although he is more generally accepted by others as an assertive woman. One implication here is that while men are expected to be cooperative and socially adept, women are not, and the more 'difficult' their behaviour the more likely it is that they will be admired and even loved. Clearly, *Tootsie* shows a range of sometimes conflicting attitudes towards feminist debates but they are arguably located more pertinently in the world of 1982 than 2010, and the apparently safe ideological ground its makers chose is in reality a minefield of possible criticisms.

Arguably, *Tootsie* shows Shakespearean influence through genre, but the subject needs to be treated with a light touch, if only because the movie is not especially as profound or self-critical as Shakespeare's play. As I have argued of most films after the 1950s, the most obvious references are to other movies, so that the Shakespearean influence is even more indirect than in the earlier movies. This is especially so in this case, since its primary indebtedness is to *Some Like It Hot* itself and perhaps *Sylvia Scarlett* (1935), a film directed by George Cukor in which Katharine Hepburn disguises herself as a boy in a fraudulent ruse. The plot motifs and generic patterns from Shakespeare have already been absorbed into the new medium of cinema and exist by now at second hand, but are also probably completely invisible to the film-makers. However, we are led back again to a 'composite' version of Shakespeare's genre of romantic comedies. In this instance, the original comic writer,

Larry Gelbart, was acquainted with classical literature and would certainly have known Shakespeare's works, since he had adventurously adapted Jonson's *Volpone* into a successful Broadway show called *Sly Fox* (1976). He had adapted a book by Robert Louis Stevenson into the movie *The Wrong Box* (1966), and was co-librettist for *A Funny Thing Happened on the Way to the Forum* (1966) having written the book on which it was based, ransacking both Plautus and Shakespeare's *Julius Caesar* for aspects of plot and many familiar details. There is an obvious difference between Shakespeare's comedies and *Tootsie* in that it is a man disguising as a woman rather than the other way around, though the plot complications and some thematic issues are similar and besides, on the Elizabethan stage males played females, and Michael Dorsey is nothing if not an actor (as is Hoffman 'beneath' the character). But accepting this as a variation of the genre that uses cross-dressing, we can say that elements are borrowed from the three major comedic heroines in Shakespeare. Like Viola in *Twelfth Night* the disguise acts as a trap, since Dorsey as Dorothy is unable to pursue the heterosexual relationship he desires with Julie, and he also attracts unwanted desire from two same-sex figures. The same could be said of Rosalind who, disguised as a man, is seen as a potential love partner by Phoebe, and in this sense the historical origin lies in Sidney's *Arcadia*, from which Shakespeare often borrowed. In this comic romance, the male disguised as female, Pyrocles, is on the one hand disabled from revealing his gender to the woman he loves, while at the same time he is pursued by an older man (Duke Basilius) and also by an older woman, Basilius's wife Gynecia, who sees through the disguise. In *As You Like It* Rosalind's disguise as Ganymede is as liberating as Dorsey's disguise as Dorothy, giving both a social freedom to speak their minds and relish the opportunity for role playing that becomes available. When Rosalind at the end of the play is required to shed her disguise and to take her place as a woman, she conspicuously loses the 'voice' she has gained while acting as a man but simultaneously becomes eligible to marry Orlando. In a comparable way, when Dorsey must stop playing Dorothy he can no longer indulge the freedom of speaking as a woman, though he also can now pursue a heterosexual relationship with Julie. There is also a conspicuous pastoral interlude in *Tootsie* that operates the same way as in *As You Like It*. When Dorothy and Julie visit the latter's widowed father on his farm, where the frenetic pace of the film mellows into bucolic relaxation (Dorothy even milks a cow, with comic results), the characters may share contemplative and (almost) honest communication about their emotions. The more distant and forgotten generic sources are prose romances, Sidney's *Arcadia* and Lodge's *Rosalynde*, but Shakespeare's romantic comedies are the illustrious and celebrated precedents that established the generic contours of comedy of disguise. Of course, there is no suggestion that anybody involved in making *Tootsie* was remotely aware of the eclipsed early modern antecedents, but intertextuality can have a subterranean life of its own in transmission through culture, especially through the lucky accident of Shakespeare's example.

Mrs Doubtfire (1993) may be an unexpected inclusion in a book on Shakespeare's influence on movie genres, but it shows how far the use of a brand of comedy turning on gendered disguise extends into unlikely films, and how it can be adapted to address contemporary social issues at the time the film is made, like *The Taming of the Shrew*. In this case, the prime generic source is *Tootsie*, and just as that film was a vehicle for the character acting of Dustin Hoffman, so *Mrs Doubtfire* is designed to showcase Robin Williams's chameleon comic acting versatility, though the movie is not so comic as the producers must have expected. Where *Tootsie*, as I have argued, reflected debates raging publicly in the 1970s concerning what was then known as 'women's lib', so the later film engages with a related issue that has continued since the 1990s to be topical and controversial, namely the rising incidence of divorce and consequential problems relating to child custody. With its 'hero', who is once again an unsuccessful actor, disguising this time as a middle-aged Scottish woman in order to become a housekeeper for his ex-wife so that he can spend more time with his children, the film takes a clear stance that can be briefly summed up from a feminist perspective as assertively pro-male. Indeed, it would be difficult to mount any argument from a feminist perspective that would be sympathetic to the film's premises. This is at least partly, I suggest, because a different issue from women's rights was being debated in the 1990s, paternal rights, which is at the heart of the film's concerns. The initial divorce is represented as the wife's choice, based on what are constructed as intolerant and trivial grounds, that her husband is too irresponsible and erratic even to run a children's party without causing havoc, let alone to sustain a marriage. The wife is absent from the party in a way presented as subtly culpable, and she is seen throughout as a strict disciplinarian and 'anti-fun' parent. Daniel Hilliard (Williams), however, is not only deeply loved by his three children but also is by profession a children's entertainer, and one who is very child-like himself. When the question of custody is considered (twice) by the courts, once again the film's dice are loaded against the ex-wife, who alienates audience sympathy and yet is aided by the law that deprives the father of joint custody, adding insult to injury by making his access not only minimal in time but compulsorily chaperoned. Attitudes of suspicion and hostility adopted by the mother and the law alike are exploited to make us base our judgements on the supposed manifest trustworthiness of the misunderstood father. His elaborate disguise as Mrs Doubtfire is a device to get around the legally sanctioned limited access, but more generally it is presented as the result of paternal love, commitment, and loyalty, which is respected and reciprocated by the children. After many obvious predicaments are milked for their comic potential, the resolution eventually comes predictably in the ex-wife's willing recognition that she has been 'wrong' all along. The disguise has succeeded in making her realise that the father's feelings for his children, and theirs for him, are far deeper than she had realised. She also recognises that she had drastically undervalued her ex-husband's competence even in the traditionally female realm of housekeeping, and that he is emotionally mature in ways that shame her own limitations and those of her callow new lover. So loaded against the woman are the markers in the film that one suspects some autobiographical impulse on the part of somebody, perhaps Williams himself, in making it, and it was certainly angled to provide strong ideological support to the men's lobby for paternal rights that was developing at the time. The example shows once again that an apparently hackneyed stage convention made famous by Shakespeare in his romantic comedies has also become a convention in movies extending through *Some Like It Hot* in the 1950s, *Tootsie* in the 1970s, and *Mrs Doubtfire* in the 1990s, in ways that show the genre is capable of being adapted to address new, contemporary socio-sexual problems.

Another subject related to cross-dressing and transvestism is androgyny in relation to personal identity and relationships, and Bruce Babington and Peter Evans point out that this too has its origins in *Twelfth Night*:

> At the Romantic pole of the comedy of the sexes the blurring of male and female characteristics into an image of bisexuality is presented as a thing of delicate mystery (Viola/Cesario's masculine/feminine youth – 'For they shall yet belie thy happy years / That say thou art a man'). It centres around images of youth, either a girlish boy or a boyish girl.[25]

Androgyny or the concept of hermaphroditism is an issue in most of the films I have analysed in this section, and overtly so in the 1992 film based on Virginia Woolf's novel *Orlando*, where Queen Elizabeth I herself makes an appearance. It has been an issue in various modern clothes fashions, musical movements such as 'glam rock', and cults around the figure of David Bowie and other stars using androgyny as their blazon. Consideration of this area would lead us even farther away from Shakespeare, though his disguised heroines and the ambiguous 'master mistress of [his] passion' in the *Sonnets* would deserve some part in the

Comedy of disguise and mistaken identity

discussion, alongside a reasonably consistent critical fashion since the mid-1980s for seeing his works as potentially gay.[26] I hope to have at least established that within the spectrum of historically located versions of films utilising cross-dressing and 'gender-bending', Shakespeare's romantic comedies make an important, if not often noticed, contribution to the development of the modern cinematic genre of romantic comedy based on disguise and sexual desire.

'Slumming': class, non-gendered disguise, and mistaken identity

Disguised gender in Shakespeare and in movies need not be a matter of simple appearance or clothes, since this would nowadays be dismissed as implausible by audiences accustomed to the naturalistic representations in movies. Rather, disguise in the more general sense is a form of acting, the adoption of a persona playing a role, and the equivalent psychological situation depends on mistaken identity rather than wilful duplicity. This is as true of Shakespeare's Rosalind, Viola, and Portia as the Antipholuses and Dromios of *The Comedy of Errors*, since their action of disguising as male is a visual metaphor for adopting chosen roles that may reveal their true identities while masking more superficial traits. Each of them is highborn, but *The Arcadia*'s Musidorus assumes the occupational identity of a person beneath his inherited status, and disguises himself as a shepherd. (His cousin Pyrocles represents gender disguise, impersonating an Amazon.) Perdita in *The Winter's Tale* is not consciously disguised but she is assumed to be a shepherdess. When stated in this way, the convention acquires more familiarity and frequency as a motif in films, to the extent that romantic comedy of disguise can be claimed as a sub-genre in its own right. The prince or princess, or the wealthy magnate, is seen as a pauper, either through some mistake or by choice. Because of its greater plausibility, the obscuring of one's class, wealth, and status offers an even more fertile device for modern movies than does disguised gender. It has many early modern precedents in some of the main works from which Shakespeare borrowed, such as *Arcadia* and Greene's *Pandosto* mentioned above. In Sidney's romance, the point of the young princes' disguising is partly to conceal wealth and royal blood, in an attempt to evade the Delphic oracle's prediction about the women's future marriage mates. In Shakespeare, both Viola and Rosalind, as well as disguising their gender, also act below their true class. Rosalind the duke's daughter masquerades as Ganymede, named after Jove's page, giving her emotional access to Orlando, who is a disinherited second son of a nobleman. Celia proposes to clothe herself 'in poor and mean attire' and call herself Aliena. They both end up marrying into their birth right, money, and high position. Viola is a 'lady' with enough gold to be 'bounteous'. In such cases the issue of obscured class is arguably as important, if more often overlooked, as disguised gender. This is crucial in cinema's adaptation of such conventions.

Many Hollywood films turn on such social disguises, in situations where the main impediment between potential lovers may be a radical difference in status. Either a female 'dresses down' from princess status and attracts a middle- or working-class male lover; or an impoverished, fortune-hunting male, either by design, or opportunism, or inadvertently, represents himself as or is mistaken for a man of considerable means, usually a millionaire or at least heir to a fortune – or the reverse. The adoption of a role relating to class or profession poses fewer problems for the naturalistic mode of cinema than gendered disguise, it avoids many of the inherently comic aspects of the latter, and it can apply equally easily to a man or a woman. It also reflects the dominant preoccupation with wealth and financial insecurity that has always been a hallmark of Hollywood cinema, especially during and after the Depression (*Gold Diggers of 1933* – and of 1935, 1937, and 1996), presupposing the danger of sudden impoverishment or the possibility of dramatic upward mobility. A paradox exists whereby democracy proudly proclaims equality and the unimportance of class, yet it also depends on an apparently contradictory mythology that a poor person can become enviably rich or a 'log cabin' dweller can move into the White House, and also a prevailing fear of sudden poverty no doubt based on folk memories of the Depression years when 'talking pictures' were consolidating their position in mass media entertainment. Other anxieties lurk beneath such ideas, most pertinently here the fear expressed in Thomas Hardy's novels that it is impossible to move outside one's social rank, and that wealth can dictate marriage choices, for better or for worse, if it is seen as the only marriageable commodity a person may have. Disguise, then, can be generalised as a matter of identity considered in social and economic terms, rather than narrowly defined as a question of anatomy, gender, or sexual preference. It can include many forms of making one's 'self' unrecognisable, or concealing a reality lying beneath a surface appearance. In American films especially, a persistent kind of disguise is either for the rich to feign 'ordinariness' or for the poor to conceal poverty or low status in order to pursue an otherwise out-of-reach lover. It seems peculiarly common in films from America, where markers of wealth are not necessarily publicly obvious, and curiously absent from British films where class, commonly signalled in external ways such as clothes and accent, might be more valued in the context of a perceived 'class war'.

A simple Hollywood example is provided by the wartime film, *You'll Never Get Rich* (1941), starring Fred Astaire and Rita Hayworth.

Astaire's character is a private in the army who is confined to the guardhouse because he has stolen a captain's uniform, and in this garb he impersonates an officer in order not only to meet 'Sheila' but also to pretend he is as eligible to marry her as his rival who is indeed a captain. Such deceptions in films of the time are tantamount to a form of disguise, since in the army, rank is presented as central to identity. Astaire may still be '*Private* Robert Curtis', but when he is accepted as '*Captain* Robert Curtis' he is treated very differently. Elsewhere in this film the distinction between being a rich boss or an ordinary worker is significant – Astaire's peacetime employer makes him the 'fall guy' for his own marital infidelities – and there are comparable distinctions set in a business world. Such impersonations or disguises of status account for the basic structure in many filmed romantic comedies, including musicals. One of the advantages is that such deceptions can fulfil the inner, metaphorical purposes of disguise exploited by Shakespeare, who was writing in a society where sumptuary laws regulated what one wore and was entitled to, by way of economic privilege.

Happy Go Lovely (1951) is an undistinguished but representative movie based on disguised status as adapted to suit modern times. Its plot draws on earlier backstage musicals such as *Gold Diggers of 1933* (1933), in which a wealthy but shy aristocrat effaces his class when becoming involved in (and financially bailing out) a musical theatre company. However, there are also, I suggest, less obvious links in both films with Shakespeare's comedies of disguises. Set in Edinburgh and starring the British actor David Niven, though in all other ways a Hollywood product, it is based on an initial, mistaken identity that becomes accepted as a consciously maintained disguise. The showgirl, Janet Jones (played by Vera-Ellen), mistakes for a newspaper reporter the rich but conservative and cautious bachelor, B. G. Bruno (Niven), and she not only reveals secrets to him but also falls in love. As events develop, Bruno decides not to correct her mistake, as he gradually discovers that he is in love with her. This obviously leads not only to a generous subsidy for the musical theatre company but also, in time, to marriage, so everybody benefits. The plot itself bears some comparison with *As You Like It*, substituting the world of repertory theatre for the forest as the play space, while Shakespeare's treatment of the accidental 'disguise' or mistaken status becomes a device for allowing courtship to develop gradually and to explore issues of emotional compatibility. Theatre, whether backstage or onstage, becomes like a Forest of Arden, a place for role playing, simple 'playing' in different senses, and where feelings and identities can be shed and acquired. So long as Janet does not know Bruno is a millionaire, she treats him not according to a stereotype but as an equal. This gives her the opportunity to get to know him as a 'real person' uncluttered by assumptions about his wealth, and also enables her to treat him as an emotional confidant and eventually an attainable figure of desire. In turn, this brings out in Bruno himself a new and unexpected personality, much to the surprise of his business employees, as he becomes more light-hearted and colourful in every way. This is very close to the way in which Rosalind's disguise operates in *As You Like It*, since it allows her and Orlando to get to know each other emotionally by both adopting personae that reveal new, independent aspects of personality in each, but at a safe distance without risking either rejection or damaged feelings. Furthermore, the way the initially cruel figure of authority, Oliver, is changed in the forest into a suitable marriage partner for Celia provides a similar pattern to Bruno's transformation. The backdrop of the theatrical world in *Happy Go Lovely*, which is a world alien to Bruno, equates also to the Forest of Arden, where hypothetical 'supposes' and counterfeited, acting behaviour can unlock genuine feelings. Rosalind's 'Well, this is the Forest of Arden' in Shakespeare's time was addressed to a bare stage turned by language into a place of wishing, hoping, disguising, 'playing', and all the other things that go on backstage in the movie. In the 'real' world of Shakespeare's presentation of the contrasting court, just as in the business world where Bruno 'holds court', the feelings liberated in the imaginative space are impossible to entertain, or liable to be thwarted. The mistaken class of the protagonist becomes a catalyst for revelation and emotional changes, which is the mechanism driving the plot in *As You Like It* and affects all the characters, not just Rosalind and Orlando. For Shakespeare, this kind of situation provided him with a model for a version of romantic comedy that differs from that in *A Midsummer Night's Dream*, where parental opposition and legal restrictions thwart young love.

A brace of romantic comedies starring Audrey Hepburn in the 1950s turn on similar variations of mistaken or disguised identity. In *Roman Holiday* (1953), which is briefly mentioned in Chapter 2, the adolescent Ann, crown princess of an unnamed monarchy, escapes the constricting routines of royal schedules and is found on a public wall sleeping off the influence of sleeping pills. Her saviour is a reporter (Gregory Peck) contracted to cover the royal interview scheduled for the following morning. When she refuses to accept his money for a taxi 'home', the reporter takes 'Anya Smith' back to his very modest flat. A source of comedy is what the man sees as the incongruous airs and graces in an apparently homeless commoner. Gradually he sees through Ann's assumed role, and like the reporter in *It Happened One Night*, he gradually realises he can get an exclusive, personal interview with the princess in his room. Without taking advantage of the intimacy, he manages to give Ann a memorably happy experience blossoming into a mutual love, which unfortunately cannot be continued because of their differences in status. Like a Shakespearean character who has found her way temporarily into a liberating, 'green' world where she can discover herself and fall in love, the princess, like the duke's daughter in *As You Like It*, must finally return to 'duty' in the royal way of life. But unlike Orlando in Shakespeare's play, the reporter must remain simply a reporter while the princess accepts that she is professionally destined for higher things. In the following year Hepburn starred in *Sabrina* (1954), which turns on a more physical kind of transformation, though one more universal than disguised identity – the inevitable yet unexpected biological changes as the 'chauffeur's daughter' emerges from the chrysalis state of an inconspicuous adolescence into an elegant and sophisticated woman, after a sojourn in her discovered 'green world', Paris. The two brothers who grew up with her now begin to take a new interest in her. They both fall in love with her, which is complicated by the fact that another woman loves one of the men. The convenience of the extra woman makes a double wedding easily achieved – thus adding a motif Shakespeare had experimented with in *The Two Gentlemen of Verona* and liked enough to repeat in *A Midsummer Night's Dream*. Next in Hepburn's series of such movies, in *Funny Face* (1957) an apparently plain girl selling books in a shop is 'noticed' and becomes a photographic fashion model. The transformation from ugly duckling to beautiful swan comes after elaborate makeovers akin to those in *Pygmalion* and *My Fair Lady*. The result is effectively a disguised identity that reveals lovable parts of her identity that have never been appreciated. Such plots are heirs to Shakespeare's 'disguised heroine' plots in their metaphorical interpretations, where sets of inward rather than external metamorphoses are suggested. A young woman voluntarily or accidentally discovers an unrevealed side to her personality, by either choosing or having imposed upon her a defamiliarised self-image or previously unconsidered identity. Or a man is led to value aspects of the woman he had never noticed before – all Shakespeare's comic heroines exemplify some or other part of this formula and it is so recurrent and central that it can be seen as a hinge to his conception of romantic comedy as a genre. The exception that proves the rule might be poor Helena in *All's Well That Ends Well*, since the man she loves is simply incapable of recognising her inner beauty and moral worth, until paradoxically the darkness of night is her disguise. Of course, Hepburn herself grew out of her youthfulness, and she inevitably moved away from such films where one patterning at work shows the elfin girl-woman acquiring a sexual identity through a process of obscuring an earlier self.

The possibilities are virtually endless in such forms of adaptation of Shakespearean disguise turning on class rather than clothing or gender. In *Trouble in Paradise* (1932) a female pickpocket pretends to be a countess. In *The Lady Eve* (1941) a rich but naive man falls in love with a dishonest, fortune-hunting card-sharp. After rejecting her once, he again falls in love with her in her new pretence of an English woman disguised by her accent – an example implicitly showing that love itself can penetrate a disguise by operating directly on the emotions rather than externals, as in both *Twelfth Night* and *As You Like It*. (In *The Merchant of Venice*, Bassanio's inability to see through Portia's disguise is yet another variation on the formula, in a play that reveals some scepticism about the hero's fortune-hunting motives in pursuing the woman.) *Two-Faced Woman* (1941), as its title suggests, frames a woman who deceives her husband by pretending to be her own identical twin sister – 'two-faced' in both senses, dissimulating and hypocritical. In an ironic twist on this kind of plot, Lubitsch's *The Shop around the Corner* (1940) shows a woman and man falling in love with each other while they are anonymous pen pals, even though they detest each other when in physical proximity. *By Candlelight* (1934) shows a butler pretending to be his master in order to attract the countess, a basic plot device recalling Malvolio's sorry story. In *Monte Carlo* (1930), directed again by the king of romantic comedy, Ernst Lubitsch, the heroine assumes that a count is a hairdresser, and only realises her mistake after they have fallen in love, when she sees him in the VIP box at the opera. Romantic complications in *Pillow Talk* (1959) turn on various pretences, such as Rock Hudson disguising his voice over the phone, impersonating a wealthy Texan rancher, and pretending to be effeminate (with the implication of homosexuality) to persuade Doris Day he is 'a gentleman'. In a backstage comedy musical, *Let's Make Love* (1960), directed by George Cukor, billionaire businessman Jean-Marc Clement (Yves Montand) finds himself mistaken for an actor auditioning to play his own 'real-life' character in a satirical musical based on his life. He decides to go along with this and maintains the pretence by assuming the identity of 'Alexander Dumas', because he becomes interested (as who would not?) in the production's impoverished leading lady, Amanda (Marilyn Monroe). As in *Happy Go Lovely*, he anonymously bails out the company so that the production can be staged. The twist in the narrative is that although Clement is deeply gratified that somebody can like and even love him for himself rather than his money, Amanda, far from being pleased to discover his true identity, at first refuses to believe it, and then becomes furious at the apparent betrayal of her trust. She has, besides, throughout the film been attached to an actor who is as poor as she is and he would appear to be a more equal and deserving partner, as William is for Audrey in *As You Like It*. In this case money itself becomes a disadvantage when it comes to love, and disguise is made problematical to the honest as a breach of trust. These emotional impediments sustain the story through more complications, but of course the providential rules of romantic comedy apply by the end. The film is perhaps made less formulaic than the description suggests by the indignant honesty that Monroe brings to the role, somewhat undermining the filmic intentions behind the 'happy' ending and the convention of impersonation in general.

A downward change of status can be just as effective whether practised by a man or a woman. In the screwball comedy *My Man Godfrey* (1936), Godfrey is a 'forgotten man', a victim of the Depression living on the streets. He becomes butler to a rich, idle family, and is eventually revealed as a Harvard graduate and millionaire, who saves the feckless family from ruin. He brings a reality and 'propriety' into their pampered lives, particularly that of the spoilt younger daughter. There are elements of odd-couple comedy from *The Shrew* as part of this film's generic make-up, but it also, and arguably more centrally, employs the part of romance traditions adopted by Shakespeare in depicting such characters as Viola and Rosalind, Perdita and Imogen, where social rank is an aspect of assumed or mistaken identity, and where the disguised figure brings a new emotional pattern into the lives of other characters.

Shakespeare rarely uses a convention in a formulaic or purely literal way, but rather uncovers some human emotional need through its use. He also keeps exploring and experimenting, finding new ways of deploying a plot device. Nowhere are these facets more evident than in his use of the disguised heroine. Rosalind, Portia, and Viola (as well as Julia, Helena, and Imogen) all discover within themselves unexpected, potential identities by donning a disguise, with the implication that all people hold within themselves the capacity for change and for multifarious emotional experiences. At the same time, there can be something reassuring about the fact that one can maintain a stable identity, and love, through such changes. Hollywood comedies extend the Shakespearean convention to interrogate and undermine gender categories, while other films use disguise to explore issues of class divisions and how love operates in such cases. The pattern is so fundamental and yet flexibly inventive in the films that employ disguise that it can be claimed not as a fixed 'convention' but as a genre, or at least a sub-genre of romantic comedy, and as such another part of the cinematic legacy of Shakespeare's comedy of love.

Notes

1 Rebecca Bell-Metereau, *Hollywood Androgyny* (New York: Columbia University Press, 1993).
2 Annette Kuhn, 'Sexual Disguise and Cinema', in *The Power of the Image: Essays on Representation and Sexuality* (London: Routledge & Kegan Paul, 1985), 48–73.
3 Laura Mulvey, 'Visual Pleasure and Narrative Cinema' (1975), repr. in E. Ann Kaplan (ed.), *Feminism and Film* (Oxford: Oxford University Press, 2000), 34–47.
4 Kuhn, 'Sexual Disguise and Cinema', 52.
5 Kuhn, 'Sexual Disguise and Cinema', 50.
6 Bertrand Evans, *Shakespeare's Comedies* (Oxford: Clarendon Press, 1960).
7 Louise George Clubb (ed. and transl.), *Pollastra and the Origins of Twelfth Night* (Leicester: Ashgate, 2010).
8 See Joanna Thompson, *The Character of Britomart in Spenser's 'The Faerie Queene'* (Lampeter: The Edwin Mellen Press, 2001), 72 and elsewhere.
9 See Hunter, *John Lyly*, 310–15.
10 A large body of critical work lies behind these generalisations, stemming from, modifying, or opposing Juliet Dusinberre's pioneering *Shakespeare and the Nature of Women* (New York: Macmillan, 1975) and essays in Carolyn Ruth Swift Lenz, Gayle Greene, and Carol Thomas Neely (eds), *The Woman's Part: Feminist Criticism of Shakespeare* (Urbana: University of Illinois Press, 1980). Other influential contributions include Paula Berggren, '"A Prodigious Thing": The Jacobean Heroine in Male Disguise', *Philological Quarterly*, 62 (Summer 1983), 383–402; Catherine Belsey, 'Disrupting Sexual Difference: Meaning and Gender in the Comedies', in John Drakakis (ed.), *Alternative Shakespeares* (London and New York: Methuen, 1985), 166–90; Jean E. Howard, 'Crossdressing, the Theatre, and Gender Struggle in Early Modern England', *Shakespeare Quarterly*, 39 (Winter 1988), 418–40; Michael Shapiro, *Gender in Play on the Shakespearean Stage: Boy Heroines and Female Pages* (Ann Arbor: University of Michigan Press, 1994); Stephen Orgel, *Impersonations: The Performance of Gender in Shakespeare's England* (Cambridge: Cambridge University Press, 1996). A useful anthology of some important statements is Deborah E. Barker and Ivo Kamps (eds), *Shakespeare and Gender: A History* (London: Verso, 1995).
11 I realise the assertion that Shakespeare questions rather than reaffirms notions of sexual essentialism is not accepted by all scholars who have written on the issue. For a useful summary of the different views that have been expressed, see Peter Berek, 'Cross-Dressing, Gender, and Absolutism in the Beaumont and Fletcher Plays', *Studies in English Literature 1500–1900*, 44 (2004), 359–77, fn. 4.
12 Berek, 'Cross-Dressing, Gender, and Absolutism', 366.
13 See, for example, Marilyn French, *Shakespeare's Division of Experience* (New York: Summit Books, 1981).

14 Dympna Callaghan, *Shakespeare without Women: Representing Gender and Race on the Renaissance Stage* (London and New York: Routledge, 2000).
15 Marjorie Garber, *Vested Interests: Cross-Dressing and Cultural Anxiety* (London: Penguin Group, 1993), 35. On Puritan anti-theatricalism and disguise, see also Laura Levine, *Men in Women's Clothing: Anti-Theatricality and Effeminization, 1579–1642* (Cambridge: Cambridge University Press, 1994).
16 Some of these questions are explored in my article 'Metamorphosis by Love in Elizabethan Romance, Romantic Comedy and Shakespeare's Early Comedies', *Review of English Studies*, 35 (1984), 14–44.
17 Babington and Evans, *Affairs to Remember*, 286.
18 Bell-Metereau, *Hollywood Androgyny*, 71.
19 Garber, *Vested Interests*, 227 ff.
20 Bell-Metereau, *Hollywood Androgyny*, 56.
21 Bell-Metereau, *Hollywood Androgyny*, 64.
22 Ed Sikov, 'Clothes Make the Man: *Some Like It Hot* – An Escapist Comedy', in *Laughing Hysterically: American Screen Comedy of the 1950s* (New York: Columbia University Press, 1994), 128–49.
23 Bell-Metereau, *Hollywood Androgyny*, 64.
24 Garber, *Vested Interests*, 7.
25 Babington and Evans, *Affairs to Remember*, 128.
26 For example, Joseph Pequigney, *Such Is My Love: A Study of Shakespeare's Sonnets* (Chicago: Chicago University Press, 1985); Kate Chedgzoy, *Shakespeare's Queer Children: Sexual Politics and Contemporary Culture* (Manchester: Manchester University Press, 1996).

6

'Star-crossed lovers': *Romeo and Juliet* and romantic tragedy

Romeo and Juliet has probably the most immediately recognisable plot in literary history, to such an extent that its generic influence on cinematic romantic tragedy is undeniable. The play itself is performed time and again and is obligatory in schools around the world as a text for study and for auditions. It has been filmed in relatively straightforward versions at least thirty times, and many more times in freely adapted and even off-beat versions (such as *Tromeo and Juliet* and the Swedish *Sex Lives of Romeo and Juliet*, known also as *Romeo and Juliet II*), inset within another story (as in Dickens's *Nicholas Nickleby* and *Carry on Teacher* (1959)), or mercilessly parodied (Ustinov's *Romanoff and Juliet* (1960)). More pertinently for this book, there are many films that represent the same basic narrative situation of unfortunate lovers who are compromised by cultural differences between their respective families and/or religious and ethnic groups (Anglos and Puerto Ricans in *West Side Story* (1961), Italian Catholic and Anglo-Saxon Protestant in Baz Luhrmann's *William Shakespeare's Romeo + Juliet* (1996)), to such an extent that it is possible to identify the narrative structure as a kind of genre in its own right, the 'Romeo-and-Juliet genre'. At the very least it can be claimed as a paradigm for romantic tragedy.

A major new film of *Romeo and Juliet*, sporting Shakespeare's authorship and aiming at some fidelity to the text, appears about every thirty years: Cukor's in 1936, Zeffirelli's in 1968, Luhrmann's *Romeo + Juliet* in 1996. There have been others in between (Castellani's in 1955, for example), but the three in particular have been seen as significant moments in the history of Shakespeare productions and film.[1] The thirty-year cycle seems to allow for a generation change in the younger audiences that are usually targeted. Although each has maintained its status as a classic film in its own right and of more than historical interest, yet each has dated over the ensuing thirty years, as decisively as the society for which it was made. Even one decade has seen the most recent, Luhrmann's, fade somewhat into recent history as the bleakness of 'Generation X' has given way to a more optimistic 'Generation Y',[2] but still each version continues to be marketed to a discrete generation. Those of us who were teenagers in the 1960s, with its 'make love not war' ethos, when Zeffirelli's appeared can be nostalgic about the film as a piece of our own lost youth, even as our own children and students see it as hopelessly old-fashioned. Beyond these 'watershed' films, *Romeo and Juliet* has, like *Hamlet*, generated dozens if not hundreds of 'spin-off' versions and imaginative adaptations that are still recognisable through the generic aspects of the play, which have proved powerful and durable as a film narrative basis.[3] If there is some truth in Linda Charnes's speculation that 'we must conclude that *Hamlet* – and not Hammett – offers the first fully *noir* text in Western literature, and Prince Hamlet the first *noir* detective. Or rather, the first *noir* revenger',[4] then another suggestion can be made: that Shakespeare's Romeo and Juliet, as originated in the mid-1590s, are the first tragically separated lovers in *film* history, and that their story initiated a new genre, 'the *Romeo and Juliet* film'. Making a similar claim in different terms, Lloyd Davis wrote that '*Romeo and Juliet* stages a *paradigmatic conflict* between ways of representing and interpreting desire' (my italics),[5] and this chapter will be concerned to analyse some of the ways in which the specific 'paradigm' of love blighted by societal conflict can be realised in an apparently endless series of movies proximately based on Shakespeare's play.

What interests me in this chapter is the way that the play, having (I would argue) originated a unique and recognisable genre that has been assimilated into the world of film, also holds within its blueprint a set of different possible foci, any one of which can be foregrounded according to the director's choice without obscuring the generic foundations. There is scope within Shakespeare's fable for 'repetition *and variation*', with the latter usually reflecting a preoccupation of the age in which the film happens to be made. As Deborah Cartmell points out, Zeffirelli accentuates 'the distance between old and young', 'the generation gap' created in part by the baby boomers after the Second World War, which was such a publicly discussed issue in the 1960s.[6] Meanwhile, as Barbara Hodgdon argues, Luhrmann's version largely downplays this aspect and instead locates the conflict between a world of unfeeling capital and business, exposing the social alienation of the lovers, 'their desire for a private universe', an interior space where emotions can be expressed with trust, and where the ethic of consumption driving 'global capitalism' is excluded.[7]

Wherever film has gone, so has *Romeo and Juliet*. Eddie Sammons in *Shakespeare: A Hundred Years on Film* describes over eighty versions ranging well beyond English-speaking nations to almost every country on earth, especially India and also including Italy and France (both with several silent versions), Spain, Denmark, Germany, Argentina, Belgium, Switzerland (*Romeo und Julia auf dem Dorf* (1941)), Poland (*Romeo i Julieta* (1937)), Mexico, Egypt, Russia, Mali, Bulgaria, the Netherlands, and Japan.[8] Sammons's list is certainly selective and has been augmented by films from at least Singapore, Czechoslovakia, Greece (*Agapi kai amai* (1968)), Yugoslavia, and Wales. Entries by Courtney Lehman and Douglas Lanier in Richard Burt's two-volume *Shakespeares after Shakespeare* repeat and add to the growing list of adaptations and offshoots.[9] It also makes its way unannounced into many movies. A recent example is the commercially successful 'Twilight saga' based on a series of books aimed at teenagers. Not only does the relationship between the outsider, 'white vampire' figures of Bella and Edward bear resemblance to Romeo and Juliet's, but also in *New Moon* (2009) they actually watch a version of Shakespeare's play that is on their college syllabus. Beyond these examples rears a further mountain of movies where the genre has been absorbed less explicitly, perhaps less consciously, and adapted into superficially unrelated narratives and settings. So deeply has it entered our culture that it has shaped tacitly held preconceptions, even among those who know nothing about Shakespeare, about a certain kind of impulsive, doomed young love.

Whereas in dealing with the influence of other plays on film we see the reception of a generalised genre such as 'romantic comedy' or 'green world comedy', where incidents may be appropriated indiscriminately from several plays, in the case of *Romeo and Juliet* the actual narrative stands alone as the basis for movie plots, and it is still recognisable even when there is no reference by name made to Shakespeare or his play. In this case, even though Shakespeare himself was not original but was basing his play on sources, it is undoubtedly his play's influence alone that has made such an impact on film history. Nobody to my knowledge has ever attributed the recurrence of the Romeo and Juliet tragedy in popular films to the celebrity of Arthur Brooke's *The Tragicall Historye of Romeus and Juliet* or William Painter's *The Palace of Pleasure*, let alone Matteo Bandello's *Giulietta e Romeo*, or, for that matter, 'Pyramus and Thisbe'. It is unequivocally Shakespeare's *Romeo and Juliet* that has entered popular consciousness at all levels of cultural production and consumption. Partly this is attributable to the poetry he adds to the story, so that a whole film can be largely structured, as is Luhrmann's *Romeo + Juliet* (1996), around even one memorable passage spoken by Juliet:

> Give me my Romeo, and when I [he?] shall die
> Take him and cut him out in little stars,
> And he will make the face of heaven so fine
> That all the world will be in love with night
> And pay no worship to the garish sun. (3.2.21–5)

More important even than the lyrical poetry inspired by love, however, is the basic story of 'star-cross'd lovers', who are opposed in their love by parental and traditional divisions that may represent disputes based on race, religion, ethnicity, or some other social or cultural difference. When such a story is filmed anywhere in the world it is marketed as a 'Romeo and Juliet story', even though the motivating contexts will be different. At least in this case it is not necessary to tiptoe reticently around the elusiveness of influence study, since the prime and virtually sole derivation of the generic essentials are from Shakespeare's play, and film adaptations of the play itself become the clear stepping stones leading in unexpected but undeniable directions all around the world. In this chapter I shall also be giving full force to my subtitle 'A Study in Genre and Influence', since here we can observe most clearly not only the ways in which Shakespeare's genre feeds in to modern movies but also how, by giving the play a new time and new circumstances, the movies can illuminate potential in Shakespeare's text that may have waited centuries to emerge.

Some plays seem to have a special affinity with a particular nation. *King Lear* has been filmed as the brooding soul of Russia in Kotsintsev's version and in *King Lear of the Steppes*; *Hamlet* has been a special favourite for German critics and film-makers; *Macbeth* has been refashioned by Kurosawa to embody the spirit of samurai in Japan. Even the French, who usually remain culturally aloof from English writers and have had an historically ambiguous attitude to Shakespeare, internalised *Othello* in their greatest film, *Les Enfants du Paradis*, perhaps because 'crime of passion' was considered a stronger legal defence in France than elsewhere. (There is a French version of *Romeo and Juliet* that includes scenes from the play as an integral inset, André Cayatte's *Les Amants de Vérona* (1949), but it seems to reflect a condescending attitude towards the hectic Italian race.) However, *Romeo and Juliet* is a play that seems to be transportable to almost any time and place, and subjected to apparently infinite localisation and recontextualisation. It is so recognisable that the play itself can be taken for granted and alluded to as an inset to the main plot. Given the ubiquitous success of his plays translated, adapted, and forcibly shoehorned into films in all countries during the twentieth century, it is easy to see Shakespeare as a writer who springs up in a host of countries around the world, rather than belonging to the English, and *Romeo and Juliet* is the one play that can be and has been adapted through film into virtually every culture.

Ironically the British themselves, while not disowning the play, at least have not always warmed to it as much as other nations. The stern Scotsman A. C. Bradley excludes *Romeo and Juliet* from his study of

Shakespeare's tragedies, because he had in mind a definite prototype dwelling on the fall of the flawed great man. It is more surprising that some neglect has been evident among the most English famous actors, perhaps indicative of a distaste for emotional expressiveness usually ascribed to those living in Mediterranean climes. David Garrick, the great eighteenth-century actor, played Romeo often, but only in his own adaptation that cut out much of the rhyming poetry – he clearly believed non-rhyming iambic pentameters to be the true mode of poetic drama. John Philip Kemble played Romeo only a few times, and his famous sister Sarah Siddons played Juliet only once. The greatest of them all, Edmund Kean, tried Romeo and failed. The great tragic actors, if they condescended to perform in the play at all, preferred Mercutio's role, presumably because it gave them a memorable death scene and one of the best lines in the play, 'A plague o' both your houses' (3.1.106), and in the days after doubling was practised it allowed them to slip away to the tavern early. Some of the great female actors embraced the role of Juliet, yet directors have often tried new, young, and unknown talent on debuts. The most memorable performances by women were actually in the role of Romeo – Charlotte Cushman, Ellen Tree, and Priscilla Horton among them. Although the play has been perennially popular on the stage, it has been seen more as an ensemble piece or a play for young, undiscovered actors to lift off into more conventionally 'great' character portrayals, and it is perhaps more popular in schools and amateur groups than among professionals. Generally speaking, the feeling is that *Romeo and Juliet* is not an 'English' play, and it is hard to think of a screen version from that country, successful or not (unless *Gnomeo and Juliet* (2011) can be counted). The summer in London in 1595 when it was probably first performed (alongside *A Midsummer Night's Dream*) was unusually warm, and there is a tacit sense that it belongs more comfortably in its latinate setting in Verona, or in other places where feelings run hot and public conflict is to be expected. Where it has found its twentieth-century forte is in the international medium, cinema, and here the proof is palpable. Among the first silent film adaptations, one was made in Italy in 1908, in 1911 another version – unusually long for the time – came from Film d'Arte Italiana, and in 1912 a version called *Indian Romeo and Juliet* was made in America, in which the 'Indian' reference is to Native Americans.[10] Of the four most memorable film versions, two are from Italian directors (Castellani and Zeffirelli), one from an American (Cukor), and one from an Australian (Luhrmann).[11]

As a related point, it is noteworthy that the play has always had an intimate connection with music, and this tradition also hails from the European continent rather than Britain. Peter Conrad has entertainingly traced adaptations into operas by Bellini, Keller, Delius, and Gounod, into a dramatic symphony by Berlioz, a 'fantasy overture' by Tchaikovsky, and the famous ballet by Prokofiev.[12] Contributing to a musical genre especially associated with Italy and Germany, the palpable presence of the idea of *Romeo and Juliet*'s star-crossed lovers lies in a pervasive way behind Verdi's *La Traviata* and Wagner's *Tristan und Isolde*, and it is referenced in many modern popular songs, those by Dire Straits (a rare and beautiful English contribution) and Lou Reed among the most well known. The theme music for Zeffirelli's movie, composed by Nino Rota, was top of various hit parades in 1968. *Romeo and Juliet* was also made into an Off-Broadway musical in 1970, *Sensations*. There has been at least one full-scale film musical version, *West Side Story*, in which Leonard Bernstein's musical score is the most memorable and impressive facet. From our point of view, one of the film's themes is the conflict between the Spanish-derived personality and the Anglo-Saxon, in New York as a city of immigrants. Irene Dash has emphasised the historical moment when the original musical was staged, suggesting that dividing society and countries into polarised enemies was a conscious political strategy during the Cold War in the 1950s: 'the culture of fear, distrust, bias and conflict' is clearly and strongly condemned not only in some of the songs but in the overall thematic structure.[13] Luhrmann's film launched songs that topped the charts.

In fact, if some person were unaware of its existence as a play by Shakespeare, she or he could be forgiven for thinking that *Romeo and Juliet* is in essence a musical. Although pulling against the play's emphasis on poetic language, this conclusion is not entirely surprising, since the most insistent subject of popular music composed for the mass consumption of adolescents in modern times has been melancholy love, just as it was a favoured theme of madrigals in the Renaissance. Music was in earlier periods associated with Orpheus and sometimes deemed to be therapeutic or healing in its overt aim of achieving harmony, but it was also often connected with 'mania', loss of control of the rational faculties under the spell of overwhelming emotion amounting to the feeling of possession and loss of soul – the 'twin narcissism' of modern psychoanalysis, mania, and the mass hysteria generated at some popular concerts.[14] Walter Pater may have been too sweeping in saying that 'all art aspires to the condition of music', but in the case of the play *Romeo and Juliet* he seems to have a point.

Films are made to reflect their times in order that their topicality may find a sizeable audience, preferably on many continents and among many age groups. Film is also an expensive medium: an average commercial feature film requires investment of about $50 million, preferably more. Financial backers want their money back with profits, so directors must have not only a tried and proven formula but also variations that precisely target a specific, predictable, and large group audience. Shakespeare's bare narrative of *Romeo and Juliet* provides the formula, and its name (and his) give an aura of traditional approval and educational worthiness, as well as conveying the excitement of young love.

However, in the numerous silent versions of *Romeo and Juliet* on screen, the play was often treated irreverently as burlesque. Robert Hamilton Ball traces the deliberately hilarious treatments:

> There was ... considerable filching of Shakespeare's good name in the [First World] War years, almost entirely for comic purposes. What would the film makers have done without *Romeo and Juliet*? The lovers were neither star-crossed nor piteously overthrown. There were at least nineteen short films that touched, however vaguely, on Shakespeare's play; eighteen of them were American. Sometimes the heroine's name was not Juliet, as in *Ethel's Romeo* or *Martha's Romeo*. The first was a one-reel farce which had no other discernible relationship to Shakespeare; the second, a boarding-house comedy in which an actor assumes Romeo's garb and climbs to a window to woo the cook ... In *A Seashore Romeo* the hero overcomes the opposition of his sweetheart's father by apparently saving her from drowning; in *A Prairie Romeo*, Billy Bones, a lovable old drunkard, serenades his love at her window and has potato peelings dumped on his head. There was *A Roaming Romeo* and *A Reckless Romeo*, and, to change the point of view, *Roping her Romeo*, with glance at a balcony scene in the first ... A review by Margaret I. MacDonald in the *Moving Picture World* of November 24, 1917, is headed: 'Prominent Sculptor in Film. Helena Smith Dayton Appears on the Screen Introducing an Animated Clay Figure Production of *Romeo and Juliet* Fashioned by Her Hand.' ... Another kind of animation was a split-reel cartoon film called *Romiet and Julio* but this was about a couple of cats.[15]

Did Tom Stoppard know about *Ethel's Romeo* when he hypothesised *Romeo and Ethel the Pirate's Daughter* in the more recent *Shakespeare in Love* (1998)? In the latter, Shakespeare wrestles with his new conception for a play called 'Ethel and the Pirate's Daughter' and he is finally put right by Marlowe who suggests the basis for *Romeo and Juliet* instead, which also has the functional echo of a play-within-a-play in the main plot in reflecting Shakespeare's amatory predicament. (The ploy of creatively 'interfering' with Shakespeare's compositional process is used elsewhere in the time-bending *Time Flies* (1944), which may well have been a source for the better-known and clever episode of *Doctor Who* entitled 'The Shakespeare Code' (aired on British television on 7 April 2007).) At least we can conclude that in the early stages of cinema history, Shakespeare's name was not considered so sacred that his plays could not be affectionately sent up in the nickelodeons in which cinema began its life, and the odd, silent versions are early evidence of a recognisable 'Romeo-and-Juliet genre' that could be presupposed as within the audience's repertoire.

There are many strange versions, such as openly pornographic appropriations like the Swedish *The Secret Sex Lives of Juliet* and *Romeo and Juliet II*; the 1990s 'grunge' version, *Tromeo and Juliet*; and the loose adaptation, *Romeo Must Die* (1994), which owes its style to Hong Kong cinema, gangster movies, hip-hop, and kung fu. Many films that are loosely based on *Romeo and Juliet* do not declare the origin in their titles: for example, *Fire with Fire* (USA, 1986), in which Lisa is a Catholic schoolgirl and Joe a juvenile offender in a boot camp, and *The Punk and the Princess* (Australia, 1993), based on love between a rich girl and a street boy. *Lost and Delirious* (2001) is a rather disjointed and even hysterical Canadian film made for television. Set in a college, it foregrounds an emotionally disturbed female student who compulsively identifies with Shakespeare's characters. It contains much overt Shakespearean material, especially from *Twelfth Night* ('I will build me a willow cabin ...'), and there emerges in microcosm a lesbian version of *Romeo and Juliet*. In its depiction of adolescent passion and isolation the movie dwells on love (the topic for discussion in class) as something socially alienating but capable of giving immortalising longings: 'once you are up there, looking down on everybody else, you are there forever'. Accordingly, the 'heroine' follows her death wish by jumping from the roof of the school building in an act of ecstatic suicide. Such films hail from all over the world, and their existence proves that the feelings represented in Shakespeare's play can be localised to suit any city or country divided by ethnic, dynastic, or religious factors, where young lovers will be caught in the crossfire. There have been staged performances from Belfast in Northern Ireland (C21 Theatre Company) and a documentary made by a Canadian director and filmed in Bosnia and Herzegovina, *Romeo and Juliet in Sarajevo* (1994), to name but two out of many set in civil wars. As the play says, a rose by any other name would smell as sweet, and no matter where they are placed or whatever they are named, they remain Romeo and Juliet.

Landmark versions

Four adaptations in particular helped to establish *Romeo and Juliet* in the panoply of Hollywood classics, and to lay down the bases of a genre of cinematic romantic tragedy. Issues of age, or rather youth, are at the heart of the genre. Of these three major cinematic adaptations using Shakespeare's text, two at least positively changed youth consciousness in their respective eras, while the other at least reflected its audience to some extent even while shifting the emphasis away from youth. In 1936 George Cukor cast on the basis of star quality actors who, even at the time, were considered too old for the roles: Trevor Howard (aged thirty-nine) as Romeo, Norma Shearer (aged thirty-six) as Juliet, John Barrymore (aged fifty-four) as Mercutio, and Basil Rathbone (aged forty-two) as Tybalt. Presumably the film was made for audiences over thirty, the generation with enough money to go to the cinema during the Depression, and they would no doubt have been comforted to feel that age did not wither them nor custom stale their infinite variety since they were not precluded from identifying with youthful passion. But still, the fact that reviewers were critical demonstrated that Shakespeare's play turns on contrasts between the young characters and the older, the Friar and Nurse as much as the Montague and Capulet parents. The set was lavish, again reflecting the taste of movie-goers encouraged by film escapism to aspire to wealthy lifestyles: 'At enormous expense an entire replica, based on first-hand photographs, of an Italian Renaissance city was constructed on a Hollywood back lot ... The Capulet ballroom scene rivalled a Busby Berkeley musical extravaganza.'[16] Despite superficial visual references to Italy, the film is overwhelmingly within a British or Anglo-American tradition of acting and conceiving Shakespeare. An American academic, Professor Strunk from Cornell University, was employed to ensure the text was scrupulously Shakespeare's, and at 126 minutes' length (including credits) it is almost exactly the 'two-hours' traffic of our stage' described by the Prologue. There may not be any direct evidence of the political and economic background of the Depression and anxiety about Nazi Germany, but those contexts are still relevant insofar as film in the 1930s could release people from their fears and anxieties.[17] The sumptuous wealth of the ballroom scene and emotional projection into the personal tragedy of young lovers could transport and divert audiences away from everyday concerns into what they saw as more universal emotional crises – and this is the function given to 'Shakespeare' at the time in the theatre and on film. The film initiated some ideas that were to become conventions for later adaptations. Barrymore's Mercutio as the older, rakish figure with a touch of gay decadence became Zeffirelli's John McEnery, also conspicuously older than Romeo. He is even more of an emaciated roué than Barrymore, and carries a quite explicit air of the lover abandoned for women by Romeo. By the time of Luhrmann's version, Mercutio has become ostentatiously transsexual, black, and takes the drug ecstasy. Another evolving filmic convention can be seen at the beginning of each film. The 1936 version shows credits over a mock Renaissance map of Verona; *West Side Story* has credits over a long helicopter view of the 'Hell's Kitchen' area on the West Side of Manhattan; which Luhrmann has telescoped into a dizzying and deafening few seconds of a helicopter apparently about to crash into the high-rise part of the city whose skyscape is marked by two office towers on the West Side of Manhattan, specifically billboarded as the companies of Montague and Capulet respectively. The larger meaning of this repeated choreography of the camera may be that the tragedy of Romeo and Juliet is being played out in many households in any city, and that they are examples of a trend rather than isolated victims.

One film version that, in hindsight, looks rather tame and old-fashioned was in its time innovative, and pointed to the future. Renato Castellani in 1954 directed *Romeo and Juliet* with the kind of close attention to outdoor, visual detail that would mark Zeffirelli's movie. Whereas previous versions had used sets elaborately built for the occasion, Castellani filmed on location in Italy and produced a work that has been described as 'extraordinarily rich and voluptuous, photographed in the golden remnants of the High Renaissance in Verona, Venice, and Siena, and with costumes by Leonor Fini that are derived from works of art by Piero della Francesca, Pisanello, Carpaccio, and Fiorenzo di Lorenzo'.[18] Chiaroscuro, picking up on the many references to light and dark in the play, marks the interior and night-time scenes, bright whites the external and daytime. As well as carrying these quintessentially Italian, painterly references, the outdoor setting brings burgeoning nature to the fore, not just as a visual spectacle but as a symbol for the young lovers' relationship to natural forces. It is a shame that technical advances in colour make Technicolor, so magically realistic in the 1950s, now seem pastel and watery. The casting was designed to appeal to a much younger audience, although John Gielgud frames the action as a mature Chorus, recalling older acting traditions, and Flora Robson, the great English character actress, is an elderly, fussy Nurse. In casting the lovers, Castellani was very different from Cukor. Laurence Harvey (twenty-six at the time) as Romeo was in the same year the lead actor in the evocatively titled *The Good Die Young* (1954) and was to become associated with the ambitious, 'angry young man' stereotype in *Room at the Top* (1959) and *Life at the Top* (1965), a fact that makes a point about the social ostracism of the lovers. He was packaged as the English version of James Dean. Susan Shentall, aged twenty, was the youngest Juliet to that date, and as a non-professional actor she was expected to convey innocence and some naivety. The choices demonstrate how casting is significant in creating a general reading of the play, although at the same time the very Englishness of the actors and the restrained traditions they work from pull against the Mediterranean light that threatens to overwhelm them. On the other hand, it is impossible for us not to see with hindsight, and the film appears slow and under-acted only because the later versions are so hyperactive. In its own right Castellani's film is wonderfully sensual, colourful, and sumptuous, in ways that his fellow Italian, Zeffirelli, clearly developed.

By the 1960s a new function was given to Shakespeare in films. He could galvanise hearts and minds to comment on events of the time when the film was made, and rectify social injustices. In the words of a very influential book's title, he became 'Shakespeare our Contemporary'.[19] Two quite remarkable adaptations of *Romeo and Juliet* in that decade illustrate the capacity of his texts to be aligned with a social conscience and progressive politics. One of these, *West Side Story* (1961), capitalised on the way the underlying generic aspects can be adapted to changing places and times, and will be dealt with in the next section. The second is Franco Zeffirelli's *Romeo and Juliet*, which he first directed on the stage and later turned into a film. This was released in 1968 at the height of the 1960s youth revolution, student unrest, 'flower power', and calls for sexual freedom. He cast actors of seventeen (Leonard Whiting, with Beatles haircut) and fifteen (Olivia Hussey), and clearly angled his film at teenagers, the first wave who already had commercial power and media glamour. The great debates of the times from their point of view were being misunderstood by parents; the issue of twenty-year-old youths in some countries who did not even have the vote being conscripted to fight a war in Vietnam created and perpetuated by their parents; and the emergence of a new ethic encapsulated in the phrase 'make love not war'. Zeffirelli consciously draws on these debates, invariably intervening on the side of youth, and he makes the tragedy turn on the fact that family conflict reflects inter-generational tension between teenagers and their corrupted parents' generation. The film is perhaps the most didactic of the various versions: the lovers are seen as genuinely innocent victims, whose poignant deaths lead to ending the family feud. 'Make love not war' could stand as an epigram for the film, and Mercutio's cry, 'a curse on both your families', in his unforgettable death scene, rings out as a rejection of society. In his film, Zeffirelli vigorously takes Shakespeare out of the hands of traditionalists, and turns the play into a genuine film. One of the surprising effects, in the light of Hussey's tender years, is that she is directed in such a way that Juliet seems to age and mature from a sparkling child to a prematurely experienced and tragic young woman. Whiting's Romeo, on the other hand, does not seem to move emotionally. The exquisitely photographed film (by Pasqualino de Santis, who won an Oscar) constantly places the young characters in relation to lush vegetation, aligning them with nature in a way that is a far cry from the deliberately sterile urban setting of Luhrmann's 1990s film. The guiding spirit is voluptuously Verdi, and Italian opera in general, which Zeffirelli had directed on film, and the haunting musical score by Nino Rota can still raise a surreptitious tear on the age-ravaged cheeks of those who were fifty-something in the mid-1990s. Their children may have generally been unmoved, because in 1996 they had their own *Romeo and Juliet*, made especially for 'Generation X'.

Between 1968 and 1996, two watershed dates, there were no fewer than seven *Romeo and Juliet*s on film, but none so influential as those described. A cartoon version appeared in 1992, and it captures an essence of the play for very young audiences – a contemporary equivalent of Charles and Mary Lamb's *Tales from Shakespeare*. The Stratford Festival stage production was filmed in 1993, and in 1994 Thames Television in Britain produced an understated but effective version for television. In a dignified concession to passing time, the actress Jenny Agutter, remembered by many as a schoolgirl in both *The Railway Children* (1967) and Nicholas Roeg's *Walkabout* (1971), now plays Juliet's mother, and in matronly fashion abandons the field of youth to an unspectacular Geraldine Somerville and Jonathan Firth.

A colleague of Luhrmann hired his old tutor at the University of Newcastle in Australia to advise him in making *Romeo + Juliet* (1996), an opportunity that must be the secret fantasy of all Shakespeare tutors. The version is as much of its time as the others, this time showing a 1990s youth subculture based on the availability of drugs and guns, idleness enforced by unemployment, a society marked by callous indifference to emotions, contrasted with eruptions of manufactured festivity and spectacle like a Michael Jackson concert. The vision adds up to a nihilism of the senses that is set against, and ultimately caused by, profiteering multinational corporations (the families of the play are companies in the movie), seedy urban decay (Verona Beach looks like an abandoned film set), and the frustrations of a neglected generation. In some way each of the groupings is racially liminal. The Capulets are Latin American, the Montagues are Irish American, Mercutio and the Prince both black, and the setting is represented as a crucible of ethnic and class tension as befits Miami Beach, which is both playground for the rich and first port of call for Cuban refugees. In such an array of marginal groups, 'the centre does not hold', and indeed the film intentionally shows a society devoid of shared, community assumptions. There seems in the film, as presumably in its target audience, to be a confused yearning for religious symbolism but no spiritual heart, and the final scene in the church (a cathedral rather than a chapel, let alone a crypt), full of candles, flowers, and operatic music, evokes the music of the pop star Madonna, with its unique mixture of religiosity and eroticism. Here, the older generation is cynical, wilfully unaware of the consequences of their feuds, and literally beyond the law because they hide behind their alienated status of corporations. Romeo and Juliet are victims not only of an uncaring society and their own divided generation, but of the insatiable greed of news moguls who exploit 'human interest' stories such as teenage suicide – their narrative is framed in a typically disposable television news story. In its way Luhrmann's film is as morally based as Zeffirelli's, but because the picture it gives of society is so bleakly negative, and the watery moments of love between Romeo and Juliet are so rare, brief and hurried, the film tends to confirm a 'no hope' reading. The lovers die bewildered and frightened, and it seems that their fate matters to nobody, except as a quickly forgotten news item.

As a symptomatic issue, it is hard entirely to reconcile the film's general anti-consumerist ethic with the 'hard-sell' marketing of the film by Fox Studios as a commodity, with its CD music, interactive CD ROM, official and unofficial websites, overpowering advertising, and so on. These aspects of the film, together with its eclecticism of settings, costumes, and cultural groupings, its juxtapositioning of glamour, stylishness, and seediness, perhaps justify the use of that overused word 'postmodern', and make the film a genuine symptom of a generation's anxieties.[20] Of course, the other current mantra-word, 'globalisation', is an aim of the film in its search for the largest international audience possible. Glimpses of localisation are erased: Tybalt is killed under a crumbling edifice that again looks most like a crumbling film set, while Juliet lives in what could easily be an international airport hotel, complete with its private swimming pool. The Italian Mediterranean is only one of many contexts in a cultural melange whose reference is more to media conventions than to geographical locations.

The music in this film, in particular, seems to have haunted at least two star-crossed adolescent youths: one of them committed suicide in Australia, and the music CD of the soundtrack was found beside his body; and later, in America, a teenager who shot his parents and then massacred fellow students at school was obsessed with the music. It is very hard to imagine that either Castellani's or Zeffirelli's films would provoke such responses. When Luhrmann's film was first released a bishop in England prophesied that it would be an inducement to teenage suicide, and we all scoffed at the time, but subsequent tragic events such as these should sober us all into rational discussion of the issue. It is hard to blame Shakespeare's text, since Luhrmann's film uses only

50 per cent of it, and besides, there are enough checks and balances through wary internal commentators to suggest that Shakespeare gives us a wider perspective. It is surely something to do with the music, which is popular culture's instant access to emotion not rooted in reality, and to the way the director links music with impossible aspirations on the one hand and social despair on the other. But in the end even the director is simply filtering the culture around, and the real fault-line seems to be that very culture itself, where innocence, realistic optimism, and fresh hope are hard to find. In an almost terrible sense, the play's own 'moral' is vindicated: 'All are punish'd'.

The climax of Luhrmann's film, with its circling paramilitaries, helicopters, and journalists outside the cathedral, while within its hushed and sacred space a joint suicide for love is played out to the strains of Wagner's music from *Tristan und Isolde*, makes another point about intertextuality. Versions of *Romeo and Juliet*, whether played on film or stage or written about in pages of criticism, all work within certain conventions of their own. In this case, we find multi-layered references to familiar tropes, from romantic opera to films like *Bonnie and Clyde*, numerous romantic thrillers, and the nightly televising of real-life 'hostage sieges' – products of the American media imprint that all but efface Shakespeare's Italian setting. The points that emerge are corollaries: first, the inescapable influence of Hollywood conventions on contemporary versions of the play, and second, more intriguingly, the pervasive influence of Shakespeare's play on Hollywood romantic tragedy. In *Romeo and Juliet* he has forged from an earlier and unpromising source a true myth, the narrative of doomed young love, love in the face of parental disapproval or family/social/ethnic conflict, which has embedded itself so deeply in our culture that we accept it as 'natural' and literally cannot see beyond its parameters. The enduring and subtle cultural influence of the play as realised in these memorable film versions of the twentieth century not only proves that Shakespeare has always been a writer who aimed at popular audiences, but also unnervingly suggests that he may have contributed to every generation's version of its own popular culture, and even modern conceptions of love itself.

Out of America

The regular features of the 'Romeo-and-Juliet genre', as they have emerged from the major cinematic productions, can be summarised. Two groups or factions representing an older generation are public enemies, whether on grounds of family rivalry, race, status, professional competition, prevailing civil war, or for no specified reason (as in Shakespeare's version, where nobody seems able to explain the origin of the feud). A young man and a young woman from each group respectively fall mutually in love. This may come after an unsatisfactory or unrequited affair (Romeo and Rosaline), but it is instantly recognised as 'the real thing'. Various character types fulfil certain roles that, in Shakespeare's play, equate to a confidante for the young woman (the Nurse) and a wooer acceptable to the family (Paris), a close friend of the young man (Mercutio) who is accidentally killed as a consequence of the feud and his foil, a young enemy (Tybalt) who is murdered by the Romeo figure, and an elderly go-between (the Friar) who offers worldly cautions but generally supports the young lovers. The young lovers finally die as a result either of a series of tragic accidents or destiny depending on one's reading of the play, and there are educative recriminations among the warring factions that may lead to chastened reconciliation. This blueprint has proved apparently endlessly translatable into new film versions, though each will differ significantly from the prototype, in terms either of the specific time and place in which the film is set and made, or following the particular exigencies of the new plot. Some films have a 'strong' resemblance to *Romeo and Juliet* in containing all or most of these ingredients, while others have a relatively 'weak' relationship, ranging from full-blown tragedy through to satirical, comic, and even happy endings. The unstated but obvious presence of the 'Romeo-and-Juliet genre' in popular films aimed at children, most obviously *The Lion King 2: Simba's Pride* (1998), and predictably at adolescents, such as at least elements in *Twilight* (2008), shows that the influence is not necessarily restricted to particular age groups and audiences, although there is some understandable targeting of youth and college students since they are quite likely to study the play at some stage. The main thing that emerges from less obvious adaptations is a transcultural diversity to which we now turn.

West Side Story (1961) is a Hollywood musical directed by Jerome Robbins and Robert Wise. Transferred from the Broadway stage, it employs no lines from Shakespeare, though it is clearly based on his play. Instead of setting the lovers against warring families, a context that is all but non-existent in this movie, it places them in the context of youthful violent gang warfare in the slums of New York, and draws on fears of out-of-control teenage delinquency. The emphasis is not on generational gap but racial and cultural difference. The Capulets are a Puerto Rican gang called the Sharks who are clearly set up as embodying for an American audience a stereotyped 'latin' vitality and unpredictability and warm-heartedness that can erupt into violence. The Montagues are white

American 'Anglos', the Jets. This version trusts Shakespeare's narrative but not his language, as if that language would falsify the social realist emphasis. Unlike earlier versions, the film demystifies Shakespeare in order to focus the narrative on contemporary social problems. It reflects the contemporary preoccupation with street hoodlums, anarchic youth violence, gang warfare, popular music, and youth rebellion (James Dean, Elvis Presley). Also reflecting pervading fears in the 1950s, the violence is perceived partly as the result of failures of society and their absent parents to restrain and control (or even care – the only older people we see are the bigoted policeman and the isolated 'Doc' in the drugstore whose role approximates Shakespeare's Friar's). Surrounded by corrupt police, urban decay, and racial hatred between immigrant populations, youth is not integrated into the complacently idealistic dream of 'free America'. Tony, Maria, and Bernardo (Romeo, Juliet, and Tybalt respectively) are seen as casualties of these unresolved and uncontrolled tensions, a legacy of history, and it is interesting that Bernardo emerges as equal to the lovers in his victim status. The problems are seen not as family ones, but racial, social, and political, amounting to a national failure. By the end the gangs become dimly aware through the genuinely touching death of Tony (Maria does not die but survives to voice the sense of injustice) that their real enemies are defined by prejudices based on race and class. But undoubtedly the most memorable aspects of *West Side Story* are Jerome Robbins' dance choreography and Leonard Bernstein's musical score with lyrics by a young Stephen Sondheim, which generated hit after hit, including 'Maria', 'America', 'Tonight', 'There's a Place for Us', and 'I Feel Pretty'. Costing about $6 million, *West Side Story* went on to rival *My Fair Lady* (1964), *The Sound of Music*, *Mary Poppins* (1964), and *Grease* (1978) as one of the most popular film musicals in history. A direct transposition of *West Side Story* onto the Bollywood screen in India came in Mansoor Khan's *Josh* (2000), where the setting is Goa.

In the wake of *West Side Story*, *Romeo and Juliet* in an American city (often New York) became something of a niche sub-genre of films that use Shakespeare's story to explore ethnic and racial differences in an urban, potentially violent setting. There is *China Girl* (1987), which also depicts the lovers caught up in gang warfare, this time between youth from the community of Little Italy, which is shrinking in population, and the new Chinese immigrants in an expanding Chinatown. In *David and Layla* (USA, 2005), marketed as 'inspired by a true story', inter-racial and family tensions enmesh the lovers, David, a French Jew, and Layla, a Muslim refugee. The families fiercely oppose the liaison on mainly religious grounds, and Layla, an 'exotic' dancer, when faced with deportation must choose between her 'Paris' favoured by the family, a

Muslim-American from Kurdistan, and her 'Romeo', David. The clash between these two religions has always been an issue in New York, known as a city closely identified with its large Jewish community, and has become more tragically potent after 9/11 in 2001. What the lovers discover is that their mutual attraction is based not only on bodies and personalities but on the rich and ancient history they share through their respective cultures – just as, to some extent, in *Romeo and Juliet* the very thing that draws them together is what stands in their way, as Juliet recognises and laments to her Nurse:

> My only love sprung from my only hate!
> Too early seen unknown, and known too late!
> Prodigious birth of love it is to me
> That I must love a loathèd enemy. (1.5.137–40)

To David's boast that without the Jewish Einstein there would be no Microsoft, Layla retorts that the Arabs invented algebra and the number zero a thousand years before the West – without them, she points out, there would be no Einstein. 'Love your differences and enjoy life' is David's cryptic summary as he proposes to her. His love initially does not extend to converting to Islam as she suggests. He does so and the film shies away from Shakespeare's tragedy and is instead a 'feel-good' comedy, although the issues of cultural difference raised are more serious and potentially deadly than those in another New York comedy based on *Romeo and Juliet*, *Love Is All There Is*.

Love Is All There Is (made in 1994, released in 1996) appeared in cinemas in the same year as Luhrmann's *Romeo + Juliet*, but its conspicuously low budget, directors known for their comedies about marriage (Joseph Bologna and Renée Taylor), and self-consciously parodic style all sidelined it into well-deserved cult status rather than box-office success. The premise is a long-standing feud between two very different food catering businesses in a very Italian-American community in the Bronx on Coney Island, the Sicilian 'Prince Rosario Catering' run by the Capomezzo family, specialising in jumbo portions of hot and spicy food, and the Malacici's 'Royal House of Florence', which presents north Italian cuisine and prides itself on 'dainty, low fat, pastel colours, subtle flavours'. The styles of food as much as the respective restaurants' ethos and family homes mirror a stark class division between working and upper-middle classes. There is 'bad blood' between the families because they have been competing for the same clientele, and early on Shakespeare's name is invoked: 'Shakespeare once said "what's in a name?" but he was wrong 'cos Cappamezzo means half a head and Malacici means bad beans ...'; *King Lear* also does not escape parody: 'See, nuttin' from nuttin'. Let's go to bed'. To emphasise the connection with *Romeo and Juliet*, the central event is a production for a church charity of this very play in which Romeo is played by Rosario Capomezzo (Nathaniel Marston) and, after a false start in casting, Juliet comes to be played by the sixteen-year-old, sheltered, and rich daughter Regina or Gina Malacici, played in turn by none other than a fleshly young Angelina Jolie with a gloriously thick Italian accent. Not surprisingly, they fall in love literally on the stage in the middle of a performance, revealing the young man's increasingly tumescent 'dingle' to his horrified relatives. There follows a satirical version of the balcony scene that leads to sexual consummation intruded upon by his parents. On his side, the subsequent elopement is carried out as a filial rebellion against his controlling mother – 'this Romeo is a mother's boy', and he pleads, 'Ma, do you want me to be happy and live, or miserable and die?', to which she replies, 'These are my only choices?' Meanwhile, Regina is also trying to break away from her indulgent but emotionally stifling parents, whose hope is that their daughter will go to Paris to study music – 'Paris' in the geographical sense becomes the Paris of Shakespeare's play, the parental choice of a future commitment. The 'elopement' leads the lovers no further than a garden shed in which they are almost asphyxiated by fumes, which looks like precipitating the tragic catastrophe of Shakespeare's ending. However, confirming one mother's plea, 'Please don't turn this into a tragedy. It's a comedy. Look, I'm laughing …', they are saved in the nick of time by both sets of parents. They in turn are so relieved that they drop their feud and approve the marriage, after which a banquet is announced by the priest with the words, 'As Shakespeare would say, may the merry farce begin'. The riddling mantra phrase given by a spurious but effective fortune-teller is the paradox, 'Love is all there is. Love is not enough', and the solution seems to lie in the priest's finale: 'Turn business rivals into firm friends' – the amicable compromise. As a film *Love Is All There Is* is both charming and hilarious, and its success turns on 'localising' *Romeo and Juliet* into a specific ethnic context, which is presented as so laughable that it cannot be taken seriously and generically could never bear a tragic ending.

Another urban American *Romeo and Juliet*, this time set in Boston, is the unattributed adaptation *Love Story* (1970), and in this canon it is virtually an iconic tragic romance in filmic terms. As we saw in Chapter 3, the play is the most common Shakespearean reference when the subject of acting comes up, and the play has always been a mainstay for study in American colleges, an environment in which this film is partly set. This movie is based primarily on a novel by Erich Segal but the influence of *Romeo and Juliet* is implicit but obvious, and the movie draws out more clearly than others the potential for sentimentality in

Shakespeare's play. The family resistance to the love affair is based on social status and is not so much a feud as a matter of class prejudice. Oliver Barrett IV, Ollie for short (Ryan O'Neal), is a Harvard law student and a scion of a family so rich that the university's Barrett Building is named after them. Jennifer Cavalleri (Ali MacGraw) – 'no relative' to *Cavalleria Rusticana*, though the reference links her to music and the opera is about peasants – is a music student and daughter of a humble New York pastry cook. Her father holds no particular class antagonism but he does show religious prejudice as a Roman Catholic suspicious of the kind of WASP family Ollie comes from. The Barretts are ostentatiously classist and have a different girl lined up for their son. In an early moment reminiscent of Juliet's premonitions of disaster, but in this case delivered with a jokey fatalism, Jennifer predicts the affair cannot last, given their social differences:

> JENNIFER Come on, Ollie, don't be stupid, would you please, it's inevitable.
> OLIVER What is?
> JENNIFER That we're going to graduate and go our separate ways and that you're going to go on to law school.
> OLIVER What are you talking about?
> JENNIFER You're a preppy millionaire and I'm a social zero.

She sees her 'negative social status' as a prime cause for Ollie's interest and as a symptom of what she fears is short-lived, his rebellion against his disapproving father's money. The issue eats into their relationship, leading to mutual recriminations like her 'You're a heartless bastard' and his 'sometimes you are really a bitch'. The particular difference of wealth certainly causes impediments since Oliver's father (Ray Milland), who is implacably opposed to the liaison, disinherits his son, who is forced to choose between love on the one hand and future wealth and even professional status on the other, since he can no longer afford to pursue the law except with money from his father, which comes in a late moment. However, the final tragedy is not caused by family differences but – with a nod to the English *Love Story* (1944), which otherwise bears little resemblance – Jennifer acquires a fatal illness, which appears to be leukaemia but is not specified. Before this reveals itself, the lovers marry as in *Romeo and Juliet*, and Jennifer's father (John Marley) fills the role of Shakespeare's Friar in his reserved support. At the wedding the camera circles the lovers, placing them in a ring that seems almost a convention of straightforward filmed versions of Shakespeare's play deriving from the dance scene in the ballroom. The epithalamium comes not from Shakespeare but another literary source, and ironically from another 'Barrett' (again 'no relative'), Elizabeth Barrett Browning, and is clearly not only celebratory but premonitory and ominous, and seems to show the influence of *Romeo and Juliet* in its imagery and theme:

> When our two souls stand up erect and strong,
> Face to face, silent, drawing nigh and nigher,
> Until the lengthening wings break into fire
> At either curvèd point, – what bitter wrong
> Can the earth do to us, that we should not long
> Be here contented? Think! In mounting higher,
> The angels would press on us and aspire
> To drop some golden orb of perfect song
> Into our deep, dear silence. Let us stay
> Rather on earth, Belovèd, where the unfit
> Contrarious moods of men recoil away
> And isolate pure spirits, and permit
> A place to stand and love in for a day,
> With darkness and the death-hour rounding it.

The poem provides a subtext suggesting the love is too 'pure' for the earth with its 'Contrarious moods of men'. News of the impending death of Jennifer comes as the anticipated 'darkness and the death hour' rounding their brief and impoverished state of married bliss, and all the Hollywood stops are pulled out to milk the situation of its affective potential. The repeated refrain, 'Love is never saying you're sorry', provides a circuit breaker between Oliver and his father, who are reconciled through the dying heroine who had tried her hardest to heal the rift beforehand.

Hollywood's *Love Story* is still, admittedly, capable of stirring emotions, but in many ways it is also dated. The time is very clearly the late 1960s, which is established not only through clothes and music (which won an Oscar for Francis Lai and created at least one hit tune) but also contemporary references – 'She wants to bring home the troops by Christmas'. However, the inadvertent datedness of the movie is actually built into its structure in a purposeful way that once again leads back to Shakespeare. As in Zeffirelli's version, which had been widely acclaimed just two years earlier, the idea of a 'generation gap' between parents and children is emphatically central to the fable. Even the camerawork in its shots of Harvard and surrounding Boston repeatedly juxtaposes the old, ivy-clad buildings representing tradition and respectability, and modern skyscrapers and motorways looming up from the distance. Jennifer tellingly confronts her father, who is otherwise a 'modern' and enlightened figure in his personal tolerance, with bigotry when she upbraids him with 'It's a new world, Philip', met by his rather bitter riposte, 'Oh yes, it's new all right'. However, the younger generation does not get all the sympathy and the only actual quotation from Shakespeare, only vaguely spotted by the characters, is old Hamlet's Ghost's 'what a falling-off was there' as he laments his wife's behaviour after his death.

Love Story is a fairly typical Hollywood product in eliminating most complexities from *Romeo and Juliet* and building the narrative around its most emotionally affecting elements, highlighting not only the 'love story' itself and the pathos of Jennifer's death but also Oliver's rift with his father and the resulting financial and potentially career sacrifices – things that seem dear to the American heart, judging from other films. His own personal survival carries a hint that it is the reconciliation with his father and the presumed projection into a future where he will resume his profession, status, and inheritance that are the most important issues. Jennifer's death, as in *Romeo and Juliet*, is a catalyst for change and social stability, but this may suggest an unintended but palpable callousness on the part of the film, that it is her desire, posthumously achieved, to reconcile Oliver with his own father that is decisive, especially since she has already voiced a suspicion that Oliver's love for her is more of a rebellion against his father. The fact that her fatal illness is so veiled and unexplained subtly reinforces this reading. The crucial change from Shakespeare's play lies in the fact that only one figure actually dies, and not for love. This is not to deny the tear-jerking quality of the ending, but it qualifies significantly the driving motivation of 'all for love' and in a muted way returns to the moral that 'all are punish'd'.

World film

Made of much sterner stuff and revealing a strongly political potential in *Romeo and Juliet* is the dark, post-war film from Czechoslovakia, Jiří Weiss's *Romeo, Julia a tma* (1960), variously named in English *Romeo, Juliet and Darkness* and *Bright Light in a Dark Room*. The title itself picks its imagery and theme from Shakespeare's play, which, as Caroline Spurgeon pointed out as long ago as 1935, is full of references to light (especially associated with Juliet) and circumambient darkness:[21] 'O, she doth teach the torches to burn bright!' (1.5.43); 'The brightness of her cheek would shame those stars / As daylight doth a lamp' (2.1.61–2); 'not impute this yielding to light love, / Which the dark night hath so discoverèd' (2.1.146–7); 'More light and light, more dark and dark our woes' (3.5.36), and so on. In this grim movie the 'bright light' is the young Jewish woman, Hanka, while the 'dark room' is the attic in which she is hidden from the German Nazi occupiers by the young 'Prague boy', Pavel. The difference between Jew and Aryan is mentioned but is subsumed under the shared national victimhood of both – Hanka has temporarily avoided the train to the concentration camp, knowing none the less that 'They'll get me one day', while Pavel and his family and schoolmates are at the mercy of the German army. When news breaks of the assassination by the Czech underground of the governing officer, who was historically Reinhard Heydrich, there follows a brutal purging of the local populace, and in a stark final scene Hanka goes downstairs to give herself up and is shot dead off-screen. As in *Love Story*, the male lover survives, but the effect is utterly different, heightening the sense of political injustice running through the film rather than holding a sentimental colouring. Throughout the film, images and sounds carry the message of victimhood – the song of a caged bird is repeated at significant moments, a shy guinea pig with which Hanka comically identifies herself is hunted by a small dog owned by a collaborator, and the dog in turn is smothered to death by Pavel. Right at the beginning a child clings to a doll as she and her Jewish family must leave for the fateful train, and the girl innocently asks whether the family will return 'home' after their 'holiday'. All except the SS are, in some way or another, political victims, as Hanka realises: 'If they find me, they'll kill you, your mum, and all the innocent people', to which Pavel responds, 'You are innocent too!' As in Shakespeare, there are other victims. The conflict lies not inherently in the family nor between families but in the political situation in the Czech state, but problems do inevitably become internalised when Pavel's mother vehemently opposes sheltering the young woman. However, the mother herself is a victim since she is congenitally, and with good reason, anxious about the safety of her family. Resembling Shakespeare's Mercutio is Pavel's best friend, Vojta, who is taken away by the police just before Hanka is shot at the end; the fellow student Jan Bubenek, who is violently taken from the classroom because of suspicions surrounding his father; the smothered dog, or at least its treacherous drunken owner, fills the role of Tybalt who is part aggressor and part victim himself. In some ways the Friar's role is taken by Pavel's grandfather, an eccentric and senile man who obsessively rebuilds old clocks. While 'not wanting to know' he helps Pavel shelter Hanka, and with great courage tries to intervene at the end to save her life, without success. There is also a 'Rosaline' figure in Pavel's initial girlfriend from school, whom Hanka supplants in his affections. The film, which at first seems to owe only the motif of young love to *Romeo and Juliet*, reveals on closer inspection a surprising amount of coincidence with the play.

Standing for all the victims of the Nazi occupation of Czechoslovakia and state anti-Semitism, the boy and girl who gradually become lovers are the centre of attention and, as in other filmed versions, the camera circles them in their spell of emotional absorption in each other. They try imaginatively to escape from the situation represented by confinement in the small, dark attic-room. Their circling and slow dancing conjures up an outdoor scene with floating clouds, accompanied by flute music broken by an ominous drum-beat. At this stage sexual arousal leads to impulsive rejection and shame, emphasising the young ages of these figures and the fact that they are undergoing their own rites of passage into adulthood. Attempts at imaginative escape persist. Pavel's interest lies in astronomy and he speaks of the Proxima – twin stars, 'two stars revolving around the same centre of gravity' and image of their love. The only reason Hanka countenances belief in God is in her desire to escape: 'Sometimes I wish he existed. Perhaps he would nod at me and say "Come up to me, girl, they don't want you down there. Because you are Jewish …"'. Soft piano music plays as Pavel declares, 'I want you Hanka', to her 'I know', and they continue their theological musings:

– He doesn't exist anyway.
– How could he just watch, if he did?
– I'm happy you know so much.
– I'm happy you exist.
   [*they kiss*]
– We'll never part, Hanka.

In its quiet and understated way, in the light of the extreme danger confronting the characters, this film captures a pathos surrounding the isolated and markedly young and innocent figures in *Romeo and Juliet* that escapes Hollywood's *Love Story* and even many versions of the play itself. However, the movie focuses on a vision of hope in a future:

– We won't meet in the dark any more. We'll have plenty of light.
– No more silence any more. We'll sing and dance all day …

The arrival of screaming police cars at the end may have been Luhrmann's source. The invisible bird sings now ominously as the lovers speak their final duet:

– You have to live.
– In this world? It's not worth it. Not without you.
…
– There are woods, sun, and there's a river there.
– Tomorrow, Hanka, tomorrow.

After the gunshot as she is killed, the final, muted, and silent scene shows the pages of the book from which Pavel has been teaching Hanka Latin blowing softly in the wind. *Romeo, Juliet and Darkness* reveals the fable-like contours of the 'Romeo-and-Juliet genre' in its initially surprising but seamlessly apt adaptation to an anti-Nazi and anti-war theme.

India: folklore meets Shakespeare

Throughout their illustrious and colourful history, Indian film industries (pluralised because, although the Hindi 'Bollywood' alone as the best known is a diverse enterprise, there are many other traditions with different linguistic and cinematic bases) have embraced the 'Romeo-and-Juliet genre', to the extent that it has become linked with stories from the subcontinent's own folklore.[22] Harish Trivedi in a detailed summary of *Romeo and Juliet* in India speaks of a process of 'cultural hybridization', suggesting that 'Britain (and metonymically the West) raised a hegemonic house of many mansions that more and more Indians are now beginning to inhabit'.[23] Shakespeare cannot take full credit since there are similar tales (though with significant differences) about transgressive love from Indian cultural sources, such as the ancient Sanskrit play of cross-caste love by Kalidasa, *Abhijnanasakuntalam* (shortened to *Shakuntalam*), derived from the epic *Mahabharata*, which are a part of local or ethnic Indian literary representations, both oral and written. The kind of love represented in *Romeo and Juliet* is considerably more carnally physical and ripe for erotic exploitation, but this has been quite enthusiastically absorbed into recent Indian film versions. The closeness of Shakespeare's play to local stories perhaps explains why it is this play (with the unexpected addition of *The Comedy of Errors*) that has lent itself to such deep and apparently natural absorption into mainstream Hindi cinema, confining conscious adaptation of Shakespeare's other plays (even *Hamlet*) to more art-house and recognisably Westernised styles. A whole history of Indian films is based on the story, made in different languages: in particular *Laila Majnu*, *Sohni Mahiwal* (remade ten times between 1928 and 1984), *Heer Ranjha* (also remade at least ten times between 1928 and 2009), *Anjuman* (1948, remade 1986 and 1987), *Isaaq* (2013), and *Ishaqzaade* (2012), where the love is between a Hindu man and Muslim woman. All of these turn on young sweethearts divided by some variation on family opposition (not necessarily a feud between families), because the woman's parents have decided on an arranged marriage for her to a wealthy but ridiculous 'man of wax' like Paris, plunging the lovers into a life of tormented deprivation and persecution. In this sense we can see that in Indian traditional cultures, marriage customs and especially those arranged by families are in many ways closer than our own to those prevailing in Shakespeare's day. Although this generalisation again needs to be heavily qualified because 'India' itself is such a complex construct with a diversity of languages, cultures, customs, gulfs, and paradoxes, a basic comparability lends a special significance to *Romeo and Juliet* for Indian audiences.

Qayamat Se Qayamat Tak (1988), whose Urdu title has been variously translated as 'catastrophe on catastrophe', 'from apocalypse to apocalypse', and 'doom and destiny', seems to be at its heart more closely based on the Indian folktale material, but it also clearly reveals the definite analogies to Shakespeare's play. This long and epic-like film is significant in the history of Bollywood films and was extremely popular in India on its release and won many awards. Here the origin of the family feud is made clear in a lengthy flashback even before the film's title and credits come up, and it is repeated several times up to the end. Dhanraj Singh had killed the man who had caused his sister's suicide by impregnating and abandoning her, and as a result had been imprisoned for many years. When released he maintains his anger against the family of the man he murdered. Dhanraj's son Raj, now grown up, first glimpses Rashmi, the daughter of the rival family, when they meet each other at her birthday party, which Raj, like Romeo, has gatecrashed and from which he is chased away. Knowing nothing of the family feud, the lovers meet again outdoors while Rashmi is taking photographs, and they capture each other on camera, an equivalent of Shakespeare's characters becoming imprinted on each other's imagination. Telephones are another modern technology that, like the camera, both facilitates and threatens communication throughout the story. They meet again in a forest where they become lost, and later Raj rescues Rashmi from men who assault her, another element from the Indian folktale rather than Shakespeare. Their love blossoms 'now that fate has thrown us together', in her words. When the families come to know, they try to separate them, not only because of the families' animosity but also since Rashmi is promised to the family's chosen candidate, the wealthy but ridiculous Roop Singh in arranged marriage. The only helpful go-betweens from the older generation who know the origins of the feud are an uncle of Rashmi who plays something of the Friar's role in *Romeo and Juliet*, and her grandmother who is the equivalent of the Nurse, in agency if not in personality. A cousin plays the Tybalt role, betraying the lovers when they flee. Rashmi and Raj, discussing the issues raised by Shakespeare's 'what's in a name', conclude that on one hand they knew each other far better before finding out about the family situation, but on the other hand, as Raj says, 'what is destined definitely happens'. They decide that they are responsible for their own lives and not their parents' property, and elope. After spending some happy but physically deprived time together, they are eventually hunted down to a ruined fort and their lives placed under threat. Rashmi is killed, by mistake, by an assassin hired by her father to kill Raj, and in desperate grief Raj kills himself with a dagger given to him by Rashmi. The story, then, follows closely Shakespeare's, and it raises similar thematic questions around love, fate, tragic accident, and the lovers' moving deaths. The effect of the deaths on the respective families is left unexplored. The film's presentation of the family feud emphasises not only its generational basis but also the fully explained motivation behind it, unlike Shakespeare's, which is left unexplained. It becomes an image for forces by which the past determines and governs the present, a kind of destiny. The filmic device of the flashback to the initial murder, several times repeated, itself enacts the inescapability of historical transgression, even extending into future generations. Shakespeare's silence on the matter invites Western film-makers to see the feud as an unnecessary relic, something that deserves to be swept away, but *Qayamat Se Qayamat Tak*, by placing the narrative in a different cultural and religious context, insists on the interrelatedness of events and the ways in which the past cannot be escaped. It is a different dimension in the fable, implicit rather than explicit in Shakespeare, and made meaningful in adaptation into a different world-view. A more stylistic point might be made that Shakespeare's play (and his plays in general) may have a special appeal for the Indian film industry since there are many occasions for comedy and for musical interludes, which are treated generally as digressions and excrescences in Western versions (except as an opportunity for the composition of music with popular appeal like Nino Rota's) but become central in the variegated and assimilative Bollywood experiences. In *Qayamat* the melodramatic but functional music is central to its unity and appeal as a film.

Other examples show how closely the traditional Indian story of star-crossed lovers can be grafted with *Romeo and Juliet* acknowledged in its own right. Directed by the Tamil K. Balachander, *Ek Duuje Ke Liye* (1981), translated roughly as 'made for each other', was a very successful movie telling the story of love between younger members of neighbouring families who have settled in Goa, one Hindi and the other Tamil. The families are in a state of perpetual conflict on virtually all significant grounds – geographical (North Indian and South Indian), class (affluent landowners and struggling tenants respectively), professional (Sapna's father is a wealthy professor, Vasu's from humbler stock), language, diet (meat-eating and vegan; 'wheat eater ... rice-eater' are used in the film as terms of abuse), religion (Hindu and Tamil), and caste, and on a range of temperamental issues. The love between Sapna and Vasu is 'at first sight' and cuts across all these sites of conflict. Shakespeare becomes immediately relevant since, even before they meet, Sapna is seen browsing in the library:

LIBRARIAN Hullo Sapna. Good morning. What are you looking for?
SAPNA Professor Mushiran's notes.
LIBRARIAN About?
SAPNA *Romeo and Juliet.*
LIBRARIAN No, we've got *Love's Labour's Lost.*

This distinction becomes a crucial reference since, when the parents discover the love affair, they follow the lead of the women at the end of Shakespeare's comedy by condemning them to separate for a year. At this stage the tone of the film is romantic, optimistic and love-suffused. However, in the 'year off', Sapna is betrothed to another man. Vasu goes to Hyderabad and takes the trouble to learn not only Hindi but several regional variations of the language as well. Literacy and language, as Rachel Dwyer points out, make up a constant reference in the film: 'The film ... keeps displaying written Hindi, first in Roman script and then, as Vasu's competence grows, in Devanagari, allowing him to write Sapna's name in the sand on the beach and later to compose love letters; she writes a love letter on his back and his name thousands of times on her bedroom wall.'[24] When the year is up and Vasu returns to Goa, Sapna's parents are impressed by his linguistic facility, but fate intervenes through the divisive figures of Sapna's fiancé and her brother (the equivalent of Tybalt Capulet), who between them ensure that the true love is thwarted and ends in death, a denouement that was controversial with audiences and opposed by promoters as an incitement to teenage suicide. The Shakespearean references to *Romeo and Juliet* ring out ominously. Sapna is seen alone reading out loud to her father Juliet's 'what's in a name' soliloquy from a large volume titled clearly *William Shakespeare: The Complete Works*. Her scholarly father sagaciously points out that the speech applies to caste and many other things as well as name, which is 'just a label'. She ignores his long and rather boring literary interpretation and switches the light on and off to signal to Vasu next door. Then again Sapna sings to Vasu, 'We will marry no matter what the world does ... Of all the languages the language of love is universal. It's the language of Romeo and Juliet.' Otherwise, the film, which is impressive in its own right, includes all the conventions of the traditional Indian story: rough seas, deserted ruins, rape of Sapna by hoodlums hired to assassinate Vasu, and final death as they plunge together onto the rocks. But it is also an example of several films in which the traditional Indian story is combined quite explicitly with *Romeo and Juliet*. *Bobby* (1973) provides a further variation, since although the plot turns on parental opposition to young lovers on the grounds of class and religion, this time, after the couple elope, the ending is happy as the respective parents find through experience how important their children are to them and withdraw their objections.

Goliyon Ki Raasleel Ram-Leela (2013), a title translating as 'a play of bullets', in which Ram (Ranveer Singh) and Leela (Deepika Padukone) are the central characters who are bonded like their titular, hyphenated names in love, is clearly signalled as an adaptation of *Romeo and Juliet*. In a twist of fiction and truth-eliding, the phrase 'what's in a name?' became legally significant in the film's release, since the original name, *Ram-Leela*, was subject to a court case based on its irrelevant but offensive proximity to the name of the Hindu deity, Ramilla (Rama), while the central characters' initial family names had to be changed to avoid a ban in Uttar Pradesh based on them being recognisably community titles in the Kshatriya society. All this is quite ironic since the most obvious source for the plot itself is the English one, with an interesting postcolonial twist that the character in the role of Paris is represented in ridiculous light as an effete archaeologist from London. There are many direct references to *Romeo and Juliet*. There is a 'balcony scene' based in detail on Shakespeare's. The hero at one stage laments the family feud in which the lovers find themselves victims, saying 'we are star-crossed lovers' (in the English subtitled translation), and in the 'ballroom' scene (here a spectacular Bollywood dance ensemble) there is a visual equivalent of 'palm to palm is holy palmers' kiss' … 'O then, dear saint, let lips do what hands do', as Ram takes red powder from the palm of Leela and they smear it over each other's face. The sequence in the play where Tybalt kills Mercutio, who does not at first seem fatally wounded, and Romeo in impetuous retaliation kills Tybalt, is quite faithfully followed in the film, lacking only Shakespeare's language. Ram kills Leela's brother in retaliation for the death of his kinsman. The thematic point that the movie continually makes is that even the lovers, no matter how much they actively oppose the family conflicts (especially Ram who is presented as a peacemaker), cannot escape the context of virtual civil war between their families. Constant gunshots in the street are replicated in the relationship as Ram and Leela pretend to shoot each other in semi-jest, and accentuate the theme in a song with repeated phrases such as 'a game of bullets and kisses', 'this is love at war', and 'our bed is a battle field'. 'Now we are joined by blood' becomes a literal trope. Even when they elope and symbolically marry, the bickering turns into mutual recriminations and serious conflict between the two, alternating with passion. In Shakespeare this may not be an obtrusive theme, but it is implicit in the way that Mercutio is killed as a result of Romeo's attempted intervention, and Romeo is also fatally implicated through his murder of Tybalt. The movie, then, becomes an example of mutual, intertextual influence – based on *Romeo and Juliet*, its treatment draws out an often overlooked potential in the play's treatment of romantic love in an inherently violent society.

Other aspects of *Romeo and Juliet* occur in modified form in the film. First, Ram's family, like the Montagues, are dominated by men, the friends of Ram (who watch porn movies and eventually betray him) and an entirely male assembly under a 'don' who passes his power to Ram himself, while Leela's family is a matriarchy and the formidable mother is surrounded by women – a concession to the fact that in the Capulet family it is Lady Capulet who appears to hold power. Second, the go-between functions of the Nurse and Friar are for dramatic economy conflated into one person, Leela's sister-in-law, who must overcome her own feelings since it was her husband who was killed by Ram. She is mocked by Ram's friends, as is the Nurse by Romeo's, but more seriously she is assaulted by them in a scene where a major conflict is revealed as that between Rajadi males and Saneras females. The lovers are separated, and the agent of misunderstanding is not a miscarried letter but a misused cellphone, showing another facet of Shakespeare's plot adapted into a modern context. Even instagrams and tweets figure in the plot. Thereafter, every attempt at negotiating peace between the communities, now led by Ram and Leela respectively, is thwarted, in an escalation of violence and conflict leading towards a massacre of both sides. However, Ram and Leela agree to make the ultimate sacrifice by killing each other: 'A love story should not be so toxic that innocent people die', says Ram. 'With us gone the enmity in Ranjeer will end.' Just too late peace breaks out, but not before the lovers are dead. 'If anger and revenge can turn an ocean into a barren desert, then true love can also make flowers bloom there', intones the chorus. In this case, as in Shakespeare's play, the temptation to provide a happy ending is resisted. In some ways the refusal to compromise is the most interesting aspect of this adaptation because, unlike many others, the love itself comes to doom the lovers since it holds a deterministic element that means the love itself can never escape the ancient and pervading conflict as it is from start to finish represented as a kind of love-hatred.

Given the understandable divergence of Indian views on the historical British occupation of their country, there is scope for Shakespeare's legacy to be seen in a critical, postcolonial light, but so far *Romeo and Juliet* seems not to have been radically questioned or undermined. However, it might be possible to argue more positively that since Independence, and through its unique cinema industry, India has taken ownership of the 'Romeo-and-Juliet genre' in its own special way, wresting monopoly away from Anglo-American hands. This is the future that was glimpsed in Merchant Ivory's elegiac *Shakespeare Wallah* (1965), in which not only is British culture losing its grip on the public but live theatre also is giving way to popular movies.

The renowned director Vidhu Vinod Chopra at least builds some creative ambivalence into his film. He himself has acknowledged in interviews that he came rather late to English as a language, not learning it until seventh grade at school, and in particular to Shakespeare, whose works he encountered not through the educational system but only later when he entered the Film Institute in Pune.²⁵ As a result he may have avoided both poles of the political spectrum, neither revering nor reviling Shakespeare. However, having discovered the bard he was quick to exploit the plays for his own filmic purposes, and in 1994 directed *1942: A Love Story*, in which Shakespeare's *Romeo and Juliet* is copiously and unmistakably referenced in the main plot, though never actually named,²⁶ and becomes a vehicle for exploring the relationship between Indian nationalism and the struggle for independence.²⁷ Shakespeare is not set up as an easy target for dismissal or as a symbol for the superimposed English culture represented in the movie by the brutal General Douglas. Richard Burt's comment that *Romeo and Juliet* 'allows for a transgressive, cross-class romance and marriage' is equally relevant in terms of the political situation in *1942*, ambivalently poised on the side of neither the colonials nor the revolutionaries. As a play-within-the-film, an Indian production in Hindi is framed by a typical Bollywood musical sequence aimed at local Indian audiences, as though enfolding Shakespeare within local culture.²⁸ There is also a plan to assassinate Douglas during this performance. Chopra clearly sees Shakespeare as a complex and ambiguous symbolic force in Indian culture and politics, fully assimilated and yet still a product of England. *Romeo and Juliet*, true to other productions analysed here, is localised and, if anything, taken away from the English and turned against them. The plural and hybrid forms and associations are entirely in tune with Indian cinema itself, as well as consistent with the cinematic yoking of Shakespeare with Indian mythology.

A different kind of culturally eclectic version is *Mississippi Masala* (1992) directed by Mira Nair, an Indian film-maker based in New York whose aim is to probe sometimes critical international perceptions of India by expatriates. *Monsoon Wedding* and *Salaam Bombay* are critical of India but made with an insider's emotional investment. *Mississippi Masala* is rather different, made and set in America, inflected with layers of multicultural influences, but still with an Indian perspective. It deploys the 'Romeo-and-Juliet genre' with yet another application, this time focusing on the complexities of racial prejudice in both black Africa and predominantly white United States. The central consciousness is a lifelong expatriate, Mina, an Afro-Indian who is seen first in childhood as her family is forced to flee Kampala in 1972, the days of Idi Amin's regime in Uganda, and then in 1990 as an adolescent working in a motel in Greenwood, Mississippi. Her father has obsessively pursued legal claims to his property in Uganda for the intervening period, without receiving even a reply until towards the end of the film. The apparent contrasts of time and place historically have a strong racist link. In Uganda the father is told by his black African friend, 'Africa is for Africans. Black Africans', while when the family lives in America they face just as much prejudice and hostility, alongside the equally disenfranchised and victimised African-American community to which Demetrius (a good Shakespearean name), who becomes Mina's lover, belongs. Partly as a reaction against prejudice and partly as a celebration of their roots, both the Indian and black American communities express their respective family traditions. However, an inter-generational conflict also exists between the young, who try to adapt and overcome prejudice, and the older generation, who cling to their traditions. Mina sees herself as a rootless mixture of races, a 'mixed masala' defined as 'a bunch of hot spices'. All live and work in a motel, a symbolic place of transience and a place where both Indian and black Americans have to deal not only with antagonistic whites but with sordid thrill-seekers pursuing one-night stands. However, even between these equally beleaguered communities, where, as one character puts it, 'all of us people of colour must stick together ... united we stand', there exists racial prejudice, and at one stage Demetrius jokingly equates racism and 'tradition'. It is racial antagonism between the elders in ethnic sub-groups that creates the context for the Romeo-and-Juliet genre which underpins the structure of the story of love between Mina and Demetrius. Mina's mother says that Demetrius should 'know his place and stay in it' and there are frequent references to the history of slavery in America, with racist overtones, while the African-American family loses customers from their cleaning business because of the situation. We see the kind of scene reminiscent of *Guess Who's Coming to Dinner* (1967) (a film that holds a muted *Romeo and Juliet* story within itself, although offering a happy ending in which the parents are 'educated' into tolerance), with the irony that the black American man is dining with the Indian family. Meanwhile, there are characters who carry out comparable functions in *Romeo and Juliet*, for example Mina's mean-minded relative Anil, who plays a kind of ineffectual Tybalt role, and Tyrone as the flirtatious friend of Demetrius who also suffers the fate of Mercutio. Both families say to the young lovers, 'You've caused enough trouble', not seeing the irony that the conflict is not the fault of the young lovers. There are significant variations, however, on the play's events, since the family 'feud' transfers itself onto Demetrius himself. He rejects Mina, and the 'happy ending' is a sentimental cop-out. Everybody discovers and proves the adage 'home is where the heart is' – Mina's father relinquishes his aim to live again in Uganda even as it becomes possible, and the reconciled Mina and Demetrius's threat to elope reignites their parents' affections. The final images of an African child cradled by the Indian expatriate who watches native Ugandans dancing, and Demetrius dressed in African garb dancing with Mina in traditional Indian dress, suggests that harmony can be established by accepting with tolerance passing time and changing situations. Given the highly political tensions raised by the plot, this ending may come as surprisingly tame, shirking the very issues of race and generational change that have been activated, but even so it reveals a more didactic undercurrent of optimism available in *Romeo and Juliet*.

A *Welsh* Romeo and Juliet

One film, chosen from the many possible to explore in more detail the ways in which genre shapes, and also changes, adaptations, is the Welsh *Solomon and Gaenor*. Made in 1998/99, it played in independent cinemas in the UK and the DVD is accompanied with such warnings as 'Contains violence, nudity and *cultural enmity*. In English, Yiddish and Gaelic with subtitles' (my emphasis). From this alone we realise it is a strongly localised film depicting 'cultural enmity' between immigrant Jews and the Welsh community. (The warning must have been added by English promoters, since the Welsh language is never referred to as 'Gaelic' but as 'Cymraeg' by Welsh speakers and by others simply as Welsh.) It is set in 1911, but with fairly clear contemporary reference also to the socially divisive miners' strike in the mid-1980s, which had such traumatic and devastating effects on communities in the Welsh valleys, the north of England, Scotland, Kent, and elsewhere that the memory still carries a strong emotional charge. Since the film is presented as a collaboration between S4C (the Welsh-language television station), Film Four, the Arts Council of England, and the Arts Council of Wales, it is clearly a subsidised 'art house' film rather than a 'box-office' one from a commercial, multinational, or Hollywood company. Like Zeffirelli, the director, Paul Morrison, cast young and relatively little-known actors, Ioan Gruffud as Solomon and Nia Roberts as Gaenor. While there is none of Shakespeare's language, and his creative influence is not credited, yet the publicity announced: 'As timeless as young love and as tragic as *Romeo & Juliet*, SOLOMON & GAENOR is a lush Oscar-nominated romance featuring star-crossed lovers caught in a cultural crossfire.' Variations are played on some of the underpinning patterns from Shakespeare's play, such as family difference and conflict, the particular kind of desire that is represented, the subjectivity of time-awareness, and the issue of fatal causality that turns on an unresolved debate between destiny and luck, most poignantly located in the fact of two people's births from four unique parents all carrying their own societies' prejudices. This version of the 'Romeo-and-Juliet genre' has its topical relationship to its own times in the choice to centralise issues of racism within a small community, arguably one of the most prominent areas of social concern at the time when the film appeared.

Solomon is a 'packman', selling linen and sewing implements and cotton, door-to-door. Gaenor appears to have recently left school and she spends her time at home with her mother, helping also at the chapel Sunday school. Their love blossoms when, in the rather greyly coloured mining town, he chooses richly red cloth and sews it into a dress as a gift for her. However, the social problems quickly emerge. Impassable cultural and religious differences between the respective families are established through a series of juxtaposed foreign-language scenes, in which, respectively, Solomon's family converses over dinner in Yiddish, Gaenor Rees's, equally uncompromisingly, in Welsh. Solomon's rabbi uncle advises his community to learn the ways of 'this nation which we have made our home' by reading the novels of Dickens, which ironically misses the point that they are not living in a native English-speaking country. Solomon feels forced to lie to Gaenor from an early stage, pretending to be 'Sam Livingstone', the son of an English railway engineer, concealing his address, hiding his 'tzitzit' undergarment before each time they make love, and lying that his mother is ill in order to prevent Gaenor from meeting her. He attends the Protestant chapel service against his own religion, simply to see Gaenor. The church is the unlikely equivalent of the Capulets' ball, and his subterfuge is akin to Romeo's mask. When in Gaenor's company, asked directions by a Jewish vagrant family, he gives them in English (which is barely understood by the refugees), instead of Yiddish. They recognise Solomon as a fellow-Jew ('Are you a Yid?' the man asks in Yiddish), but he refuses to acknowledge this. However, it is hard to blame Solomon for his disingenuousness, even though it shows he has internalised the cultural and religious differences, bringing the 'family feud' into the love relationship. His own family condemns the liaison when they know of it: 'If you go with this girl, you will be dead to us. We will say kaddish over you.' Gaenor's brutish brother Crad, playing Tybalt's role, reveals the deep local prejudice against 'Jew boys' who 'probably got a pile of money stashed away in that cart'. Gaenor, on the other hand, is painfully truthful and open, even when one would expect her to tell white lies to her censorious family. She wears the red dress Solomon has made for her, walks arm in arm in public with him, and makes no pretence of her love. In the chapel, she is accused by Noah, the 'Paris figure' of *Romeo and Juliet* – a schoolteacher whose attentions she has spurned – of being pregnant after 'fornicating with a stranger' (spoken in Welsh). For this she is publicly humiliated but with dignity refuses to deny, conceal, or distort the truth, accepting the consequences fully. For this she is condemned: 'Shame on you, Gaenor Rees. You were an example of goodness to the young, and now, about you is the stench of deceit and evil. The trust those children placed in you – our trust – has been polluted.'

When the film appeared, reviewers were apt to condemn Solomon's apparently chronic lying to his trusting lover, but even this aspect of the characterisation has its origin in *Romeo and Juliet*. Romeo's mask gains him access to the ball where he meets Juliet, a kind of duplicity that is justified by the circumstances. However, Romeo cannot deny his family or name since these are widely known, and like Solomon he exposes both himself and his family to some danger if the courtship and marriage should become public. Mercutio and Tybalt die, and Romeo is banished, as consequences of the family feud being indirectly intensified by a clandestine love relationship. For Solomon's family, the latent, smouldering prejudice against their race is literally ignited in the community by the miners' strike as workers are laid off. Immigrant Jews are victimised as a group, wrongly rumoured to be rack-rent landlords, and racial violence is the result. Solomon's brother sees the Welsh community as '*goyische*' and his grandfather says the 'goys' are 'not our people. They're different'. Later in the film, Solomon is beaten up by Crad, and the brutality of this scene is depicted at sickening length. Soon after this, the Jewish shop belonging to Solomon's family is forcibly entered and looted by youths with Crad as ringleader, and the family is financially ruined. In an inset cameo, Solomon, hiding on a hillside, watches as Crad slaughters a sheep (an incident that has become a kind of badge of gritty authenticity in regional films such as the Italian *The Tree of Wooden Clogs* (1978)), and the scene acts as a symbol of victimisation of Jews and the lovers alike. As in *Romeo and Juliet*, these events may not be directly caused by the young lovers' affair, but they are the unavoidable markers of the larger divisions based on prejudice, violence, and cultural difference in which the love is played out. Certainly Crad's animosity to Solomon from the outset is fuelled by his recognition of the Jew's real identity. The only human response available is a level of concealment, even between the lovers, since the alternative of complete openness would make the love unsustainable, as well as potentially endangering more lives. Gaenor, in turn made resentful by Solomon's apparent ambiguity, becomes so mistrustful that she does not tell him of her pregnancy, and the cry 'Why didn't you tell me?' becomes a mutual taunt used by each. The film's point, in its nuancing of the *Romeo and Juliet* story, is that the wider 'feud' between cultures inevitably erodes trust and communication even between the lovers. Shakespeare may not stress this, since his lovers are seen as more collaborative against prevailing, external social norms, but the potential still lies in the story itself. Neither Shakespeare's play nor the film provides an unambiguously sentimental belief that love will conquer all, but rather both suggest it is doomed.

In fact the kind of love depicted in *Solomon and Gaenor* is a 'variation', to an extent that at first sight almost disqualifies it from the 'Romeo-and-Juliet genre'. Almost invariably, filmed versions of the play depict the love as overwhelmingly romantic – lushly burgeoning among exotic vines in Zeffirelli's case, cocooned in watery mesmerism in Luhrmann's, bursting irresistibly into song in *West Side Story* – but always driven by compulsive romantic idealism, epiphanic ecstasy, and time-stopping wonder contrasting with the sheer rapidity of the time scheme. By contrast, the love between Solomon and Gaenor is muted and understated, and at first not fully transgressive since it holds the promise of public acceptance after the initial secrecy. Both characters are, presumably under the pressure of their respective national characteristics, cautious, inexpressive, and without the inflammatory and incandescent poeticism of utterance between Shakespeare's lovers. As time goes on, the mistrust between the lovers and the increasing social ostracism cause the kinds of internal misunderstandings between the couple that are not an issue between Romeo and Juliet. When love does erupt into action, it is expressed in open sexual desire, which is again far from the sometimes physically coy presentation in films of the play where love exists more through lyrical utterance than action. Juliet has often been seen by critics to be franker and more realistic than Romeo, and in this vein the Juliet-figure even more decisively rejects the repressive inhibitions of her family and the repressive church society, playing a full, equal, and even initiating role in the love-making. The longer time scheme of the film, by contrast with Shakespeare's in which the entire tragedy is played out so rapidly, enforces attention not on the causes of infatuation but its consequences, which the lovers must fully face over many months of increasing isolation and distress. However, although the lineaments of the love represented are different, and the emphasis is placed on the social complexities rather than the biological imperatives of desire, yet the main aspects of *Romeo and Juliet* are retained, in a developed way. What Lloyd Davis says of desire as 'lost presence' in Shakespeare's play is equally true in the film, though it is conveyed in different ways. Davis argues that *Romeo and Juliet* 'explores the interplay between desire, death and selfhood', suggesting that it imitated and initiated other texts that 'place desire in conflict with time, recounting movements of ideal presence whose future reveals they could never have been'.[29]

Among narrative aspects of the play that the film duplicates is the apparently very Elizabethan trope of the written message that goes astray, a device that places the play paradoxically in the territory of comedy of errors rather than tragedy of fate. Again, Lloyd Davis has mused interestingly on the fate of letters in texts that 'convey and address feelings of risk, trust and curiosity prompted by a network of social relations which continues to be expanded and complicated by the carrier and postal routes along which they travel', in an age when organised mass communication was rudimentary and unreliable.[30] Shakespeare most often associated the miscarried letter with comedy, indicating luck rather than destiny, as in *Love's Labour's Lost* and elsewhere, so its occurrence in *Romeo and Juliet* poignantly highlights the generic ambivalence of the play that could so easily (as some modern films suggest) have culminated in a happy ending.[31] The equivalent of the Friar's misdirected letter in *Romeo and Juliet* is a message written by Solomon, who has been sent away by his family to Cardiff and made virtually a prisoner to officework. In it he professes love for Gaenor and gives her an address to contact him. However, her brother, Crad, intercepts and buries the letter, so she never receives it. Thinking she is rejected, she goes to see Solomon's mother, who conveys in her immigrant English language that he 'won't be back here':

> SOLOMON'S MOTHER Excuse me for saying this. You have yourself made this situation. Don't make Solomon to rescue you. Don't ruin his life.
> GAENOR I love him, He loves me. I think.
> SOLOMON'S MOTHER [*In Yiddish, to her husband*] Maybe she wants money.
> GAENOR No, please. I don't want money.
> SOLOMON'S MOTHER I am sorry, my dear. I can see you are an honest girl. I am glad Solomon found an honest girl. You'll get over it. You both will get over it. Love, when you are young, love comes and goes. You have a long life to live yet. It will heal. I wish you happiness, you and your child. Hmm. Understand?
> GAENOR He's your grandchild. Don't you understand?
> SOLOMON'S FATHER He's no grandchild of ours. He's a mistake. He's not our grandchild.

They refuse even to pass on a message from Gaenor to Solomon, and his mother writes to Solomon in these words:

> Dear Solomon, Your girl has gone away. You will never see her again. It is a good thing. You would never have been happy. You will stay in Cardiff. For a boy like you there are more opportunities in the big city. Work hard, I know you will succeed. Your ever-loving mama.

Both sets of parents are concerned to disown the unborn, illegitimate child and get it safely out of the way as an embarrassment. The undeniable feeling is that the love is simply impossible to sustain, given the ugly facts of social and familial divisions. Here there is no sense at all of Shakespeare's Friar's hope, implied at the end of Zeffirelli's version and enacted at the end of *West Side Story*, that recognition of the love might heal divisions. The love is 'star-cross'd' from without, as certainly as the unredeemably bleak and bitter ending to Luhrmann's film plays out.

Part of Shakespeare's presentation is the importance given to the relativity of time. This is also the case in *Solomon and Gaenor*, but here it holds a different significance. However, the variations between play and film are ones that demonstrate the fertility and flexibility of the original prototype, rather than denying the connection. Shakespeare tells us in the initial Prologue that the lovers will die, whereas in *Solomon and Gaenor* there is no inkling of this until late in the film. Even here, the overall effect may not be dissimilar, since the play also tempts us to see ways in which the fate is avoidable while the film gives even more possibility of genuine happiness in marriage. In neither case does an internal tension or mistake between the lovers cause their deaths, which are the result of pre-existing problems in the society they live in. There is also a variation on the ways in which time is represented in the two works. *Solomon and Gaenor* is more like Shakespeare's source, Brooke's *Tragicall Historye*, which spanned nine months, since there is enough time for Gaenor to become visibly pregnant. *Romeo and Juliet*, on the other hand, gives a notorious example of a 'double time scheme'. The action lasts no longer than five days, from Sunday to Thursday, although also, and in contradiction, the palpable impression is given of Aristotelian unity of time, in which the action takes place in the 'two-hours' traffic of the stage' as we watch, or at least over twenty-four hours, even though we know this is not so. It is the play's precipitate speed that is central to the effect of young love burning itself through from innocence to experience and then death, and much of the imagery conveys this urgency. At the same time, a much longer, inter-generational perspective is overlaid on Shakespeare's action, in the historically prolonged feud and also in the words of characters like the Nurse and Friar. The former can look back over thirteen years and more, counting the years not by dates but by events such as saint's days, birthdays, weaning of Juliet, deaths such as that of a lost Susan born in the same year as Juliet, and remembered natural happenings such as an earthquake, and others. The Capulet cousins argue at length over whether their 'dancing days' ended twenty-five years ago or thirty (1.5.32–40), to the elegiac refrain, "'Tis gone, 'tis gone, 'tis gone' (24). The Friar, who regrets and warns against haste in the hope that the lovers may live on to reach maturity, is the one who is most conscious of the potentially tragic discrepancy between the 'short time' of adolescent desire and the 'long love' of mature attachment:

> These violent delights have violent ends,
> And in their triumph die like fire and powder,
> Which as they kiss consume. The sweetest honey
> Is loathsome in his own deliciousness,
> And in the taste confounds the appetite.
> Therefore love moderately. Long love doth so.
> Too swift arrives as tardy as too slow. (2.5.9–15)

In *Solomon and Gaenor*, however, time is significant in different ways. For a start, the film's action seems to span at least three seasons, and certainly longer than the nine months of pregnancy. The seasons' changes reflect the 'inner weather' of the story's emotional movement, as fine weather (never quite sunny, but apparently warm enough to make love outdoors without clothes and without visible goosebumps), in which the lovers, like Zeffirelli's, meet in natural settings against green foliage, gives way to driving rain in the miners' strike and the vandalising of the shop, and finally deep snow and skeletal trees at the end of the film. The longer and slower time scheme of the film implies larger natural and human cycles, but also allows room for more vicissitudes, tensions, and estrangements than the play depicts – for example, Romeo and Juliet do not argue and temporarily fall apart as Solomon and Gaenor do, simply because they have no time to do so. It is their fate not to have enough time, while for Solomon and Gaenor, in some ways, they have too much time. The advice against intemperate love is delivered by Solomon's mother, who is more hostile than the well-meaning Friar: 'You'll get over it. You both will get over it. Love, when you are young, love comes and goes. You have a long life to live yet. It will heal.'

The film does not end exactly like Shakespeare's *Romeo and Juliet*, since only one lover dies and a baby appears. Gaenor is sent to her aunt's house for the birth. Solomon, after being beaten by Crad and almost dying in the snow, tracks her down. 'Don't leave me now, my love', she pleads, and she goes into the bed. He dies in her embrace. Gaenor sobs helplessly, in a scene affectively reminiscent in an understated way of Luhrmann's ending. Soft piano music (rather than an operatic aria) plays, as the camera circles above the bed, which is juxtaposed to a bleak, wintry exterior. Luhrmann's candles in the cathedral are replaced by a brave indoor plant with fresh buds on the table. The baby arrives as

Solomon lies dead. In a brief flash-forward that operates as an epilogue, we learn that Gaenor gives up the child, as planned by the family, and we see her in numbed grief, being driven home by her brother. For the screenwriter, there is a suggestion that the tragic centre of the 'Romeo-and-Juliet genre' is not only the waste of young lives that are driven by desire sacrificed to irrational and ancient grudges, but also the repetitiveness of the pattern down through the ages. Solomon's death repeats a situation she has already faced. We hear early that Gaenor had been attached to a young miner who was disabled in an accident and her family forbade the marriage since he could not 'keep' her. Her acquiescence to her parents on that occasion may have made her more determined to defy them now, but in the end the outcome is even more tragic, the physical death of her lover. In every sense, time achieves nothing, but simply returns lovers to individual isolation.

Shakespeare's *Romeo and Juliet* is still a strong cultural reference point, even in contexts that are unexpectedly remote from the play itself, and at best allusive. They can, however, indicate an intertextual complexity. Recognition of Shakespearean parallels makes us aware of where some conventions of our contemporary ceremonies have come from, such as the 'civil brawls' whose origin is long forgotten in popular memory but still destructively active. Such recognitions can also momentarily illuminate Shakespeare's text (at the very least, textual editors might investigate the social origins of biting one's thumb in Italy). In the case of *Solomon and Gaenor*, however, Shakespeare's play is not just a reference point but a clear artistic source, providing a generic masterplan that colours audience expectations from early in the film. Comparative analysis of play and film can bring an enhanced understanding of the fertile potential lying in the 'Romeo-and-Juliet genre', with its 'repetition and variation' an example of mutual influence. What has been seen unfailingly as a play that centrally explores desire and romantic love in the Western world has been revealed as having a different, equally important theme, that such love is shaped, partially created, and also destroyed by different social patterning, in this case, constraints imposed by specific perceptions of race and religion.

Star-crossed comedy and parodies

Familiarity need not breed contempt but affectionate mockery. *Romeo and Juliet*, along with *Hamlet*, has produced a large corpus of satire as a direct consequence of its early absorption into film vocabulary. We have seen this already in the frequent allusions in Hollywood musicals, where simply mentioning the names or the balcony scene can act as a shorthand for associations with Shakespeare, the classical drama repertoire, thespian acting styles, or disappointed young lovers in general. Film-makers clearly expect audiences to have *some* knowledge of the play, even if it is based only on the common misunderstanding of the line 'wherefore art thou Romeo?' (the pornographic version comes out as 'wherefore art thy pants?'). As a result, an ever-widening group of movies can flaunt radical variations, most commonly in making the ending comic, a development anticipated by Shakespeare in his own contemporary parody, 'Pyramus and Thisbe', the play-within-a-play in *A Midsummer Night's Dream* in which by the end, and despite the lovers' deaths, 'the wall is down that parted their fathers'. Lubitsch's silent comedy, *Romeo und Julia im Schnee* (1920), places the young lovers and their feuding families in an Alpine village in the nineteenth century and gives them all a happy ending.[32] At the other end of the time scale, the Russian *Van I Ne Snilos* (1980) also presents the Romeo and Juliet story with a happy ending. However, as Douglas Lanier argues in 'Will of the People: Recent Shakespeare Film Parody and the Politics of Popularization',[33] the process of parodying Shakespeare on film became especially prominent in the 1990s. Lanier's explanation is not the common one that 'parody is often seen as a symptom of a genre's senescence, a means for reviving what has become exhausted or irrelevant',[34] but rather he argues that the 'pop Shakespeare hybrid' or 'Shakespop parodies' are a familiar part of postmodern hybridisation, offering a '"double access" – a facility under a mask of irony, with both low and high culture'.[35] It reveals contradictory goals of simultaneously popularising Shakespeare while preserving his 'cultural authority from the pernicious effects of mass culture'. Although my examples will come from the 1990s, I am not convinced that it is a distinctively postmodern tendency, since it can be traced right back to *Shake Mr Shakespeare*, and such versions exist from the silent beginnings of film history, especially concerning *Romeo and Juliet*. Rather, my analysis continues to emphasise the perhaps less complex argument that Shakespeare's play created a recognisable and unique genre in its own right that can then – like westerns or Dracula movies – be presented either straightforwardly or parodied. Furthermore, these versions also underline the capacity of the genre to penetrate apparently into any local community in the world.

The Singaporean version of *Romeo and Juliet* is *Chicken Rice War* or *Jiyuan qiaohe* (2000), where the central situation is so similar to the one in *Love Is All There Is* that there is clearly both influence and intertextual referencing not only to that film but also Luhrmann's movie and to *Shakespeare in Love* (1998). As in other examples noted in this book, whereas earlier films often reference Shakespeare directly, in later times it is more common to echo a previous, well-known film version. There is an excellent essay on the film written by Li Lan Yong, 'Romeos and Juliets, Local / Global', which examines as a source of comedy in the film various cultural intersections between an affirmation of the universal suggested by Shakespeare, the global world of commodities, and the mundanely local; or the canonical and the popular, and even the perfect 'It girl' and the girl-next-door embodied in an amateur actress playing Juliet.[36] The rival family businesses are Singaporean Chinese hawker stalls that compete for diners over their 'special' chicken rice recipes, which ironically is more or less a national or at least universally available dish in Singapore, as common as Shakespeare is in the educational system. The vendetta extends to sabotaging the competitor's cooking by sending rats to the other stall or poisoning the food, and also by offering very different forms of musical entertainment, popular and Chinese opera (sung by 'The Fat Lady'), respectively. Meanwhile, the chicken-seller, acting as the Chorus, fans the flames, since he profits from the increased sales of chickens to the rival families. The young lovers caught in the crossfire of the twenty-year-old family feud are Fenson Wong and Audrey Chan, who are rehearsing the roles of Romeo and Juliet for an amateur production. Yet again, the dialogue at the masked ball is filmed to music with the camera circling the characters, evoking the romantic atmosphere of other versions, but the aura is undermined by the mundane lecture theatre where they rehearse in the anonymous educational context of the Singaporean university. What makes the film a comedy or parody is the regular pattern of returning from, as Yong puts it, 'Juliet and Romeo' to the 'everyday selves' of the two inveterately local Singaporean teenagers. There are many wry ironies such as the fact that Audrey, who is herself Chinese so there is no ethnic difference in this instance, is surprised to find she can 'share the same thoughts about romance and Shakespeare' with a Chinese boy whom she had assumed would be like other Chinese male 'geeks' and 'squares', 'into their maths and science'. When she passionately kisses him, he cautiously asks 'was that real or just acting?'. The young lovers also consciously decide to end the family squabble by each spilling the information about the other family's 'secret ingredient' in their chicken rice recipes: 'we can change things'. At the performance of the play, the patriarchs of the Wong and Chan families, both inappropriately dressed up in competition with each other, first effectively watch their children enacting their own family squabble and end up ruining the performance with their intrusive bickering. The comedy also springs from linguistic impositions as 'high' literary English jostles with the dialect of 'Singlish' or Singaporean English, in a community where Cantonese, Mandarin, Hindu, and Malay are also spoken. In the action the constantly emphasised gap between Shakespeare's story and the petty animosities in the hawkers' centre not only creates comic incongruities but also raises questions about Shakespeare's text being used simultaneously as an icon of institutionally sanctioned values and as mass appeal entertainment, or as a symbol of British colonialism wrestling with local customs, language, and attitudes. This melting pot of cultural forces is inevitably at work to some extent in the multitude of variations, tragic or comic, on the 'Romeo-and-Juliet genre' tested in a multitude of nationally and socially diverse settings.[37]

Genre at heart is a matter of expectations. Early on in a narrative we expect to know where we are and where we are heading, and Shakespeare's play of tragic, young love provides one of the most immediately recognisable structures in dramatic and subsequently filmic experience. In essence, the 'Romeo-and-Juliet genre' turns on the pathos of innocence impaled on experience, young love crossing boundaries that have been created by some ancient internecine conflict. Beyond that, the conflict is usually inter-generational but it also signifies a broader clash based on socially constructed difference – religious, political, national, ethnic, professional, and so on, apparently without end. It can result in pointless tragedy and chastened admonition of the warring parties that have lost a generation:

> Where be these enemies? Capulet, Montague,
> See, what a scourge is laid upon your hate,
> That heaven finds means to kill your joys with love.
> And I, for winking at your discords, too
> Have lost a brace of kinsmen. All are punishèd. (5.3.290–4)

Or it can lead through loss and shame to reconciliation when they are faced with the 'Poor sacrifices of our enmity'. Alternatively, tragedy can be averted altogether and the apparently tragic story turned into comedy or parody, a concession to the fact that it turns on randomly accidental events as much as either personal destiny or providence. The rich but miscellaneous body of filmic works canvassed here are linked by one connection, which is the only thing they have in common, the influence of Shakespeare's play as their prototype.

Notes

1. I have briefly surveyed the field up to 2000 in 'Romeo and Juliet: A Mediterranean Love Story', *Shakespeare and the Classroom*, 10 (2002), 45–54.
2. See Rebecca Huntley, *The World According to Y* (Sydney: Allen & Unwin, 2006).
3. James N. Loehlin suggests that at least behind Zeffirelli's film lies a 'rebellious adolescent' convention evident in films such as *The Blackboard Jungle* and *Rebel without a Cause*, but even Loehlin's brief words tend to suggest what I would argue, that behind the plot lies *Romeo and Juliet* itself. See James N. Loehlin, '"These Violent Delights Have Violent Ends": Baz Luhrmann's Millennial Shakespeare', in Mark Thornton Burnett and Ramona Wray (eds), *Shakespeare, Film, Fin de Siècle* (London: Palgrave, 2000), 121–37, esp. 122.
4. Linda Charnes, 'Dismember Me: Shakespeare, Paranoia, and the Logic of Mass Culture', *Shakespeare Quarterly*, 48.1 (1997), 1–16, 4.
5. Lloyd Davis, '"Death-Marked Love": Desire and Presence in *Romeo and Juliet*', *Shakespeare Survey*, 49 (1996), 57–67, 59.
6. Deborah Cartmell, *Interpreting Shakespeare on Screen* (London: Palgrave, 2000), 44.
7. Barbara Hodgdon, 'Baz Luhrmann's *William Shakespeare's Romeo + Juliet*', in R. S. White (ed.), *Romeo and Juliet: Contemporary Critical Essays* (London: Palgrave, 2001), 129–46.
8. Sammons, *Shakespeare: A Hundred Years on Film*, 112–32.
9. Burt, *Shakespeares after Shakespeare*, vol. I, chs 3 and 4.
10. See Ball, *Shakespeare on Silent Film*; Rothwell, *Early Shakespeare Movies*, and other books.
11. For a brief but excellent history of performance of *Romeo and Juliet*, see Jill Levenson, *Shakespeare in Performance: Romeo and Juliet* (Manchester: Manchester University Press, 1987).
12. Peter Conrad, *To Be Continued: Four Stories and Their Survival* (Oxford: Oxford University Press, 1995).
13. Dash, *Shakespeare and the American Musical*, ch. 3.
14. See, for example, Gary Tomlinson, *Music in Renaissance Magic: Toward a Historiography of Others* (Chicago and London: University of Chicago Press, 1993), ch. 5.
15. Ball, *Shakespeare on Silent Film*, 217–18.
16. Kenneth S. Rothwell and Annabelle Henkin Malzer, *Shakespeare on Screen: An International Filmography and Videography* (New York: Neal Schuman Publishers Inc., 1992), 249. See also Rothwell, *A History of Shakespeare on Screen*.
17. See Bruce Babington, *Blue Skies and Silver Linings: Aspects of the Hollywood Musical* (Manchester: Manchester University Press, 1985).
18. CD-ROM, *Cinemania 5* (Microsoft).
19. Kott, *Shakespeare Our Contemporary*.

20 For an aspect of this large area, see Timothy Murray, *Drama Trauma: Specters of Race and Sexuality in Performance, Video, and Art* (London and New York: Routledge, 1997), esp. 1–9, where Luhrmann's film is used to illustrate cultural 'traumatophilia'. I am grateful to Gail Jones for pointing out this essay.
21 Caroline Spurgeon, *Shakespeare's Imagery and What It Tells Us* (Cambridge: Cambridge University Press, 1935).
22 I am grateful to Poonam Pandit from the University of Rohtak and Shalmalee Palekar at the University of Western Australia for some information in this account, though they are not responsible for my errors or misunderstandings.
23 Harish Trivedi, 'Colonizing Love: *Romeo and Juliet* in Modern Indian Disseminations', in Poonam Trivedi and Dennis Bartholomeusz (eds), *India's Shakespeare: Translation, Interpretation, and Performance* (New Delhi: Dorling Kindersley, 2006), 66–81, 65.
24 Rachel Dwyer, *100 Bollywood Films* (London: British Film Institute, 2005), 92.
25 Chopra makes the point in various published interviews, for example in *The Hindu*, 12 April 2015, 'I Have a Munnabhai in Me: Vidhu Vinod Chopra'.
26 Trivedi, 'Colonizing Love', 75.
27 See Rosa Maria García Periago, 'Quitting India, Quitting Shakespeare? The Curious Case of *1942: A Love Story*', *Proceedings of the 34th International ADEAN Conference*, Almeira (2010), 1–6.
28 Richard Burt, 'All That Remains of Shakespeare in Indian Film', in Dennis Kennedy and Yong Li Lan (eds), *Shakespeare in Asia: Contemporary Performance* (Cambridge: Cambridge University Press, 2010), 73–108, 97–8.
29 Davis, '"Death-Marked Love"'. The article has been reprinted several times: Dana Ramel Barnes (ed.), *Shakespearean Criticism* (Detroit: Gale, 1998), vol. 38, 31–40; Kathy D. Darrow and Michelle Lee (eds), *Shakespearean Criticism* (Detroit: Gale, 2000), vol. 51, 236–45; R. S. White (ed.), *Romeo and Juliet: Contemporary Critical Essays* (London: Palgrave, 2001), 28–46.
30 See Lloyd Davis, 'Living in the World: Communication and Culture in Early Modern England', in Philippa Kelly (ed.), *The Touch of the Real: Essays in Early Modern Culture* (Perth: University of Western Australia Press, 2002), 202–20, 214.
31 See R. S. White, 'The Rise and Fall of an Elizabethan Fashion: Love Letters in Prose Romance and Romantic Comedy', *Cahiers Elisabéthains*, 30 (1986), 35–47.
32 For some discussion of parodies, see Guneratne, *Shakespeare, Film Studies*, 158–9.
33 Douglas Lanier, 'Will of the People: Recent Shakespeare Film Parody and the Politics of Popularization', in Diana E. Henderson (ed.), *A Concise Companion to Shakespeare on Screen* (Oxford: Blackwell Publishing, 2006), 176–96.
34 Lanier, 'Will of the People', 195.

35 Lanier, 'Will of the People', 195.
36 In *Shakespeare's Local Habitations*, ed. Krystyna Kujawińska-Courtney and R. S. White (Łódź: Łódź University Press, 2007), 135–54.
37 See L. E. Boose and R. Burt, 'Totally Clueless: Shakespeare Goes Hollywood in the 1990s', in L. E. Boose and R. Burt (eds), *Shakespeare the Movie: Popularizing the Plays on Film, TV, and Video* (London and New York: Routledge, 1997), 8–22.

Conclusion

drame / drama: The amorous subject cannot write his love story himself. Only a very archaic form can accommodate the event which he declaims without being able to recount.
                            (Roland Barthes, *A Lover's Discourse: Fragments*)

Genres bear an odd, analogical resemblance to phrases we consider clichés, and both might be more important to our emotional lives than is given credit. Despite the assumption that the sentiments clichés convey are trite, insincere, and rendered vacuous from overuse, yet when pitched at just the right moment an apt if hackneyed saying can be profoundly reassuring: 'time heals all wounds', 'laughter is the best medicine'. Phrases like 'time will tell' or 'it's a matter of time' have the power to carry us through dark periods of uncertainty. Such apparent platitudes can help us face adversity with optimism – 'the darkest hour is before the dawn' – or to cooperate in some common endeavour – 'all for one and one for all', 'united we stand, divided we fall'. Most stem from 'time immemorial' but many can be traced back to written origins – somebody said them first and recorded the words – and here Shakespeare plays his part with attributions such as 'all's well that ends well', 'much ado about nothing', 'a rose by any other name would smell as sweet', and so on. He was almost certainly building on oral or biblical proverbial sayings coined long before, but we think not of the precursors but of his encapsulations in memorable language, occurring in a certain dramatic context but capable of being used out of context. The more eloquent or witty the wording of the expression, the more a presumed banality may acquire the flavour of a truism, 'what oft was thought but ne'er so well expressed' (to offer what has become another near-cliché, this time from Alexander Pope). The word itself is derived from the professional vocabulary of printing, since in French 'cliché' referred to the function (and 'click' sound) of a printing plate, as the basis for all that it could subsequently print – 'a metal stereotype of a wood-engraving used to print from', 'a process of copying' (both from *Oxford English Dictionary*), a mould, a 'matrix', which itself means 'a place or medium in which something is originated ... a point of origin and growth' and is derived from Latin *mater* for 'breeding female' and the late Middle English word for 'womb'. As a unit of thought a cliché is the *fons et origo* for all that is shaped into existence thereafter by using it. We live by clichés, and often we die by them, in the sense that they can reconcile us to the inevitableness of mortality: 'all that lives must die', intones Hamlet's mother, though in context her words are of little comfort to her grieving son; or 'ripeness is all'.

Genres, like clichés, are also created for human purposes, and as a kind of structural equivalent they can bear surprisingly similar functions. The writer's choice of genre is a starting point for a work of art, its pattern of expectations as yet awaiting content. It is the mould into which a story will be poured, the matrix that exists before words are supplied, and it will determine the emotional register of the experience (funny or sad? the bitter-sweet of tragi-comedy?). It anticipates a certain kind of closure, which may be satisfied or thwarted but still operates as a sustained expectation. The larger significance is that genre definition can provide reassurance that experiences are shaped towards certain ends in an orderly and providential universe, guided by an omniscient writer and detected by the reader or audience on the pulses. We are in safe hands, knowing in advance what kind of a journey to expect, and realising that although surprises along the way are expected, the ending is not in doubt. To quote a couple more clichés from Shakespeare that could be applied directly to genre, 'journeys end in lovers meeting' and 'the course of true love never did run smooth'. Feelings of either hope or fear, or the wide range of subtle possibilities between the two, that are generated by an awareness of genre keep us engaged, shape our experience, and give momentum and significance to the emotional logic to follow. Courtship between lovers (they hope) will lead to a happy ending of consummation, while the tribulations of lovers living in a violently divided society point to a violent destiny for them as sacrifices to others' hatred. Romantic comedy and romantic tragedy are born from and depend upon such hopes and fears. Even apart from narratives of love, as Diana Henderson points out, 'Tragedy in art has the compensation of giving shape and meaning to suffering',[1] and it can dignify pain by placing it in an aesthetically structured pattern so subject to repetition and variation that it seems culturally naturalised, perceived as universal despite its fictive and contextually bound nature. Assumptions of poetic justice, a moral apportionment of rewards and punishments, play a part also, and even when violated, as it is in Cordelia's fate, the rupture of expectations is a strongly determining part of the effect. *Love's Labour's*

Lost springs a surprise at the end, although we are never in doubt that we are in a comic world and all will be well eventually. The deferral of the expected betrothals makes us question whether the men in this case, having broken their oaths, are actually ready for 'the world without end bargain' of marriage, and that some gratifications are 'too long for a play', but it remains as a promise for future gratification.

Reduced to a sentence, the argument of this book has been that Shakespeare's experiments with genres often lie behind and influence the emotional and narrative logic of genres adopted in movies. The 'green world' has an almost exact equivalent in 'Tinseltown' and on 'the silver screen', which is now multicoloured. Correlatively, noticing this subtly transmitted historical influence can inform new understandings of Shakespeare's plays, thus adding a dimension to plays and movies alike in a mutual way. This process of reciprocal enlightenment is particularly visible in narratives dealing with love. Through the medium of movies, Shakespeare's conventions of genre have unobtrusively become the equivalent of structural clichés in movies, contributing to our most accessible modern matrices for living and loving. In the volatile and unpredictable world of love we probably need all the guidance we can get, and to know what kind of play we are living through can be helpful. If King Lear and Cordelia, or Antony and Cleopatra, had ended their stories at the moment of their moving reconciliations, their reprieve from tragedy would have provided comic closure, and if Othello and Desdemona had been given time enough to open the door to the knocking Aemilia then their tragedy could have swiftly turned to comedy as well.

A quick browse through the Internet reveals many titles from popular psychology along the lines of '5 types of love stories we experience' (or 7, 10, 25 – pick a number), and these regularly include categories such as love at first sight, friend-to-lover, secret crush, hate at first sight, 'opposites attract', 'the old flame relit', forbidden love, doomed love, and so on. Most are elaborations on the tripartite analysis of stages of love offered most prominently by the cultural anthropologist Helen Fisher, with help from neuroscience and the chemistry of the brain – infatuation, romance, and attachment (or passion, intimacy, and commitment).[2] But in the terms of this book, it is noteworthy first that the various kinds of love experiences available have a close relationship to the stories we are exposed to through films, and that are gathered into major genres and sub-genres like romantic comedy of courtship, 'bitter-sweet' ups and downs of melodrama, 'beauty and the beast' incongruous love, love 'second time around', screwball comedy of forceful individuals who bond through conflict, romantic tragedy based on 'forbidden love' that cannot be fulfilled in the society in which the lovers exist. Music is invariably involved in manipulating audience moods to expect which of these genres we are watching, and films in which music and dancing are dominant can amalgamate disparate genres into 'the musical' with its own set of sub-genres. It does look at least likely that our lives are constructed to fit the taxonomies used by the movie industry, that we expect and replicate patterns of love we see played out through repetition and variations in cinematic narratives. This is no doubt initially a Western phenomenon, but given the global reach of Hollywood it is surely becoming more international, either effacing local variations or fusing with them.

A second conclusion, if the drift of argument offered in this book is broadly accepted, is that behind these narratives of love encoded in film genres lie Shakespeare's plays, as a powerful but neglected influence. We can, then, reformulate the major kinds of genres based on love as stemming from the relationships he portrays, some of which have appeared above and others not presented in quite this way: Demetrius and Helena (transient infatuation), Viola and Orsino (secret crush), Helena and Bertram (pursuit and resistance), Titania and Bottom (beauty and the beast), Rosalind and Orlando (friendship to love), Petruccio and Katherina ('hate at first sight'), Benedick and Beatrice (love constructed socially by others), Leontes and Hermione ('second time around' melodrama), Romeo and Juliet (forbidden love). Both Shakespeare and the movies collaborate in mutual fashion to construct our living narratives of love with its joys and constraints, the stories we live by, telling us at any stage whether we are living through a romantic comedy, a comedy of errors, an odd-couple comedy, melodrama, or a doomed tragedy of love. It is a shame that, more often than not, life changes the script, though even surprises can lead to new and equally comforting (or discomforting) closures if we choose to change our script to suit another genre.

Notes

1 Diana E. Henderson, 'Introduction', in Diana E. Henderson (ed.), *A Concise Companion to Shakespeare on Screen* (Oxford: Blackwell Publishing, 2006), 2.
2 Fisher has written extensively on the subject: see especially *Why We Love: The Nature and Chemistry of Romantic Love* (New York: Henry Holt, 2004).

Bibliography

Adams, Michael, *'Who's Afraid of Virginia Woolf?': Barron's Book Notes* (New York: Barron's Educational Series, 1985).
Albee, Edward, *Who's Afraid of Virginia Woolf?* (Harmondsworth: Penguin Plays, 1962).
Allen, Richard, 'Comedies of Errors: Shakespeare, Indian Cinema, and the Poetics of Mistaken Identity', in Craig Dionne and Parmita Kapadia (eds), *Bollywood Shakespeares* (New York: Palgrave Macmillan, 2014), 165–92.
Altman, Rick, *The American Film Musical* (Bloomington: Indiana University Press, 1987).
—. *Film/Genre* (London: British Film Institute, 1999).
Anderegg, Michael, *Cinematic Shakespeare* (Lanham, MD: Rowman & Littlefield, 2004).
Armstrong, Richard, *Senses of Cinema: Billy Wilder*. Online: http://archive.sensesofcinema.com/contents/directors/02/wilder.html (accessed 12 September 2009).
Babington, Bruce, *Blue Skies and Silver Linings: Aspects of the Hollywood Musical* (Manchester: Manchester University Press, 1985).
Babington, Bruce and Peter William Evans, *Affairs to Remember: The Hollywood Comedy of the Sexes* (Manchester: Manchester University Press, 1989).
Ball, Robert Hamilton, *Shakespeare on Silent Film: A Strange Eventful History* (London: Allen & Unwin, 1968).
Barber, C. L., *Shakespeare's Festive Comedy* (Princeton, NJ: Princeton University Press, 1959).
Barker, Deborah E. and Ivo Kamps (eds), *Shakespeare and Gender: A History* (London: Verso, 1995).
Bell, Robert H., *Shakespeare's Great Stage of Fools* (London: Palgrave Macmillan, 2011).
Bell-Metereau, Rebecca, *Hollywood Androgyny* (New York: Columbia University Press, 1993).
Belsey, Catherine, 'Disrupting Sexual Difference: Meaning and Gender in the Comedies', in John Drakakis (ed.), *Alternative Shakespeares* (London and New York: Methuen, 1985), 166–90.

Benjamin, Walter, 'The Work of Art in the Age of Mechanical Reproduction', in *Illuminations: Essays and Reflections*, ed. Hannah Arendt, transl. Harry Zohn (New York: Schocken Books, 1968).

Bennett, Susan, *Performing Shakespeare: Shifting Shakespeare and the Contemporary Past* (London: Routledge, 1996).

Berek, Peter, 'Cross-Dressing, Gender, and Absolutism in the Beaumont and Fletcher Plays', *Studies in English Literature 1500–1900*, 44 (2004), 359–77.

Bergan, Ronald, 'Obituary: Irving Brecher', *Guardian*, 12 March 2009.

Berggren, Paula, '"A Prodigious Thing": The Jacobean Heroine in Male Disguise', *Philological Quarterly*, 62 (Summer 1983), 383–402.

Bloom, Harold, *The Anxiety of Influence: A Theory of Poetry* (New York: Oxford University Press, 1973).

Boose, Lynda E. and Richard Burt (eds), *Shakespeare the Movie: Popularizing the Plays on Film, TV, and Video* (London and New York: Routledge, 1997).

—. (eds), *Shakespeare the Movie II: Popularizing the Plays on Film, TV, Video, and DVD* (London and New York: Routledge, 2003).

Boose, Lynda E. and Richard Burt, 'Totally Clueless: Shakespeare Goes Hollywood in the 1990s', in Lynda E. Boose and Richard Burt (eds), *Shakespeare the Movie: Popularizing the Plays on Film, TV, and Video* (London and New York: Routledge, 1997), 8–22.

Bottoms, Stephen J., *Albee: Who's Afraid of Virginia Woolf?* (Cambridge: Cambridge University Press, 2000).

Bradbrook, Muriel, *The Growth and Structure of Elizabethan Comedy* (London: Chatto & Windus, 1955).

Brantlinger, Patrick, *Bread and Circuses: Theories of Mass Culture as Social Decay* (Ithaca, NY: Cornell University Press, 1983).

Brissenden, Alan, *Shakespeare and the Dance* (Atlantic Highlands, NJ: Humanities Press, 2001 [1981]).

Bristol, Michael D., *Shakespeare's America, America's Shakespeare* (London: Routledge, 1990).

Britton, Andrew, *Katharine Hepburn: Star as Feminist* (London: Studio Visa, 1995).

Brown, Daniel, 'Wilde and Wilder', *PMLA*, 119.5 (2004), 1216–30.

Buchanan, Judith, *Shakespeare on Film* (Harlow: Pearson Longman, 2005).

—. *Shakespeare on Silent Film: An Excellent Dumb Discourse* (Cambridge: Cambridge University Press, 2009).

Buhler, Stephen M., 'Musical Shakespeares: Attending to Ophelia, Juliet, and Desdemona', in Robert Shaughnessy (ed.), *The Cambridge Companion to Shakespeare and Popular Culture* (Cambridge: Cambridge University Press, 2007).

Burt, Richard, 'Afterword: Te(e)n Things I Hate about Girlene Shakesploitation Flicks in the Late 1990's, or Not-So-Fast Times at Shakespeare High', in Courtney Lehman and Lisa Starks (eds), *Spectacular Shakespeare: Critical Theory and Popular Cinema* (Teaneck, NJ: Fairleigh Dickinson University Press, 2002).

—. 'All That Remains of Shakespeare in Indian Film', in Dennis Kennedy and Yong Li Lan (eds), *Shakespeare in Asia: Contemporary Performance* (Cambridge: Cambridge University Press, 2010), 73–108.
Burt, Richard (ed.), *Shakespeares after Shakespeare: An Encyclopedia of the Bard in Mass Media and Popular Culture*, 2 vols (Westport, CT and London: Greenwood Press, 2007).
Callaghan, Dympna, *Shakespeare without Women: Representing Gender and Race on the Renaissance Stage* (London and New York: Routledge, 2000).
Cartelli, Thomas and Katherine Rowe, *New Wave Shakespeare on Screen* (Cambridge: Polity Press, 2007).
Carter, Tim, *Oklahoma!: The Making of an American Musical* (New Haven, CT: Yale University Press, 2007).
Cartmell, Deborah, *Interpreting Shakespeare on Screen* (London: Palgrave, 2000).
Cartmell, Deborah and Imelda Whelehan, *Screen Adaptation: Impure Cinema* (London: Palgrave Macmillan, 2010).
Cavell, Stanley, *Cavell on Film*, ed. William Rothman (New York: State University of New York, 2005).
Cavell, Stanley, *Contesting Tears: The Hollywood Melodrama of the Unknown Woman* (Chicago: University of Chicago Press, 1996).
—. *Pursuits of Happiness: The Hollywood Comedy of Remarriage* (Cambridge, MA: Harvard University Press, 1981).
Channan, Michael, *The Dream That Kicks: The Prehistory and Early Years of Cinema in Britain* (London and New York: Routledge, 1996).
Charlton, H. B., *Shakespearian Comedy* (London: Methuen, 1938).
Charnes, Linda, 'Dismember Me: Shakespeare, Paranoia, and the Logic of Mass Culture', *Shakespeare Quarterly*, 48.1 (1997), 1–16.
Chedgzoy, Kate, *Shakespeare's Queer Children: Sexual Politics and Contemporary Culture* (Manchester: Manchester University Press, 1996).
Clubb, Louise George (ed. and transl.), *Pollastra and the Origins of Twelfth Night* (Leicester: Ashgate, 2010).
Coates, Paul, *Film at the Intersection of High and Mass Culture* (Cambridge: Cambridge University Press, 1994).
Colie, Rosalie, *The Resources of Kind: Genre-Theory in the Renaissance* (Berkeley: University of California Press, 1973).
Conrad, Peter, *To Be Continued: Four Stories and Their Survival* (Oxford: Oxford University Press, 1995).
Cook, David A., *A History of Narrative Film* (New York: Norton, 1996).
Corrigan, Timothy, *Film and Literature: An Introduction and Reader* (Upper Saddle River, NJ: Prentice Hall, 1989).
Coursen, H. R., *Shakespeare Translated: Derivatives on Film and TV* (New York: Peter Lang, 2005).
Crowl, Samuel, *Shakespeare and Film: A Norton Guide* (New York: W. W. Norton & Co., 2008).
—. 'Shakespeare and Film Genre in the Branagh Generation', in Anthony R. Guneratne (ed.), *Shakespeare and Genre: From Early Modern Inheritances to Postmodern Legacies* (London: Palgrave Macmillan, 2012), 191–203.

Dash, Irene G., *Shakespeare and the American Musical* (Bloomington: Indiana University Press, 2010).
Davies, Anthony and Stanley Wells, *Shakespeare and the Moving Image: The Plays on Film and Television* (Cambridge: Cambridge University Press, 1994).
Davis, Lloyd, '"Death-Marked Love": Desire and Presence in *Romeo and Juliet*', *Shakespeare Survey*, 49 (1996), 57–67.
—. 'Living in the World: Communication and Culture in Early Modern England', in Philippa Kelly (ed.), *The Touch of the Real: Essays in Early Modern Culture* (Perth: University of Western Australia Press, 2002), 202–20.
Deleyto, Celestino, *The Secret Life of Romantic Comedy* (Manchester: Manchester University Press, 2009).
Derrida, Jacques, *Specters of Marx: The State of the Debt, the Work of Mourning, and the New International*, transl. Peggy Kamuf (London: Routledge, 1994).
Dika, Vera, *Recycled Culture in Contemporary Art and Film: The Uses of Nostalgia* (Cambridge: Cambridge University Press, 2003).
Dillon, Janette, *Shakespeare and the Solitary Man* (London: Macmillan, 1981).
Dionne, Craig and Parmita Kapadia (eds), *Bollywood Shakespeares* (New York: Palgrave Macmillan, 2014).
Dirks, Tim, 'Film Genres: Origins and Types'. Online: www.filmsite.org (accessed 5 March 2009).
Dixon, Wheeler Winston (ed.), *American Cinema of the 1940s: Themes and Variations* (New Brunswick, NJ: Rutgers University Press, 2006).
Donaldson, Peter S., *Shakespearean Films/Shakespearean Directors* (Boston: Unwin Hyman, 1990).
Duffin, Ross W., *Shakespeare's Songbook* (New York and London: W. W. Norton & Co., 2004).
Dusinberre, Juliet, *Shakespeare and the Nature of Women* (New York: Macmillan, 1975).
Dwyer, Rachel, *100 Bollywood Films* (London: British Film Institute, 2005).
Eastwood, Adrienne L., 'Between Wedding and Bedding: The Epithalamic Sub-Genre in Shakespeare's Comedies', *Exemplaria*, 22 (2010), 240–62.
Eisenstein, Sergei, 'Dickens, Griffith, and Ourselves' (alternatively titled 'Dickens, Griffith, and Film Today'), *Film Form* (1942), repr. Leo Braudy and Marshall Cohen (eds), *Film Theory and Criticism* (New York: Oxford University Press, 2004 [1974]).
Evans, Bertrand, *Shakespeare's Comedies* (Oxford: Clarendon Press, 1960).
Fermanis, Porscha, *John Keats and the Ideas of the Enlightenment* (Edinburgh: Edinburgh University Press, 2009).
Fiedler, Leslie A., *The Stranger in Shakespeare: Studies in the Archetypal Underworld of the Plays* (New York: Stein and Day, 1972).
Fisher, Helen, *Why We Love: The Nature and Chemistry of Romantic Love* (New York: Henry Holt, 2004).
Folkerth, Wes, 'Popular Music', in Richard Burt (ed.), *Shakespeares after Shakespeare: An Encyclopedia of the Bard in Mass Media and Popular Culture* (Westport, CT: Greenwood Press, 2007), vol. I, ch. 5.

French, Marilyn, *Shakespeare's Division of Experience* (New York: Summit Books, 1981).
Fritzer, Penelope Joan, *Jane Austen and Eighteenth-Century Courtesy Books* (Westport, CT: Greenwood Press, 1997).
Frow, John, *Genre* (London: Routledge, 2006).
Frye, Northrop, *A Natural Perspective: The Development of Shakespearean Comedy and Romance* (New York: Columbia University Press, 1965).
Garber, Marjorie, *Vested Interests: Cross-Dressing and Cultural Anxiety* (London: Penguin Books, 1993).
Gay, Penny, *As She Likes It: Shakespeare's Unruly Women* (London: Routledge, 1994).
Gehring, Wes D., *Romantic vs. Screwball Comedy: Charting the Difference* (Lanham, MD: The Scarecrow Press, Inc., 2002).
Glitre, Kathrina, *Hollywood Romantic Comedy: States of the Union 1934–65* (Manchester: Manchester University Press, 2006).
Goldsmith, R. H., *Wise Fools in Shakespeare* (East Lansing: Michigan State University Press, 1955).
Gooch, Bryan N. S. and David Thatcher (eds), *A Shakespeare Music Catalogue*, 5 vols (Oxford: Oxford University Press, 1991).
Grant, Barry Keith, *Film Genre: From Iconography to Ideology* (London: Wallflower Press, 2007).
Grant, Barry Keith (ed.), *Film Genre Reader* (Austin: University of Texas Press, 1993).
Granville-Barker, Harley, *Prefaces to Shakespeare: First Series* (London: Sidgwick & Jackson, 1927).
Guneratne, Anthony R., *Shakespeare, Film Studies, and the Visual Cultures of Modernity* (New York: Palgrave Macmillan, 2008).
—.(ed.), *Shakespeare and Genre: From Early Modern Inheritances to Postmodern Legacies* (London: Palgrave Macmillan, 2012).
Gurr, Andrew and Farah Karim-Cooper (eds), *Moving Shakespeare Indoors: Performance and Repertoire in the Jacobean Playhouse* (Cambridge: Cambridge University Press, 2014).
Guyon, William (ed.), *The Routledge Companion to Film History* (London: Routledge, 2011).
Hansen, Adam, *Shakespeare and Popular Music* (London: Continuum, 2010).
Hartnoll, Phyllis (ed.), *Shakespeare in Music: A Collection of Essays* (London: Macmillan, 1966).
Harvey, James, *Romantic Comedy in Hollywood: From Lubitsch to Sturges* (New York: Da Capo Press, 1998).
Henderson, Diana E. (ed.), *A Concise Companion to Shakespeare on Screen* (London: John Wiley & Sons, 2006).
—. 'A Shrew for the Times', in Lynda E. Boose and Richard Burt (eds), *Shakespeare the Movie: Popularizing the Plays on Film, TV, and Video* (London and New York: Routledge, 1997), 148–68.
Hindle, Maurice, *Studying Shakespeare on Film* (London: Palgrave Macmillan, 2007).

Hirschhorn, Clive, *The Hollywood Musical* (London: Octopus Books, 1981).

Hischak, Thomas, 'Shakespeare Musicals', in *The Oxford Companion to the American Musical: Theatre, Film, and Television* (Oxford: Oxford University Press, 2008), 669–70.

Hodgdon, Barbara, 'Baz Luhrmann's *William Shakespeare's Romeo + Juliet*', in R. S. White (ed.), *Romeo and Juliet: Contemporary Critical Essays* (London: Palgrave, 2001), 129–46.

Hopkins, Lisa, *Relocating Shakespeare and Austen on Screen* (London: Palgrave Macmillan, 2009).

Howard, Jean E., 'Crossdressing, the Theatre, and Gender Struggle in Early Modern England', *Shakespeare Quarterly*, 39 (Winter 1988), 418–40.

Howard, Tony, 'Shakespeare's Cinematic Offshoots', in Russell Jackson (ed.), *The Cambridge Companion to Shakespeare on Film* (Cambridge: Cambridge University Press, 2000), 295–313.

Hunter, G. K., *John Lyly: The Humanist as Courtier* (London: Routledge & Kegan Paul, 1962).

—. 'The Making of a Popular Repertory: Hollywood and the Elizabethans', in John Batchelor, Tom Cain, and Claire Lamont (eds), *Shakespearean Continuities: Essays in Honour of E. A. J. Honigmann* (Basingstoke: Macmillan Press, 1997), 247–58.

Huntley, Rebecca, *The World According to Y* (Sydney: Allen & Unwin, 2006).

Jackson, Russell (ed.), *The Cambridge Companion to Shakespeare on Film* (Cambridge: Cambridge University Press, 2000).

Jaffe, Ira, *Hollywood Hybrids: Mixing Genres in Contemporary Films* (Lanham, MD: Rowman & Littlefield, 2008).

Jardine, Lisa, *Reading Shakespeare Historically* (Hoboken, NJ: Taylor & Francis, 1996).

Jenkins, Harold, '*As You Like It*', *Shakespeare Survey*, 8 (2002), 40–51.

Jenkins, Linda, 'Locating the Language of Gender Experience', *Women and Performance: A Journal of Feminist Theory*, 2 (1984), 5–20.

Jess-Cooke, Carolyn, *Shakespeare on Film: Such Things as Dreams Are Made of* (London: Wallflower Press, 2007).

Jorgens, Jack J., *Shakespeare on Film* (Lanham, MD: University Press of America, 1991).

Karnick, Kristina Brunovska and Henry Jenkins (eds), *Classical Hollywood Comedy* (New York: Routledge, 1995).

Keyishian, Harry, 'Shakespeare and Movie Genre: The Case of *Hamlet*', in Russell Jackson (ed.), *The Cambridge Companion to Shakespeare on Film* (Cambridge: Cambridge University Press, 2000), 72–84.

Kishi, Tetsuo, *Shakespeare in Japan* (London: Continuum, 2005).

Kott, Jan, *Shakespeare Our Contemporary* (London: Methuen, 1965).

Kuhn, Annette, 'Sexual Disguise and Cinema', in *The Power of the Image: Essays on Representation and Sexuality* (London: Routledge & Kegan Paul, 1985), 48–73.

Kujawińska-Courtney, Krystyna, 'From Kott to Commerce: Shakespeare in Communist and Post-Communist Poland', in Krystyna Kujawińska-Courtney and R. S. White (eds), *Shakespeare's Local Habitations* (Łódź: Łódź University Press, 2007), 13–33.

Lane, Joan (ed.), with medical commentary by Melvin Earles, *John Hall and His Patients: The Medical Practice of Shakespeare's Son-in-Law* (Stratford-upon-Avon: The Shakespeare Birthplace Trust, 1996).

Langford, Barry, *Film Genre: Hollywood and Beyond* (Edinburgh: Edinburgh University Press, 2005).

Lanier, Douglas, '"I'll Teach You Differences": Genre, Literacy, Critical Pedagogy, and Screen Shakespeare', in Anthony R. Guneratne (ed.), *Shakespeare and Genre: From Early Modern Inheritances to Postmodern Legacies* (London: Palgrave Macmillan, 2012), 257–70.

—. 'Shakespearean Rhizomatics', in Alexa Huang and Elizabeth Rivlin (eds), *Adaptation, Ethics, Value* (London: Palgrave Macmillan, 2014), 21–40.

—. 'William Shakespeare, Filmmaker', in Deborah Cartmell and Imelda Whelehan (eds), *The Cambridge Companion to Literature on Screen* (Cambridge: Cambridge University Press, 2007), 61–74.

Lent, Tina Olsin, 'Romantic Love and Friendship: The Redefinition of Gender Relations in Screwball Comedy', in Kristina Brunovska Karnick and Henry Jenkins (eds), *Classical Hollywood Comedy* (New York: Routledge, 1995), 314–31.

Lenz, Carolyn Ruth Swift, Gayle Greene, and Carol Thomas Neely (eds), *The Woman's Part: Feminist Criticism of Shakespeare* (Urbana: University of Illinois Press, 1980).

Levenson, Jill, *Shakespeare in Performance: Romeo and Juliet* (Manchester: Manchester University Press, 1987).

Levine, Laura, *Men in Women's Clothing: Anti-Theatricality and Effeminization, 1579–1642* (Cambridge: Cambridge University Press, 1994).

Lindley, David, *Shakespeare and Music* (London: Thomson Learning, Arden Critical Companions, 2006).

Loehlin, James N., '"These Violent Delights Have Violent Ends": Baz Luhrmann's Millennial Shakespeare', in Mark Thornton Burnett and Ramona Wray (eds), *Shakespeare, Film, Fin de Siècle* (London: Palgrave, 2000), 121–37.

Logan, Robert A., *The Influence of Christopher Marlowe on Shakespeare's Artistry* (Aldershot: Ashgate, 2006).

Loomba, Ania, *Shakespeare, Race, and Colonialism* (Oxford: Oxford University Press, 2002).

Lynch, Stephen J., *Shakespearean Intertextuality: Studies in Selected Plays and Sources* (Westport, CT: Greenwood Press, 1998).

McKernan, Luke and Olwen Terris, *Walking Shadows: Shakespeare in the National Film and Television Archive* (London: British Film Institute, 1994).

McQuade, Paula, 'Love and Lies: Marital Truth-Telling, Catholic Casuistry, and *Othello*', in Dennis Taylor and David N. Beauregard (eds), *Shakespeare and*

the Culture of Christianity in Early Modern England (New York: Fordham University Press, 2003), 415–38.
Maltby, Richard, 'Comedy and the Restoration of Order', in Jeffrey Geiger and R. L. Rutsky (eds), *Film Analysis: A Norton Reader* (New York: W. W. Norton & Co., 2005), 216–37.
Moine, Raphaëlle, *Cinema Genre*, transl. Alistair Fox and Hilary Radner (Oxford: Blackwell Publishing, 2008).
Mulvey, Laura, 'Visual Pleasure and Narrative Cinema' (1975), repr. in E. Ann Kaplan (ed.), *Feminism and Film* (Oxford: Oxford University Press, 2000), 34–47.
Munakata, Kuniyoshi, *'Hamlet' Noh Style: Collected Versions 1982–1990* (Tokyo: Kenkyusha, 1991).
Murray, Timothy, *Drama Trauma: Specters of Race and Sexuality in Performance, Video, and Art* (London and New York: Routledge, 1997).
Naylor, Edward W., *Shakespeare and Music* (London: J. M. Dent & Sons, 1896).
Neale, Steve, *Genre and Hollywood* (London and New York: Routledge, 2000).
Nicoll, Allardyce, *Film and Theatre* (London: George G. Harrap, 1936).
Orgel, Stephen, *Impersonations: The Performance of Gender in Shakespeare's England* (Cambridge: Cambridge University Press, 1996).
Parsons, Elinor, 'The Framing of the "Shrew": Screen Versions of "The Taming of the Shrew"', unpublished PhD thesis, Royal Holloway, University of London (2008).
Pasternak, Boris, 'From "Notes of a Translator"', in Carl J. Proffer (ed.), *Russian Poets on Poetry* (Ann Arbor, MI: Ardis, 1976).
Pequigney, Joseph, *Such Is My Love: A Study of Shakespeare's Sonnets* (Chicago: Chicago University Press, 1985).
Periago, Rosa Maria García, 'Quitting India, Quitting Shakespeare? The Curious Case of *1942: A Love Story*', *Proceedings of the 34th International ADEAN Conference*, Almeira (2010), 1–6.
Pfister, Manfred, 'Germany Is Hamlet: The History of a Political Interpretation', *New Comparison: A Journal of Comparative and General Literary Studies*, 2 (Autumn 1986), 106–26.
Poague, Leland, 'Cavell and the Fantasy of Criticism: Shakespearean Comedy and *Ball of Fire*', *CineAction*, 9 (Summer 1987), 47–55.
Poggioli, Renato, *The Oaten Flute: Essays on Pastoral Poetry and the Pastoral Ideal* (Cambridge, MA: Harvard University Press, 1975).
Radner, Hilary, 'Film as Popular Culture', in William Guyon (ed.), *The Routledge Companion to Film History* (London: Routledge, 2011).
Rickman, Gregg (ed.), *The Film Comedy Reader* (New York: Limelight Editions, 2001).
Rothwell, Kenneth S., *Early Shakespeare Movies: How the Spurned Spawned Art* (Chipping Campden: International Shakespeare Association, Occasional paper No. 8, 2000).
—. *A History of Shakespeare on Screen: A Century of Film and Television* (Cambridge: Cambridge University Press, 1999).

Rothwell, Kenneth S. and Annabelle Henkin Malzer, *Shakespeare on Screen: An International Filmography and Videography* (New York: Neal Schuman Publishers Inc, 1992).
Rowe, Eleanor, *Hamlet: A Window on Russia* (New York: New York University Press, 1976).
Rowe, Kathleen, 'Comedy, Melodrama and Gender: Theorizing the Genres of Laughter', in Kristina Brunovska Karnick and Henry Jenkins (eds), *Classical Hollywood Comedy* (New York: Routledge, 1995), 39–59.
Said, Edward, 'On Originality', in *The World, the Text, and the Critic* (Cambridge, MA: Harvard University Press, 1983).
Salamansky, S. I., '*Bringing Up Baby* (1938): Screwball and the Con of Modern Culture', in Jeffrey Geiger and R. L. Rutsky (eds), *Film Analysis: A Norton Reader* (New York: W. W. Norton & Co., 2005), 282–99.
Salingar, Leo, *Shakespeare and the Traditions of Comedy* (Cambridge: Cambridge University Press, 1974).
Sallitt, Dan, 'Ernst Lubitsch: The Actor vs the Character', repr. in Gregg Rickman (ed.), *The Film Comedy Reader* (New York: Limelight Editions, 2001), 154–8.
Sammons, Eddie, *Shakespeare: A Hundred Years on Film* (London: Shepheard-Walwyn, 2000).
Sanders, Julie, *Shakespeare and Music: Afterlives and Borrowings* (Cambridge: Polity Press, 2007).
Schalkwyk, David, 'Music, Food, and Love in the Affective Landscapes of *Twelfth Night*', in James Schiffer (ed.), *Twelfth Night: New Critical Essays* (London and New York: Routledge, 2011), 81–98.
Schiffer, James (ed.), *Twelfth Night: New Critical Essays* (London and New York: Routledge, 2011).
Seng, Peter J., *The Vocal Songs in the Plays of Shakespeare: A Critical History* (Cambridge, MA: Harvard University Press, 1967).
Shakespeare, William, *The Complete Works*, 2nd edn, ed. Stanley Wells and Gary Taylor (Oxford: Clarendon Press, 2005).
Shapiro, Michael, *Gender in Play on the Shakespearean Stage: Boy Heroines and Female Pages* (Ann Arbor: University of Michigan Press, 1994).
Shaughnessy, Robert (ed.), *The Cambridge Companion to Shakespeare and Popular Culture* (Cambridge: Cambridge University Press, 2007).
Sidney, Sir Philip, *A Defence of Poetry*, in Katherine Duncan-Jones and Jan van Dorsten (eds), *Miscellaneous Prose of Sir Philip Sidney* (Oxford: Oxford University Press, 1973).
Sikov, Ed, *Laughing Hysterically: American Screen Comedy of the 1950s* (New York: Columbia University Press, 1994).
Spadafora, David, *The Idea of Progress in Eighteenth-Century Britain* (New Haven, CT: Yale University Press, 1990).
Spurgeon, Caroline, *Shakespeare's Imagery and What It Tells Us* (Cambridge: Cambridge University Press, 1935).
Sternfeld, F. W., *Music in Shakespearean Tragedy* (Abingdon: Routledge, 2005 [1963]).

Thompson, Ann (ed.), *The Taming of the Shrew* (Cambridge: The New Cambridge Shakespeare, 1984).

Thompson, Joanna, *The Character of Britomart in Spenser's 'The Faerie Queene'* (Lampeter: The Edwin Mellen Press, 2001).

Tibbetts, John C. and James M. Welsh (eds), *The Encyclopedia of Novels into Movies* (New York: Facts on File Inc., 1998).

Tilney, Edmund, *Briefe and Pleasant Discourse of Duties in Marriage, Called the Flower of Friendshippe* (1568), repr. *The Flower of Friendship: A Renaissance Dialogue Contesting Marriage* (Ithaca, NY: Cornell University Press, 1992).

Tolstoy, Leo, *On Shakespeare and on Drama* (1903), transl. V. Tchertkoff (New York: Funk & Wagnalls Company, 1906).

Tomlinson, Gary, *Music in Renaissance Magic: Toward a Historiography of Others* (Chicago and London: University of Chicago Press, 1993).

Trigg, Stephanie, 'Transparent Walls: Stained Glass and Cinematic Medievalism', *Screening the Past*, 26 (2009). Online: www.latrobe.edu.au/screeningthepast/26/early-europe/stained-glass-cinematic-medievalism.html.

Trivedi, Harish, 'Colonizing Love: *Romeo and Juliet* in Modern Indian Disseminations', in Poonam Trivedi and Dennis Bartholomeusz (eds), *India's Shakespeare: Translation, Interpretation, and Performance* (New Delhi: Dorling Kindersley, 2006), 66–81.

Troost, Linda and Sayre Greenfield (eds), *Jane Austen in Hollywood*, 2nd edn (Lexington: University of Kentucky Press, 2001).

van Laan, Thomas F., *Role-Playing in Shakespeare* (Toronto: University of Toronto Press, 1978).

Verma, Rajiva, 'Shakespeare in Hindi Cinema', in Poonam Trivedi and Dennis Bartholomeusz (eds), *India's Shakespeare: Translation, Interpretation and Performance* (New Delhi: Dorling Kindersley, 2006), 276–9.

Wade, Barrie and John Shepherd, 'Shakespeare in the Curriculum: Direction by Content' (dealing with the Newbolt Report), *Educational Studies*, 19 (1993), 267–74.

Welsford, Enid, *The Fool: His Social and Literary History* (London: Faber & Faber, 1935).

White, R. S., 'Functions of Poems and Songs in Elizabethan Romance and Romantic Comedy', *English Studies: A Journal of English Language and Literature*, 68.5 (1987), 392–405.

—. *Let Wonder Seem Familiar: Endings in Shakespeare's Romance Vision* (London: Athlone Press, 1985).

—. 'Metamorphosis by Love in Elizabethan Romance, Romantic Comedy and Shakespeare's Early Comedies', *Review of English Studies*, 35 (1984), 14–44.

White, R. S. (ed.), *Romeo and Juliet: Contemporary Critical Essays* (London: Palgrave, 2001).

—. '*Romeo and Juliet*: A Mediterranean Love Story', *Shakespeare and the Classroom*, 10 (2002), 45–54.

Wilson, Christopher and Michela Calore (eds), *Music and Shakespeare: A Dictionary* (London: Bloomsbury, 2005).

Wilson, John Dover, *Shakespeare's Happy Comedies* (London: Faber, 1962).
Wray, Ramona and Mark Thornton Burnett, 'From the Horse's Mouth: Branagh on the Bard', in Mark Thornton Burnett and Ramona Wray (eds), *Shakespeare, Film, Fin de Siècle* (London: Palgrave, 2000).
Young, D. P., *The Heart's Forest: A Study of Shakespeare's Pastoral Plays* (New Haven, CT: Yale University Press, 1972).
Younger, Prakash, 'Film as Art', in William Guyon (ed.), *The Routledge Companion to Film History* (London: Routledge, 2011).

Index

10 Things I Hate About You (1999) 23, 40, 68, 123

Abhijnanasakuntalam 201
Abramov, A. 109
Adam's Rib (1949) 13, 59, 60
Adventures of Priscilla, Queen of the Desert, The (1994) 159
Agapi kai amai (1968) 180
All About Eve (1950) 63, 68
All Night Long (1962) 3
All That Heaven Allows (1955) 32
Allen, Richard 144
Allen, Woody 92, 93
Altman, Rick 15, 71, 113, 114, 115, 129
American in Paris, An (1951) 95
Anchors Aweigh (1945) 121
Anderegg, Michael 63
Angelic Conversation (1985) 23
Angoor (1982) 144
Animated Shakespeare, The (1994) 23
Anjuman (1948, 1986, 1987) 201
Aristotle 15
Arthur, Jean 43
Astaire, Fred 83, 115, 119, 170, 171
Austen, Jane 9, 10, 28
avant-garde 23
Awful Truth, The (1925, 1929, 1937) 13

Babes in Toyland (1934) 159
Babes in the Woods (1964) 123
Babington, Bruce 168

Bade Miyan Chote Miyan (1998) 145
Bakhtin, Mikhail 77
Balachander, Tamil K. 203
Ball, Robert Hamilton 14, 184
Ball of Fire (1941) 106
Bandello, Matteo 180
Barber, C. L. 73
Barrymore, Drew 105
Barrymore, Ethel 124, 125
Barrymore, John 123, 186
Beaumont, Francis 152, 153, 157, 176
Becoming Jane (2007) 10
Beethoven, Ludwig van 157
Bell-Metereau, Rebecca 148, 157, 160, 164
Bellini, Vincenzo 183
Bend It Like Beckham (2002) 158
Berkeley, Busby 115, 117, 186
Berlioz, Hector 183
Bernhardt, Sarah 20
Bernstein, Leonard 122, 183, 193
Better than Chocolate (1999) 23
Birdcage, The (1996) 159
Black Narcissus (1947) 134
Blake, William 28, 29
Bloom, Harold 8
Blue Lagoon, The (1980) 134
Bluebeard's Eighth Wife (1938) 54
Bobby (1973) 204
Body and Soul (1947) 28
Bollywood 18, 22, 24, 31, 78, 143, 144, 146, 193, 201, 202, 203, 205, 207

Bollywood/Hollywood (2002) 31
Bonnie and Clyde (1967) 191
Borges, Jean Luis 24
Bowie, David 168
Boys from Syracuse, The (1940) 142, 143, 146, 147, 148, 149
Bradbrook, Muriel 84
Bradley, A. C. 181
Branagh, Kenneth 14, 21, 109, 119, 120, 122
Brando, Marlon 134
Breakfast at Tiffany's (1961) 31, 80
Bride and Prejudice (2004) 10
Bringing Up Baby (1938) 13, 78, 89, 91, 92, 106
Brook, Peter 97, 119
Brooke, Arthur 180, 214
Brooks, Mel 14
Brown, Joe E. 123, 162
Browning, Elizabeth Barrett 196
Buchanan, Judith 12
Burt, Richard 5, 6, 180, 207
Burton, Richard 47, 48, 66, 68
Butch Jamie (2007) 157
By Candlelight (1934) 174

C21 Theatre Company 185
Cabaret (1972) 80, 159
Caesar and Cleopatra (1945) 134
Cagney, James 117, 128
Capote, Truman 80
Caron, Lesley 95, 96
Carousel (1956) 77, 130, 132
Carpaccio, Vittore 187
Carry on Teacher (1959) 178
Cartelli, Thomas 15
Cartmell, Deborah 3, 5, 7, 179
Casablanca (1942) 103, 119
Casanova in Burlesque (1944) 123
Catch My Soul (1974) 123
Cavalleria Rusticana (1955, 1982) 196
Cavell, Stanley 12, 14, 51, 85, 88, 91
Cayatte, Andre 181
Chan, Audrey 218
Chaplin, Charlie 135, 159

Charlton, H. B. 84
Chiaroscuro 187
Chicken Rice War (2000) 22, 217
children's animations 23
China Girl (1987) 193
Cleese, John 63
Cleopatra (1963) 47
Clueless (1995) 10
Colbert, Claudette 56
Cold War 130, 183
Collins, J. 115
Comedy of Errors, Angoor (1988) 21
Congreve, William 41
Conrad, Peter 182
Conscience of the King, The 29
Cornell, Katharine 122
Corrigan, Timothy 7
Cowboy and the Shrew, The (1911) 40
crime and gangster 23
cross-dressing 74, 77, 83, 152, 153, 157, 159, 160, 162, 166, 168, 169
Crowl, Samuel 5, 15, 76, 119
Cukor, George 182, 186
cult 23, 168, 194
Curtis, Tony 79, 103, 159
Cushman, Charlotte 182
Czinner, Paul 98

Dam Dama Dam (1998) 145
Dancing Master, The (1943) 159
Dash, Irene G. 50, 111, 124, 140, 183
David and Layla (2005) 193
Davis, Bette 63, 64, 66, 84
Davis, Lloyd 179, 212, 213
Day, Doris 174
Dead Poets' Society (1989) 96
Dean, James 187, 193
Deleuze, Gilles 15
Deliver Us from Eva (2003) 40
Derrida, Jacques 8
Dickens, Charles 4, 178
Dika, Vera 21
Dil Bole Hadippa! (2009) 23, 158

Dire Straits 183
Dirks, Tim 22
disaster 23, 24
disguise 2, 8, 33, 44, 48, 61, 62, 71, 74, 77, 79, 80, 81, 83, 89, 98, 99, 104, 105, 117, 120, 121, 136, 140, 146, 148–77
Disney 157
Dixon, Wheeler Winston 54
Do Dooni Char (1968) 144
Doctor Who 29, 184
Donovan 112
Dorsey, Michael 163, 164, 165, 166
Double di Trouble (2014) 145
Double Indemnity (1944) 79
Double Life, A (1947) 3, 23
Dream (1935) 97
Dryden, John 12
Duffin, Ross, W 111, 112, 122
Dufy, Raoul 95
Dumas, Alexander 174
Dunne, Irene 43, 52
Dwyer, Rachel 204

Eddie, Nelson 115
Eisenstein, Sergei 4
Ek Duuje Ke Liye (1981) 203
Elizabeth I, Queen of England 168
Emma (1996) 10
epic 17, 20, 23, 114, 116, 201, 202
erotic and pornographic 23, 24, 91, 156, 185, 190, 217
Ethel's Romeo (1915) 184
Evans, Bertrand 149
Evans, Peter 168
Exorcism, The (1973) 66
Eyes in the Night (1942) 30

Fairbanks, Douglas 46
farce 16, 32, 52, 68, 81, 114, 117, 141, 142, 143, 184, 195
Faulkner, William 28
Fawlty Towers 63
Fermanis, Porscha 9
Fielding, Henry 156

film noir 4, 23, 30, 92, 103, 115, 179
fin de siècle 21
Fini, Leonor 187
Fire with Fire (1986) 185
First a Girl (1935) 1, 2, 13, 157
First World War 122, 126, 157, 184
Fitzgerald, F. Scott 27, 31
Fletcher, John 29, 152, 153, 157
Flintstones, The 141
Foch, Nina 95
fool 6, 75, 78, 84, 88, 104, 118, 136, 142, 154
Forbidden Planet (1956) 23
Force of Evil (1948) 28
Foster, Preston 58
Fox Studio 190
Framing of the Shrew, The (1929) 40
Francesca, Piero della 187
Frankenstein (1931) 103
Freiligrath, Ferdinand 25
Freud, Sigmund 84
Frid, Yan 109
Frow, John 21
Frye, Northrop 54, 73, 75, 76, 113, 114
Funny Face (1957) 173
Funny Thing Happened on the Way to the Forum, A (1966) 166

Gable, Clark 56
Garber, Marjorie 157, 164
Garland, Judy 101
gay 1, 2, 23, 24, 89, 169
Gehring, Wes D. 53, 82
generation gap 179, 197
Gershwin, George 95, 96, 119
Get Over It (2001) 97
Gielgud, Sir John 187
Gipsy Blood in America (1918) 79
Glen or Glenda (1953) 159
Glitre, Kathrina 110
Globe, The 110
Gnomeo and Juliet (2011) 182
Godard, Jean-Luc 14
Goethe, Johann Wolfgang (von) 25

Gol Maal (1979) 144
Gold Diggers of 1933 (musical 1933) 171
Goliyon Ki Raasleel Ram-Leela (2013) 205
Good Die Young, The (1954) 187
Goodbye to Berlin (1939) 80
Grant, Barry Keith 17
Grant, Cary 79, 86, 89, 99, 159
Granville-Barker, Harley 76, 84, 109
Grayson, Kathryn 49
Great Expectations (1946) 134
Greene, Robert 142, 169
Greer, Germaine 163
Gregory's Girl (1981) 158
Grewal, Gippy 146
Gruffud, Ioan 209
grunge 23, 185
Guattari, Pierre-Félix 15
Guess Who's Coming to Dinner (1967) 208
Guneratne, Anthony R. 12
Guys and Dolls (Broadway musical 1955) 132, 133, 135

Hamlet (1948) 22
Hamlet in Rock (2008) 124
Hammer, Mike 4
Hammerstein, Oscar 129, 130, 140
Happy Go Lovely (1951) 171, 172, 174
Hardy, Thomas 170
Hart, Lorenz 129, 130, 140
Havilland, Olivia de 117
Hayworth, Rita 61, 83, 170
Heer Ranjha (also remade at least ten times between 1928 and 2009) 201
Heliodorus 142
Henderson Diana E. 39, 48, 224
Henry V (1944) 23, 122
Hepburn, Audrey 80, 103, 104, 172, 173
Hepburn, Katharine 14, 43, 59, 86, 89, 99, 165

Her Majesty's Theatre, London 19
Hervey, Irene 141
His Girl Friday (1940) 13
Hitler, Adolf 79
Hodgdon, Barbara 179
Hoffman, Dustin 163, 164, 166, 167
Hoffman, E. T. A. 146
Hoffman, Michael 21, 97
Holiday (1938) 99, 100
Hollywood 7, 13, 14, 17, 18, 19, 21, 22, 26, 27, 28, 30, 31, 32, 46, 51, 53, 54, 61, 71–3, 76, 82, 85, 95, 97, 102, 110–13, 116–19, 128–30, 148, 156, 164, 170–1, 175, 185, 186, 191–2, 197–8, 200, 209, 216, 226
Hopkins, Lisa 10
horror 23, 24, 103
Horton, Priscilla 182
Howard, John 86
Howard, Trevor 186
Hudson, Rock 174
Humphries, Barry 159
Hunter, G. K. 27, 28, 44, 73
Hussey, Olivia 188

I Am a Camera (1955) 80
I Married a Witch (1942) 85
I Was a Male War Bride (1949) 159
Ich möchte kein Mann sein (I Don't Want to Be a Man) (1918) 157
Indian Romeo and Juliet (1912) 182
Internet Movie Database (IMDb) 3, 41
Iron Strain, The (1915) 40
Isaaq (2013) 201
Ishaqzaade (2012) 201
Isherwood, Christopher 80
It Happened One Night (1934, 1958, 2017) 13, 56, 57, 68, 172

Jackson, Michael 189
Jackson, Russell 5
James I, King of England 153
James Bond films 31

James, Sid 14
James, Stewart 86
Jameson, Frederic 21
Japanese Noh 10, 25
Jazz Singer, The (1929) 113, 124
Jennings, Humphrey 122
Jess-Cooke, Carolyn 14, 24
Jones, Allan 141
Jonson Benjamin 166
Josh (2000) 193
Jubal (1956) 23
Juliet and Darkness and *Bright Light in a Dark Room* 198, 200
Julius Caesar (1953) 23, 47, 116, 132

Kean, Edmund 182
Keats, John 5, 9
Keel, Howard 49
Kelly, Gene 95, 96, 115, 121, 124
Kemble, John Philip 182
Keyishian, Harry 14
Keystone Cops (1915) 135
King and I, The (1956) 130
King Is Alive, The (2000) 23
King Lear (1987) 23
Kirk, James T. 14
Kiss Me, Kate (Broadway musical 1948) 33, 40, 123
Kiss Me Kate (1953) 23, 48, 50
Kotsintsev, Grigori 26, 181
Kott, Jan 26
Kuhn, Annette 149
Kurosawa, Akira 25, 181

La Cage aux Folles (1978) 159
La Mort de Jules César (1907) 14
Lady Eve, The (1941) 13, 173
Lady Oscar (1979) 157
Lady Windermere's Fan (1925) 79
Laila Majnu, Sohni Mahiwal (remade ten times between 1928 and 1984) 201
Lamb, Charles and Mary 189
Langford, Barry 21
Lanier, Douglas 5, 14, 15, 180, 217

Last Time I Saw Paris, The (1954) 31
Laurel, Stan 159
Lean, David 134
Lemmon, Jack 159
Lent, Tina Olsin 51, 52
Les Amants de Vérona (1949) 181
Les Enfants du Paradis (1945) 3, 181
lesbian 23, 24, 151, 165, 185
Let's Make Love (musical 1960) 174
Levant, Oscar 95
Life at the Top (1965) 187
Lion King (1994) 23
Lion King 2: Simba's Pride, The (1998) 192
Listen to Britain (1942) 122
Locke, John 9
Lodge, Thomas 73, 151, 166
Logan, John 27
Logan, Robert A. 8, 11
Lombard, Carole 43, 57, 58
Lorenzo, Fiorenzo di 187
Lost Weekend, The (1945, 1950) 31, 79, 103
Love Before Breakfast (1936) 52, 58
Love Is All There Is (1996) 194, 195, 217
Love Story (1970) 195, 196, 197, 199, 200, 207
Love's Labour's Lost (2000) 119
Lubitsch, Ernst 54, 79, 157, 174, 217
Luhrmann, Baz 21, 123, 178, 179, 180, 182, 183, 186, 187, 189, 190, 191, 194, 200, 212, 214, 215, 217
Lyly, John 16, 80, 115, 150, 151, 153, 157, 162

Macbeth (1948) 23
McCarthy, James P. (General) 31
McCartney, Sir Paul 112
McDonald, Jeanette 115
MacDonald, Margaret I. 184
MacGraw, Ali 196
Made for Each Other (1939) 57
Magnificent Obsession (1954) 32
Mahabharata (1933, 1965, 2013) 201

Maltby, Richard 53, 54, 73
Mankiewicz, Joseph 47, 63, 66, 116, 132
Marley, John 196
Marlowe, Christopher 8, 184
marriage 13, 16, 39–69, 71, 85, 87, 88, 91, 99, 100, 101, 104, 113, 114, 118, 199, 120–2, 133, 134, 143, 156, 158, 167, 169, 170–2, 194, 195, 201, 202, 207, 211, 214, 216, 225
Martha's Romeo (1915) 184
Mary Poppins (1964) 193
Mayer, Louis B. 29
Meet Me in St. Louis (1944) 77, 101, 102
Méliès, George 14, 20
melodrama 13, 16, 23, 24, 32, 57, 75, 81, 113, 203, 225, 226
Men of Respect (1991) 23
Mendelssohn, Felix 117
Merchant Ivory 31, 206
metatheatre 75, 78, 129
MGM 28, 29, 118, 124
Midsummer Night's Dream, A (1909) 19
Midsummer Night's Dream, A (1935) 98, 128
Midsummer Night's Dream, A (1999) 21
Midsummer Night's Rave Party, A (2002) 85, 96
Midsummer Night's Sex Comedy, A (1982) 92, 93
Milland, Raymond 196
Miller, Ann 49
Millett, Kate 163
Milton, John 30
Mississippi Masala (1992) 207
Molière 26, 113
Monroe, Marilyn 63, 160, 174
Monsoon Wedding (2001) 207
Montand, Yves 174
Monte Carlo (1930) 174
Morrison, Paul 209

Mortal Coil 29
Mozart, Wolfgang Amadeus 157
Mrs Doubtfire (1993) 167, 168
Much Ado About Nothing (1993, 2011) 23
Mulan (1998) 157
Mulvey, Laura 149
murder 23, 31, 32, 55, 63, 127, 159, 192, 202, 203, 205
Murder with Pictures (1936) 31
musicals 8, 23, 24, 50, 72, 75, 76, 78, 82, 83, 85, 95, 110–19, 122–7, 129, 130–2, 136, 142, 151, 171, 193, 216
My Fair Lady (1964) 103, 106, 173, 193
My Man Godfrey (1936) 175
My Own Private Idaho (1991) 23

Nair, Mira 207
National Theatre 112
Naylor, Edward W. 111
Neale, Steve 82, 115
Never Been Kissed (1999) 105
new comedy 113, 114
New Moon (2009) 180
Newbolt Report (1921) 25
Nicoll, Allardyce 5
Ninotchka (1939)
Niven, David 171
Nolan, Doris 99
Nosferatu (1922) 117
Not Another Teen Movie (2001) 40

O (2001)
O'Connor, Donald 125
O'Neal, Ryan 196
Of Human Bondage (1934) 66
Oklahoma! (1955, 1979) 130, 140
Olivier, Laurence 14, 22, 47, 98, 122, 134
On The Town (1949) 120, 121, 122
Orlando (1992) 158
Othello (1952) 3, 23
Oyster Princess, The (1919) 157

Padukone, Deepika 205
Painter, William 180
Paris When It Sizzles (1964) 31, 103
Parson, Elinor 40, 52
Pasternak, Boris 10, 25
pastoral 16, 17, 91, 92, 98, 99, 100–5, 110, 123, 130, 150, 166
Pater, Walter 183
Peck, Gregory 104, 172
Perils of Pauline, The (1947) 126
Philadelphia Story, The (1940) 13, 85, 86, 88, 89, 92, 93
Pickford, Mary 45, 46, 47, 48
Pillow Talk (1959) 174
Pisano, Antonio di Puccio 187
Planet of the Apes (1968, 2001) 31
Plautus 16, 141, 142, 166
Polanksi, Roman 23
Pollastra (Giovanni Lappoli) 150
Polonsky, Abraham Lincoln 28, 29
Pope, Alexander 223
Porter, Cole 14, 40, 49, 119
Powell, Dick 95, 117, 134
Prairie Romeo, A (1917) 184
Presley, Elvis 193
Pride and Prejudice (1940, 2003, 2005) 10
Prokofiev, Sergei 183
psychological thrillers 3, 16, 23, 24, 191
Punch and Judy 42, 60
Punk and the Princess, The (1993) 185
Purcell, Henry 116
Pygmalion (1935, 1937, 1938) 173
Pygmalion (by G. B. Shaw) 106
Pygmalion, myth 103

Qayamat Se Qayamat Tak (1988) 202, 203

Radner, Hilary 20
Railway Children, The (1967) 189
Reckless Romeo, A (1917) 184
Red Shoes, The (1948) 95

Reed, Lou 183
Regan, Ronald 162
Reinhardt, Max 25, 64, 79, 92, 93, 97, 117, 128
Remember Me 29
Renoir, Jean 92
Renoir, Pierre-Auguste 95
Reynolds, Debbie 124
Richard III (1908, 1912, 1996) 23
road movies 23, 24
Roaming Romeo, A (1916, 1920, 1928, 1933) 184
Robbins, Jerome 122, 192, 193
Roberts, Nia 209
Robin Hood (1922, 1935, 1935,1973, 1991, 2010, 2013) 46
Robson, Flora 187
Rockabye Hamlet (1976) 123, 124
Rocky Horror Show, The (1975) 159
Rodgers, Richard 129, 130, 140
Rodin, *The Thinker* 91
Roeg, Nicholas 189
Roman Holiday (1953) 104, 172
Romanoff and Juliet (1960) 178
romantic comedy 2, 3, 8, 9, 13, 16, 23, 33, 39, 42, 44, 50, 53–6, 61, 71–106, 109–16, 119, 120, 121, 125, 127, 130, 134, 136, 143, 148, 151–4, 159, 165, 168, 169, 171–5, 180, 218, 224–6
romantic tragedy 8, 23, 33, 78, 159, 178–219, 224–6
Romeo, Julia a tma (A Bright Light in a Dark Room; Romeo, Juliet and Darkness) (1960) 198
Romeo + Juliet (1996) 123, 178, 180, 189, 194
Romeo and Juliet (1936, 1968) 23, 97, 98, 188
Romeo and Juliet in Sarajevo (1994) 185
Romeo i Julieta (1937) 180
Romeo Must Die (1994) 185
Romeo und Julia auf dem Dorf (1941) 180
Romeo und Julia im Schnee (1920) 79

Index

Room at the Top (1959) 187
Rooney, Mickey 117, 118
Roping her Romeo (1917) 184
Rota, Nino 47, 183, 189, 203
Rothwell, Kenneth 5, 19
Roualt, Georges 95
Rowe, Katherine 15
Rowe, Kathleen 41, 77
Runyon, Damon 132

Sabrina (1954) 173
Said, Edward 14
Salaam Bombay (1998) 207
Sallitt, Dan 79
Sammons, Eddie 179
samurai 23, 181
Sanders, Julie 109, 111
Sartre, Jean Paul 14
scapegoat 75, 78, 116
Schlegel, Karl Wilhelm Friedrich 25
Schwarzenegger, Arnold 14
science fiction 23, 29
screwball comedy 8, 16, 51–8, 66, 71, 81, 88, 89, 99, 157, 163, 175, 225
Seashore Romeo, A (1915) 184
Second Best Bed (1938) 52
Second World War 59, 61, 72, 87, 113, 122, 130, 141, 179
Segal, Erich 195
Seneca 16
Seng, Peter 111
Sensations (musical 1970) 183
Seven Brides for Seven Brothers (1954) 76
Sex Lives of Romeo and Juliet (Romeo and Juliet II) (1969) 178, 185
Sex, Lies, and Videotape (1989) 3
Shake Mr Shakespeare (1936) 118
Shakespeare, William
  All's Well That Ends Well 79, 82, 89, 173
  Antony and Cleopatra 41, 55, 225
  As You Like It 2, 6, 16, 45, 52, 54, 72, 75n.14, 80, 82, 98–106, 101, 110, 112, 116, 127, 128, 148, 149, 151, 152, 156, 157, 159, 166, 171, 172, 174, 175
  Comedy of Errors, The 21, 111, 130, 140, 142, 143, 144–7, 169, 201
  Cymbeline 85, 156
  Hamlet 2, 4, 6, 8, 14, 16, 20–3, 26, 29, 32, 84, 110, 118, 123–5, 134, 164, 179, 181, 198, 201, 216, 224
  Henry IV 23, 110
  Henry V 16, 23
  Henry VI 123
  Julius Caesar 23, 132, 166
  King Lear 16, 23, 127, 181, 194, 25
  Love's Labour's Lost 17, 71, 73, 74, 77, 82, 109, 115, 120, 121, 213, 224
  Macbeth 23, 31–2, 63, 70, 84, 100, 124, 127, 181
  Measure for Measure 95
  Merchant of Venice, The 2, 16, 72, 81, 82, 84, 127, 148, 149, 152, 155, 157, 158, 159, 174
  Merry Wives of Windsor, The 75, 154
  Midsummer Night's Dream, A 2, 21, 23, 25, 71–106, 116, 117, 127, 131, 148, 154, 155, 172, 173, 182, 217
  Much Ado About Nothing 3, 41, 42, 55, 62, 71, 81, 82, 83, 89, 91, 110–37, 140
  Othello 3, 23, 60, 91, 101, 108n.34, 123, 127, 181, 225
  Pericles 130, 131
  Rape of Lucrece, The 2
  Richard II 2
  Richard III 20, 23, 133
  Romeo and Juliet 2, 3, 21, 23, 33, 82, 83, 91, 97, 99, 100, 105, 113, 114, 118, 122, 123, 125, 126, 131, 178–226

Shakespeare, William (*cont.*)
  Taming of the Shrew 3, 23, 31, 39–69, 80, 82, 88, 89, 95, 97, 99, 123, 175
  Tempest, The 23, 85, 101, 130, 131, 142
  Timon of Athens 127
  Twelfth Night 2, 23, 62, 72, 73, 74, 79, 81, 83, 84, 99, 106–37, 140, 142, 143, 148, 149, 150, 151, 152, 157, 158, 159, 160, 161, 166, 168, 174, 185
  Two Gentlemen of Verona, The 2, 62, 85, 110, 123, 151, 154, 155, 157, 173
  Two Noble Kinsmen, The 29, 110
  Venus and Adonis 55, 89, 123
  Winter's Tale, The 12, 16, 51, 56, 85, 88, 130, 131, 132, 142, 156, 169
Shakespeare in Love (1998) 22, 157, 217
Shakespeare Wallah (1965) 31, 206
Shaw, G. B. 106
She Done Him Wrong (1933) 118
She's the Man (2006) 23, 157, 158
Shearer, Norma 186
Shentall, Susan 187
Shop around the Corner, The (1940) 174
Show of Shows, The (1929) 123
Siddons, Sarah 63, 64, 182
Sidney, Sir Philip 16, 73, 82, 142, 150, 151, 153, 155, 160, 166, 169
Sikov, Ed 162
Simpsons, The 29
Sinatra, Frank 121, 134
Singer, Isaac Bashevis 158
Singh, Ranveer 205
Singin' in the Rain (1951) 124, 125, 126, 127, 129
Sly Fox (1976) 166
Solomon and Gaenor (1998/99) 209, 212, 214, 216

Some Like It Hot (1959) 79, 159, 160, 161, 162, 165, 168
Something to Sing About (1937) 128
Sondheim, Stephen 193
Sound of Music, The (1964) 193
South Pacific (1958) 130
Spadafora, David 9
Spenser, Edmund 150, 151, 155
sports films 23, 24
Stage Door (1937) 77
Stage Door Canteen (1943) 122–3
Stalin, Joseph 25
Star Trek 29
Star Wars 29
Stars Over Broadway (1935) 118
State Fair (1945, 1962) 130
Sternfeld, Frederick, W. 111
Sterry, J. A. 40
Stevenson, Robert Louis 166
Stoppard, Tom 184
Streisand, Barbra 158
Sunset Boulevard (1945) 31, 79
supernatural 23, 24
Supple, Tim 160
Sylvia Scarlett (1935) 158, 165

Taming of the Shrew, The (1929, 1967, 1999) 39–69, 167
Tattoo Brute (1958) 4
Taylor, Elizabeth 47, 48, 66, 68
Taylor, Sam 46
Tchaikovsky, Pyotr Ilyich 183
teen-flick 23
Tempest, The (1979) 23
Thank God It's Friday (1978) 123
Theodora Goes Wild (1936) 52
Thief of Baghdad, The (1940, 1961, 1965, 1977) 46
Thine Own Self 29
This Is the Army (1943) 122
thrillers 3, 16, 23, 24, 191
Throne of Blood (1957) 23
Time Flies (1944) 184
To Be or Not to Be (1942) 79
Tolstoy, Leo 25, 28

Tootsie (1982) 162, 165, 166, 167
Toulouse-Lautrec, Henri de 95
Tracey, Spencer 59
Tree of Wooden Clogs, The (1978) 211
Tree, Ellen 182
Tree, Herbert Beerbohm 19
Trigg, Stephanie 11
Trivedi, Harish 201
Tromeo and Juliet (1996) 23, 178, 185
Trouble in Paradise (1932) 174
Twilight (2008) 192
Two-Faced Woman (1941) 174
Tynan, Kenneth 112

Ugly Truth, The (2009) 61
Ulta Palta (1997) 145
Undiscovered Country, The 29
Ustinov, Peter 178
Utrillo, Maurice 95

Van Gogh, Vincent 95
Van I Ne Snilos (1980) 217
Vera-Ellen 171
Verdi, Giuseppe 183
Victor Victoria (1982) 158
Viktor and Viktoria (1933) 1
vitagraph 19, 20
Voltaire 26

Wagner, Richard 183, 191
Walkabout (1971) 189
war 13, 23, 24, 29, 39, 48, 59, 61, 87, 95, 113, 119, 120–2, 126, 129, 130, 141, 150, 157, 159, 179, 183–5, 188, 192, 198, 200, 205
Warm Bodies (2013) 23
Warner Brothers 95, 116, 117, 118, 123

Weill, Kurt 140
Welles, Orson 3, 14, 27, 28
Were the World Mine (2008) 23, 97
West, Mae 71, 118
West Side Story (musical 1961) 23, 114, 122, 123, 135, 178, 183, 187–8, 192–3, 212, 214
westerns 23, 40, 82, 103, 157, 203, 217
What Ever Happened to Baby Jane (1962) 66
Whelehan, Imelda 3, 5, 7
Whiting, Leonard 188
Who's Afraid of Virginia Woolf? (1966) 66, 68
Wilde, Oscar 144
Wilder, Billy 30, 79, 106, 159, 162
Williams, Robin 97, 167, 168
Wilson, John Dover 84
Witch Hunt (1993) 31
Woman, A (1915) 159
Wong, Fenson 218
Woolf, Virginia 168
Words for Battle (1941) 122
Writers Guild of America 26, 27
Wrong Box, The (1966) 166

Yentl (1983) 158
Yidl Mitl Fidle (1936) 158
You Were Never Lovelier (1942) 61, 83, 84
You'll Never Get Rich (1941) 170

Zeffirelli, Franco 46–8, 62, 178–9, 182–3, 186–90, 197, 209, 212, 214, 215
zombies 23
Zorro (1998) 46

EU authorised representative for GPSR:
Easy Access System Europe, Mustamäe tee 50,
10621 Tallinn, Estonia
gpsr.requests@easproject.com

www.ingramcontent.com/pod-product-compliance
Lightning Source LLC
Chambersburg PA
CBHW070237240426
43673CB00044B/1823